GW00322600

Statistics for Business

Related titles in the series

Accounting
Advertising
Auditing
Book-keeping
Business and Commerical
   Law
Business and Enterprise
   Studies
Business French
Business German
Business Italian
Commerce
Cost and Managment
   Accounting
Economics

Elements of Banking
Financial Management
Information Technology
Law
Management Theory and
   Practice
Marketing
Office Practice
Personnel Management
Psychiatry
Social Services
Statistics for Business
Teeline Shorthand
Typing

Statistics for Business

Rex Ingram and
Ken Hoyle, BSc (Econ)

MADE SIMPLE
BOOKS

Made Simple
An imprint of Butterworth-Heinemann Ltd
Linacre House, Jordan Hill, Oxford OX2 8DP

$\mathcal{R}$ A member of the Reed Elsevier plc group

OXFORD   LONDON   BOSTON
MUNICH   NEW DELHI   SINGAPORE   SYDNEY
TOKYO   TORONTO   WELLINGTON

First published 1991
Reprinted 1992, 1994

© Rex Ingram and Ken Hoyle 1991

All rights reserved. No part of this publication
may be reproduced in any material form (including
photocopying or storing in any medium by electronic
means and whether or not transiently or incidentally
to some other use of this publication) without the
written permission of the copyright holder except in
accordance with the provisions of the Copyright,
Designs and Patents Act 1988 or under the terms of a
licence issued by the Copyright Licensing Agency Ltd,
90 Tottenham Court Road, London W1P 9HE.
Applications for the copyright holder's written permission
to reproduce any part of this publication should be addressed
to the publishers.

British Library Cataloguing in Publication Data
Ingram, Rex
   Statistics for business.
   I. Title   II. Hoyle, Ken   III. Series
   650.1

ISBN 0 7506 0207 4

Phototypeset by Key Graphics, Aldermaston, Berkshire
and printed in Great Britain by Clays Ltd, St Ives plc

Contents

Preface

This book provides a sound background in statistics for those studying up to intermediate levels on a wide variety of business courses. The book is practical rather than theoretical, and is sure to meet the needs of all those in the technical colleges and polytechnics who are preparing to enter the business field, and pursuing either BTEC National Courses or professional courses such as those for the Association of Accounting Technicians, the Chartered Institute of Management Accountants, the Institute of Management Services, the Institute of Statisticians, the Market Research Society and similar bodies. It will also be of interest to students on A level, first year degree and Higher National Courses who need plenty of practice in statistical work because their mathematics background is rusty.

The book will be particularly of use to entrepreneurs seeking to build their backgrounds in statistical techniques of use in business and to make sense of the increasingly quantitative presentations of banks, public companies, official bodies, venture capitalists and others active in the enterprise field.

The book is student-orientated, with plenty of exercises on each aspect of statistics dealt with and a comprehensive answer section. It embodies the authors' many years' experience in teaching statistics in further and higher education.

Every effort has been made to ensure the accuracy of the answer section, but in complex texts of this sort it is not unknown for the odd error to creep through. The authors hope that in drawing such errors to their attention students and staff will be careful to check their workings first, and ensure that only genuine complaints are drawn to the publisher's attention.

We should particularly like to thank all colleagues, students and secretarial staff who have cooperated in the production and checking of the typescript. We must also thank the publishers for their forbearance and patience.

Rex Ingram
Ken Hoyle

1

Introduction to statistics

1.1 The meaning of statistics

The word statistics was originally applied to numerical facts collected for the state and was concerned initially with population, tax revenue, government expenditure, agricultural output, and so on. Today its meaning has been widened to include not only any set of numerical data, but also the processes used in the collection, presentation, analysis and interpretation of this data.

Statistics can therefore denote either a collection of numerical data which provides the raw material for the statistician (such as population statistics or production statistics) or a body of scientific methods which can be applied to a study of the data. In this book we shall be largely concerned with the procedures used in statistics. They will be considered under two heads.

Descriptive statistics

This is the term given to the techniques which are used to organize and present the data. These include tabulation, diagrams, graphs and certain numerical procedures, all of which have as their objective the orderly summarization of the material in a form which will display its distinctive features and aid its analysis.

Inferential statistics

This branch of statistics is largely concerned with the analysis and interpretation of data obtained from samples. It is most unlikely that the data being used by the statistician will comprise the entire relevant data (called the **population** or **universe**), but rather a small part of it (called a **sample**). Yet on the basis of this sample, providing that it is representative of the population, inferences can be drawn about the population as a whole. Such inferences cannot be absolutely certain because they will be based on part of the data only, and so will have to be expressed in terms of probability. It is this aspect of statistical work which has developed so much during this century, and has led to its expansion into many fields of human endeavour, and to an increasing appreciation of the value of statistical techniques in ever-increasing fields of activity.

1.2 The importance of statistics

No one today can afford to be without some knowledge of statistical methods. As citizens we will be expected to contribute numerical facts to the state, the local authority, the bank, insurance company, etc., and we should be aware of the use to which they are put and by whom. In any working situation you will have placed before you considerable information obtained from samples, e.g. market research polls, whose value you should be able to assess. The hospital patient, the consumer of cigarettes, the motorist, all may have to depend for their lives on the validity of inferences drawn from statistical investigations. The factory worker may be faced with activity sampling, or be offered wages negotiated with reference to the index of retail prices. Statistical relationships between training and earning prospects may be a feature of recruitment in some industries. All these topics vitally affect your standard of living, and some understanding of statistical techniques would be useful in evaluating them.

If statistics are important to us in our individual lives, how much more important must they be in industry and in government, where enormous projects have to be undertaken, affecting the interests of great companies and entire nations. Vast sums of money are allocated to projects which later prove totally abortive, e.g. in such fields as defence, scientific research, new town development, agricultural development, forestry, etc. Blocks of flats, now being blown up as unfit for human habitation, were only 20 years ago being awarded architectural prizes for their innovative techniques. A more careful statistical analysis of these projects would probably have revealed at least some of the weaknesses inherent in them. Scarce capital could have been put to other, more profitable uses.

1.3 Criticisms of statistics

We live in a cynical age and it is fashionable to be particularly cynical about statistics. The well-known phrase, attributed to Disraeli, 'There are lies, damned lies, and statistics' may no longer generate amusement, but it is widely believed. Professional statisticians are entitled to be unhappy about this, since they take great pains to ensure that the pronouncements they make are as accurate as they possibly can be, given the resources that have been devoted to the exercise. Why then is there such a public distrust of statistics? The answer lies in the difficulties that must be faced in the collection and interpretation of data. In this introductory chapter it is advisable to mention some of the pitfalls facing the statistician, both in the collection of data and their interpretation. You will find it helpful in preparing your own statistical material if you critically appraise all the statistics presented to you, and examine them for the faults listed in the following section. An appreciation of the difficulties others have faced, or the weaknesses they have failed to overcome, will improve your own chances of presenting reliable data and of giving considered reports about any enquiry you are asked to conduct.

1.4 Sources of statistics

There are a number of points to note about the source of statistics. By the word 'source' we mean the place from which they originated, or the manner in which they were collected. If the source is a published source, we should state it – for example, in the form *Source: Monthly Digest of Statistics, January 1990*. For many purposes statistics can be quoted from official sources and a reasonable degree of confidence can be placed upon them. This is because they have been collected using a well-established process by trained statisticians who presumably have used their expertise to avoid the more obvious errors. Even so it may be necessary to turn up the definitions used in the process, which are usually published as a separate booklet. Thus the *Monthly Digest of Statistics* referred to above is a mass of statistics collected by official agencies using definitions published in a Supplement to the Digest called *Monthly Digest of Statistics – Definitions and Explanatory Notes*. This supplement is published annually and may be ordered by telephone on 071 873 9090, or by post from Her Majesty's Stationery Office, PO Box 276, London, SW8 5DT.

Two very useful guides to United Kingdom Statistics are *Government Statistics, a Brief Guide to Sources* and *United Kingdom in Figures*. These are free, are updated annually and may be obtained either by writing to or preferably phoning to the Information Services Division, Cabinet Office, Great George St, London SW1P 3AL (071 270 6363).

An example of the incorrect use of a source would be to base an argument about the growth in numbers of the family motorcar on statistics for 'road vehicles'. The definition of 'road vehicles' would almost certainly be much wider than the definition of 'family motorcars' and a quite misleading figure might be used as a result. The careful definition of terms used is essential before any enquiry can begin.

Many sets of official statistics are based upon records collected for quite different purposes. For example, the Inland Revenue records about taxpayers give a vast mass of statistical material which can be used for many other purposes, provided it is used with caution. Since many people do not pay tax at all (perhaps because they have a family to support, which removes them from the taxable bracket), the tax statistics would be inadequate for many purposes, particularly enquiries about family expenditure, where many of the families under discussion would not be included. Because the costs of the collection of statistics are high, it is economical to use statistics gathered for other purposes, but we must always do so with caution.

If the enquiry is to be pursued by collecting original data – by sending out questionnaires, for example – the enquiry may need to be conducted with a **representative sample** of the population. The choice of a sample is in itself a major statistical exercise, which balances the type of sample against the costs of collection. If the choice of sample is narrowed to keep down the costs, it cannot be as representative as a completely random sample. For example, an enquiry about United Kingdom family expenditure based on citizens living in Westminster will be less representative of the total population than one based on citizens of London, or the Home Counties or the entire nation. Interviewing 1 000 citizens in Westminster presents few problems, and even 1 000 Londoners are reasonably accessible, but 1 000 citizens from the Home Counties, or the entire country, will involve greater travelling costs and much more time.

Bias

Sources can be **biased**. This means that instead of the statistics being completely objective, some subjective consideration causes them to lean in a particular direction. A survey asking smokers how many cigarettes they smoke daily is likely to understate the level of consumption. A feeling of guilt causes a smaller total than the actual to be put forward.

Bias can occur for a number of reasons, the most common of which is vested interest. Politicians from the two major parties in the United Kingdom have a vested interest in claiming that '90 per cent of the population do not wish to see a change in the electoral system'. If there was to be such a change, their own influence would be diminished.

No doubt we have all listened to those animated discussions in which one politician gives the 'facts' on unemployment, to the simulated horror of another politician from a different party, who replies with a completely different set of 'facts'. In this particular case, one may question the objectivity of the presenter of the data, but, equally, many of these seemingly opposed statistics are caused by the lack of precise definition of the terms used – does unemployment include temporarily laid-off workers, part-time staff, school leavers, etc.? It is incumbent on the statistician to define his data clearly, to obtain all the data relevant to the investigation and to present it as clearly and concisely as possible.

The reader will be well aware that 'guesstimates' posing as facts are often used in industry and by governments to support propositions which in reality are not statistically valid. This does not of itself make such propositions incorrect, because, after all, statistics are not an end in themselves but only a means to an end. They are merely an aid to the process of decision-making, and although they may have an important part to play, they will only be one stage in the procedure.

When examining a source, it is always important to know who is supplying the information, why he is supplying it, and how he obtained it. Is it well founded, or is it just a guess? The unreliability of the sources is certainly one reason for the popular distrust of statistics.

False reasoning

Another reason for the distrust of those who use statistics is the false reasoning which is often applied to statistical information.

Even if there is no bias in the information used, it is relatively easy to arrive at an incorrect conclusion. In order to avoid this, students are urged to be ruthlessly logical. An enquiry may show that there is a 50 per cent increase in the sale of a particular brand of margarine. Would it be right to conclude that each housewife is buying half as much again as previously? Clearly it would not. Perhaps more outlets now stock the brand so that more housewives buy it. The amount bought per housewife might even have diminished. It will frequently be the case that an enquiry will reveal a situation which could have developed in several different ways, or be caused by a combination of factors which have together produced the effects observed.

Statistical reasoning is really a special case of the general scientific method, and needs to be as rigorous as any other branch of scientific reasoning. What is unfortunate though is that, since it is largely used to describe human affairs, and particularly economic affairs, it necessarily suffers from the defects inseparable from descriptions of human activity. For example, we cannot predict human activity with the same certainty that we can predict chemical activity, so that the too confident prognostications of statisticians are often proved wrong by events.

1.5 Discrete and continuous variables

The things which statisticians seek to measure – height, weight, wages, unemployment, prices, etc. – are known as **variables**. As the term implies, variables are studied because some variation in their value is anticipated. An investigation into the height of all 11-year-old schoolboys in England would not give the result that they were all of the same height. There will be many heights, because the schoolboys studied vary in the heights they have attained.

Variables are divided into two types: **discrete variables** and **continuous variables**. Those variables which are discrete increase or decrease in definite 'units'. For example, if the number of baby rabbits in a litter is the subject of investigation, the numbers recorded will be 1, 2, 3, 4, 5, etc. It is not possible to have 2.75 rabbits or 2.9, 4.86 or 7.72. The units therefore are single rabbits in this example, though in some enquiries the unit might be a group: we count armies in regiments, and military aircraft in squadrons, for example.

Continuous variables do not have a unitary composition. Instead there is a continuous path of increase or decrease. If one is measuring the number of kilometres which a homing pigeon flies before coming to rest, any fraction of a kilometre is possible. The pigeon may fly 2.746 km or 28.527 km or even 257.25757 km.

As explained later this distinction between discrete and continuous data is of importance when choosing the limits of classes in any classification of data, for example, in tabulation.

1.6 Collection of data

Statistics used by investigators are of two types: **primary** and **secondary.** Primary statistics are collected by the investigator when he/she searches out new information. Secondary statistics are those which an investigator obtains from other sources. Most of these will be published statistics and the government is an active supplier of information in this form.

Of course, at some stage all statistics have to be collected from original sources. Such collection involves the investigator in a number of decisions. The following are points which have to be considered when about to embark upon an enquiry:

1 What is the precise purpose of the enquiry?
2 What definitions must we lay down if the investigators are to be clear about the classification of the responses they receive?
3 How is the enquiry to be conducted and how can we make it as foolproof as possible? This usually requires the preparation of a questionnaire, and decisions about sampling.

Let us consider these points in more detail:

The nature of the enquiry

The first and most obvious point is that a clear statement of the problem must be made. In other words, what is the investigation setting out to probe? Results which emerge from surveys can be rendered useless because investigators did not have a *precise* view of the problem at the heart of the operation. 'Writing maketh an exact man', and the reduction of the purpose of the enquiry to a clear statement in a short paragraph will clarify matters enormously and make the second problem, the definition of terms, easier.

Defining terms

In any enquiry there will be terms to be defined. A recent report about 'Small Firms' defined them as firms employing fewer than 200 persons. To the sole trader keeping a village shop 200 employees does not sound 'small', but for the purpose of the enquiry it was judged to be appropriate.

In relation to enquiries about unemployment, what is meant by the term 'unemployed'? Does it refer to *everyone* without a job? Is it applicable only to those registered as unemployed? What about housewives? What about the disabled and the sick? Are people receiving training unemployed? All these points need clarification before an investigator has a reasonable chance of working out which questions to ask.

Method of procedure

The collection of statistics must be systematic, and to limit costs it should be reduced to a simple procedure so that highly qualified investigators are not needed. Provided investigators are reasonably alert and persevering, there is no need for them to be trained statisticians.

Most statistical information is collected by means of a **questionnaire**, and the investigator may favour this method, but there are alternatives. It might be that the researcher will decide to interview personally everyone considered capable of giving information relevant to the enquiry. This has the advantage of giving high-quality information, but has a very small field of coverage. Another method is for interviewing to be delegated to teams of researchers or to agencies which specialize in collecting information. In either case a number of trained personnel take a standardized schedule and specific instructions, often to preselected interviewees. Such a method also gives high-quality information and a fairly wide coverage, but it is very expensive.

The postal questionnaire is popular because it reaches a potentially larger number of respondents and is also relatively cheap. It does, however, have a number of drawbacks, among which is the uncertainty of responses. Unless the return is compulsory – as with government census surveys – a large number of people are likely to ignore the questionnaire altogether. In addition, those who do return the forms duly completed are probably those most interested in the problems with which the survey deals, and are by self-selection therefore biased. There is also no guarantee that respondents have understood the questions asked, and replies might be suspect.

Despite these problems, because of coverage and cost, postal question-naires are still favoured by many investigators.

It is highly unlikely that the investigator will be able to contact every member of the group in which he/she is interested. Such a group in total is known as the **population**. The word 'population' is used here in a special technical way, and does not have its ordinary meaning of the entire nation. Thus in an enquiry about artists the 'population' would include only those who earned their living in this way. The investigator would probably have to be satisfied with a selection drawn from this population – a **sample**. Such a sample may form a very small proportion of the total population, maybe one in every 5 000, and it is therefore important that the sample is **representative** of the population as a whole.

In order to avoid bias in the sample a technique known as **random sampling** is used. *A random sample is defined as one which ensures that every item within the population has an equal chance of selection for the sample.* One of the easiest ways to do this is to give a numerical value to items and then programme a computer to select some of the numbers in an unbiased fashion.

Ensuring that the sample is free from bias is not just a matter of avoiding obvious leanings. For example, a survey designed to show the educational attainment of the United Kingdom population would not take its sample solely from a number of universities, for it is obvious that this would overstate the degree of achievement. It is also a requirement that bias of an unconscious nature is not included. Thus, conducting a survey by questioning the first 5 000 persons encountered in Oxford Street may not build in known bias, but is unlikely to be representative of the whole population of the United Kingdom. It is to overcome such a problem that random samples are used.

It is important to note that although random sampling will give a method of sample selection which is free from bias, it cannot guarantee that the items in the sample itself will be similarly free from bias. Mr Jones, who happens to be selected in a random sample, may have very biased views on the matter in hand.

1.7   Types of sample

There are some situations in which it may prove impossible to use the technique of random sampling. For example, the total population may not be known, or if known it may be too expensive to contact a widely dispersed random sample. When taking a sample, the key element is to obtain a representative sample, a sample that truly represents the populations as a whole. A second element is the cost of arriving at the sample, since our resources are always limited. We have to sacrifice perfection for economy, to some extent. We can achieve a reasonably satisfactory result by adapting random sampling in some way, depending upon the enquiry. Every adaptation of random sampling many include some element of bias or variability from the perfect result, but it may increase the representativeness of the sample, which is our key aim, and at the same time reduce costs. The types of sampling method available are described below:

1   *Quota sampling*   Instead of having to approach a whole dispersed group in a random sample, the interviewers conducting the survey are often instructed to fill **quotas** of given types. For example, twenty mothers with blue eyes, forty mothers with brown eyes, etc. Once the interviewers have sufficient numbers for one of their types, the quota has been met and that type is not sought out further. Such a method is cheaper than a random sample.

2   *Multi-stage sampling*   This technique uses frequent subdivision of the population, but on a random basis. For example, a small number of counties may be selected by random sample. Within these counties a further random sample may give a number of district councils and within these district councils yet another random sample may reveal a number of parish council areas. Interviewers can then be sent to these local areas to conduct the survey. Because of the concentration of observations within a few areas, the method is less expensive than random sampling.

3   *Cluster sampling*   This is used to overcome a particular problem – lack of knowledge of the population. Again, small areas of the country are selected and interviewers sent into them with the object of collecting information from every person who fits a particular description, e.g., from every peroxide blonde.

4   *Systematic sampling*   This method gives a virtual random sample. All the population is listed and then a percentage of the list taken. For example, if the sample is to be 5 per cent, then every twentieth item is taken from the list. Providing that there is no regular variation on each twentieth item (e.g. every twentieth firm was an engineering company), the sample should be almost as good as a random one.

5   *Stratified sampling*   Unlike the previous methods, stratified sampling is superior to random sampling, since it reduces the possibility of bias. If a population is homogeneous, it will not give a biased result, but if the population is heterogeneous, and consists of general strata, it could give a biased result. A random sample of the school population of the UK *might* be composed entirely of sixth formers and would therefore have given a biased result, but a stratified sample composed of representatives of each age group at school could not be. The essence of a stratified sample is that it selects at random from the various strata which comprise the total population.

It is therefore important to know (*a*) the total population and (*b*) the proportion that each subgroup, or stratum, bears to the total population. For example, if the total population in a survey were 10 000 units and one stratum was 1 000 units, the random selection within the stratum of 1 000 should amount to 10 per cent of the total sample (since 1 000 is 10 per cent of the total population of 10 000).

1.8   Approximation and error

When statisticians present figures they have collected or calculated, it is usual for such figures to be rounded to a suitable degree of of accuracy. If raw data relate to hundreds of thousands of pounds sterling, it is inconvenient to record every single penny. Instead, an **approximation** of the value will be given. If the real figure is £2 127 135.20, then a number of alternatives are open to the researcher:

1   The figure can be rounded down to the nearest pound, i.e. to £2 127 135. When rounding in business statistics, it is normal to round up for values above 0.5 and down for values below 0.5. Values of exactly 0.5 are rounded to the nearest even number. Thus 4.25 would be rounded to 4.2, but 4.35 would be rounded to 4.4.
2   The figure can be rounded to some other convenient grouping such as £'000, or £0 000, or £'00 000 or £m. The earlier example would thus become successively

	2 127	(£'000s)
or	213	(£'0 000s)
or	21	(£'00 000s)
or	2	(£m)

3   The figure can be stated in decimal form – for example, £2.1m.

All these approximations instill small errors into the figures, but if the degree of approximation is adequate to the enquiry in hand, the errors are trifling. One thing must be noted, that rounded figures do not necessarily add up exactly. Thus where a table of statistics includes a number of percentages which have been rounded, they may not add up to 100 per cent, and should not be made to do so. If they add up to 99.9 per cent or 100.2 per cent it is clear that the error is a **rounding error** and only to be expected. On average, rounding errors are **compensating errors**: they cancel one another out to a considerable extent though this may not eliminate all errors in a total.

Some rounding errors though are not compensatory in nature. Instead the degree of error in the figures can be compounded by the method of rounding used. For example, if all rounding undertaken with a set of figures is rounding up, then all the errors introduced will be positive. When added together, the absolute error could be large. Similarly, if all the rounding undertaken is rounding down, the negative errors, when taken together, could be equally large. For such reasons statisticians dislike rounding in one direction only.

Calculations can be made which assist statisticians to discover the amount of error which their approximations have introduced into the figures. Such calculations rest upon the ideas of **absolute** and **relative** error.

An **absolute error** is the difference between the true figure and the approximate figure. Where the true figure is known, there is no problem. For example, if the true figure is £2172 and the approximate figure £2000, then the absolute error is £2172 – £2000 = £172.

However, it is often the case that the true figure is not known, and in such circumstances absolute error has to be expressed within sensible boundaries. For example, suppose that the approximate figure is £2150 to the nearest £50. The absolute error cannot be greater than £25 since the true figure must ie between £2125 and £2174.99.

Relative error is the absolute error expressed as a percentage of the approximate figure. For example, if the approximate figure is £2150 with a maximum absolute error of £25, then the maximum relative error is

$$\frac{25}{2\,150} \times \frac{100}{1} = 1.16\%$$

There are four basic calculations – addition, subtraction, multiplication and division – and each has to take account of the potential error introduced by approximation. Let us consider each in turn.

Addition

Consider the following example:

Example 1.1 Add up the following numbers, each of which is approximate to the extent shown. What is the possible error on the total?

    1 270 (correct to the nearest 10 – maximum error ± 5)
    1 200 (correct to the nearest 100 – maximum error ± 50)
137 000 (correct to the nearest 1 000 – maximum error ± 500)

139 470 Total

What is the maximum possible error on the answer? Clearly if all the approximate numbers had the maximum error possible, the error in the total would be the sum of the errors. This is ± 555. So the sum of the numbers is $139\,470 \pm 555$.

When adding approximate numbers the maximum possible error in the answer is found by taking the sum of the maximum possible errors in the original approximate numbers.

Subtraction

Here the position is the same as with addition. The maximum possible error in the difference is arrived at by adding together all the maximum possible errors of the component parts of the calculation.

Example 1.2 $2\,270 \pm 5$ is subtracted from $24\,200 \pm 50$. What is the answer? What is the possible error in the answer?

$$
\begin{array}{rr}
24\,200 & \pm 50 \\
-2\,270 & \pm 5 \\
\hline
21\,930 & \pm 55
\end{array}
$$

When subtracting approximate numbers, the maximum possible error in the difference is the sum of the maximum possible errors in the original numbers.

Can you see why? Suppose the two approximate numbers both had positive errors (one of 50 and one of 5); when subtracted the error would only be 45. But if one number had a positive error and the other had a negative error, the error could be as much as $+50$ or -5. The difference of the two errors could therefore be as great as 50 minus $-5 = 50 + 5 = 55$. So the maximum error possible in subtracting two approximate numbers in the *sum* of the possible errors.

Multiplication

The maximum possible error from a multiplication calculation can be found by adding together the *relative errors* of the component parts.

Example 1.3   In a certain enquiry the figure of $60\,000 \pm 5\,000$ has to be multiplied by another figure 450 ± 5. Do the calculations and state the degree of error in the answer.

60 000   Absolute error $\pm 5\,000$

Relative error $\dfrac{5\,000}{60\,000} \times 100 = 8.3\%$

$\times$ 450   Absolute error ± 5

Relative error $= \dfrac{5}{450} \times 100 = 1.1\%$

27 000 000

The maximum error in the answer is the *sum* of the relative errors $= 9.4\%$. Since 9.4% of $27\,000\,000 = 2\,538\,000$, the answer is

$$27\,000\,000 \pm 2\,538\,000$$

Division

Division calculations also involve adding together separate relative errors in order to arrive at the maximum possible error.

Example 1.4   In a certain enquiry one statistic $2\,000 \pm 5$ has to be divided by another 120 ± 5. What is the answer and what is the possible error in it?

2 000   Absolute error ± 5

Relative error $\dfrac{5}{2\,000} \times 100 = 0.25\%$

120   Absolute error ± 5

Relative error $\dfrac{5}{120} \times 100 = 4.17\%$

$\therefore$ $2\,000 \div 120$
$= 16.67$ with a relative error of 4.42%
$= 16.67 \pm 0.74$ (which is 4.42% of 16.67)

Significant figures

Statisticians often express the results of their calculations in terms of significant figures. Significant figures are those digits which convey accurate information. The accuracy of any figure depends upon the extent to which the figures *it was calculated from* were themselves rounded. For example, the figure 47.17 has only 4 significant figures even though it may be a summary of 47.172153. Had the degree of accuracy related to only 2 significant figures then 47 would represent this.

When calculating with rounded figures, it is important to remember that the results cannot be more accurate that the *least* accurate rounded figure used. Therefore $47.7123 \times 10\,000$ (rounded to the nearest 1 000) cannot be accurate to more than 2 significant figures – *10* 000 in 10 000. The result 477 123 has only 2 significant figures and should be expressed as 480 000. The addition of 274, 1320 and 400 (to the nearest 100) cannot be stated as of greater accuracy than 2 000, i.e. to the nearest 100.

Any attempt to be more specific than the rounded figures in the calculation warrant is known as being 'spuriously accurate'. In the calculation above, the addition would have been spuriously accurate had it claimed 3 or 4 significant figures: 1990 or 1994.

1.9   Simple mathematical symbols

Hardly anyone would consider repeatedly writing 'Her Majesty's Stationery Office' in lists of publications. Instead we use the abbreviation HMSO, because it saves time and it is so commonly used that everyone knows what it means. However, people who are happy with HMSO might not understand Σ (pronounced sigma), which merely means the sum of (or total of), and is a convenient shorthand way of saying this.

$$\Sigma\ 8\ 12\ 16\ \text{means}\ 8 + 12 + 16 = 36$$

There are other useful symbols of 'mathematical shorthand'. The following are some of those which will appear in this textbook:

$\simeq$ means an approximate equal, or almost equal.
n means the number of items.
f means the frequency, or the number of times an item occurs.
$\bar{x}$ means 'the arithmetic mean' or 'arithmetic average'.

1.10   Questions on Chapter 1

1   Explain what is meant by:

   (*a*)   Population
   (*b*)   Quota sampling
   (*c*)   Multi-stage sampling
   (*d*)   Random sampling
   (*e*)   Stratified sampling?

2   What is bias? How does bias arise, and what can be done to overcome it?

3   Point out the advantages and disadvantages of collecting information by the following methods:

(a)   The telephone
(b)   Direct observation
(c)   Interview
(d)   Postal questionnaire

4   What is meant by the term 'rounding off'? Why is rounding off undertaken?

5   Rounding off can be biased or unbiased. What do these terms mean?

6   What is meant by compensating error? Round the following figures to one decimal place in such a way that any error introduced is compensating: 7.33, 6.86, 7.78, 4.33, 5.57.

7   What is the absolute error in the following instances?

	True figure	Approximate figure
(a)	2 242	2 000
(b)	1 726	1 700
(c)	6 421	7 000
(d)	1 787	1 780

8   How would you express the absolute error inherent in the following figures?

(a)   2 750 correct to nearest 50
(b)   1 600 correct to nearest 100
(c)   7 000 correct to nearest 1 000
(d)   2 765 correct to nearest 5

9   What is meant by relative error? Calculate the relative error for the following (give your answer correct to two decimal places):

(a) $2 100 \pm 50$
(b) $2 250 \pm 25$
(c) $1 725 \pm 2.5$
(d) $10 700 \pm 50$

10 Add the following sets of figures:

(a) $1 370 \pm\ \ 5$ (b) $1 575 \pm 2.5$
      $1 200 \pm\ \ 50$ $1 300 \pm 50$
   $147 000 \pm 500$ $1 400 \pm 50$

11   Subtract from $27\,200 \pm 50$ the following figures:

   (a) $2\,170 \pm 5$
   (b) $2\,100 \pm 50$
   (c) $1\,855 \pm 2.5$

12   Multiply the following sets of figures:

   (a) $40\,000 \pm 500 \times 350 \pm 5$
   (b) $2\,700 \pm 50 \times 175 \pm 2.5$

13   Divide $2\,150 \pm 25$ by the following figures:

   (a) 125 ± 2.5
   (b) 140 ± 5

1.11   Summary of Chapter 1

1   The term 'statistics' can be used in two ways. It may denote a collection of numerical data (population statistics, labour statistics, etc.) or a body of scientific methods which can be used to study the data and present them lucidly to interested parties.
2   Statistics fall into two main groups – descriptive statistics which describe a particular situation and inferential statistics which infer general conclusions from the study of samples.
3   The importance of statistics lies in their widespread use in all societies to decide policies about output, distribution, marketing, social behaviour, taxation, etc.
4   Statistics are collected in many different ways, both privately (for an individual researcher, firm or company) and officially (by Government agencies of various sorts).
5   In collecting statistics we must be careful to avoid bias, whether intentional or unintentional. False reasoning can also lead to wrong conclusions. Statistical reasoning is a special case of scientific reasoning and must be rigorous in its search for truth.
6   The things which statisticians seek to measure are called variables. They can be discrete (increasing or decreasing in whole units, like a bitch giving birth to 2, 3 or 4 puppies) or they may be continuous (like a record breaker running 37.256 kilometres).
7   Before beginning a statistical inquiry we need a clear definition of the nature of the enquiry, we need to define its terms (what do we mean by households, large firms, disabled persons, etc.), and finally we need to set out the chosen methods of study in some detail.
8   If we are to study the problem by sampling, we must choose the sample type; random sampling, quota sampling, multi-stage sampling, cluster sampling, systematic sampling or stratified sampling.

9 Figures must usually be approximated (since the full figures are usually too unwieldy). When approximating figures, it is possible for errors to creep in. The difference between the real figure and the corrected version is called the absolute error, but the relative error may be more important, i.e. how significant is the error introduced relative to the total size of the figure given. When approximated figures are added, subtracted, multiplied or divided, the errors are enlarged, and great care must be taken to avoid wrong impressions about accuracy.

2
More about the collection of data

2.1 Sources of data

A prerequisite to any statistical enquiry is a clear statement of its purpose and objectives, because this will determine the type of data we require to collect and its sources, which may be primary or secondary. Primary data are statistics collected by the investigators themselves or by businesses within their own organizations, e.g. monthly sales figure, stock records, vehicle usage records, market research data, company accounts, etc. Secondary data are statistics collected by others outside the organization and usually for some other purpose, e.g. trade statistics from trade magazines, home and foreign government publications, other companies' published accounts, tax records, etc. Let us compare and contrast these sources.

Primary data: advantages

1 This data should be accurate, because we have collected it ourselves and its accuracy can be checked if necessary.
2 It should be relevant to the investigation, since we know exactly how it was collected.
3 It will use our own terms of reference and units of measurement, which have been clearly defined.

Primary data: disadvantages

1 It may be expensive to obtain and therefore not cost-effective.
2 It may take some time to collect and therefore may be out-of-date or too late for the investigation in hand.

Secondary data: advantages

1 It may be the only source available to us, e.g. many employment and trade statistics are only collected by and published by Government departments.

2 It can often be obtained easily and quickly.
3 It may be cheaper than collecting our own information.
4 It may be useful as a check on the accuracy of our own collected data.

Secondary data: disadvantages

1 It may have been collected for some purpose which is not entirely relevant to our own investigation.
2 It may not be up-to-date.
3 The accuracy of the data may be suspect, but we shall not be able to check it in any way.
4 Units of measurement and terms of reference may not have been clearly defined.

Let us take a specific example. Suppose we are manufacturers concerned with the profitability of the various lines we and our main competitors produce. Our own cost figures, **primary** data, will be readily available, and if the accuracy of some item is suspect, it can be carefully checked. However, we will be dependent on **secondary** data, such as trade journals and our competitors' own disclosures, in order to obtain information about their cost structure. This cannot be checked, and may be based upon different units of measurement or terms of reference. In addition, we may well be forced to turn to that major source of secondary data, Government statistical publications, for some supplementary information to back up other results. Although a fruitful source, Government statistics must be treated with some caution because they are dependent to a large extent on the conscientious form-filling activities of diverse people in many organizations. Completing a form can take some time and therefore be costly, often boring and consequently haphazardly done, compiled by junior staff with a limited knowledge of the terms used and the purpose for which the data is sought. Nevertheless, providing that these limitations are borne in mind, Government statistics can be useful in indicating patterns and trends against which other data can be assessed and developed.

2.2 To sample or not to sample?

In any investigation we can either collect all the relevant data, called the **population** or **universe**, or some part of the data, called the **sample**. For example, if we record for each machine in a factory the daily output for a month, then we have the population data, but if we only record the information for a few of the machines, we have sample data. In general, conclusions based on all the data (the population) will be more reliable than those based on a sample, and yet we usually use samples.

The reasons are:

1   They are much cheaper.
2   The results are obtained quickly.
3   It may be the only method available because the population may be unknown, e.g. there will be no complete list of the purchasers of a particular brand of soap powder.
4   It may be the only practical method, e.g. one could test the specification that a lamp bulb has a life of 1 000 hours by burning each one for that length of time but clearly one would never have a product fit for sale.

A sample will only be useful if it can be shown that sample results fulfil their purpose of being good predictors of population results. For example, a count of the number of vehicles using a car park during a 7-day period will only be of use if the week chosen was representative of the normal situation. An opinion poll, which is usually a sample, will only be of value if its results fairly reflect the results which would have been obtained by asking everyone. **The sample must be representative of the population from which it has been chosen so that the information collected from the sample will also be representative of the population.**

2.3   Sampling methods

In attempting to provide a representative sample there are two problems to consider: first, how to obtain an unbiased selection procedure so that each member of a population will have the same chance of being chosen and, second, how to obtain a representative selection so that conclusions based on sample results can be applied to the population as a whole. Random sampling will supply the unbiased selection procedure but not necessarily the representative sample. In fact we cannot be certain that the sample we have chosen is representative, and therefore our conclusions must reflect this uncertainty and be given the terms of probability. Sometimes random sampling is called probability sampling, and it can be subdivided into three types.

Simple random sampling

A sample can be said to have been chosen in a random manner if every member of the population has an equal chance of being picked. To make sure that such equality of opportunity exists may not be as simple as it may appear at first sight, but there are two basic procedures.

Each member of the population is represented by a number written on a piece of paper, the papers are placed in a container, well mixed and one paper drawn. This process is repeated, taking care to mix thoroughly after each selection, until the required numbers for the sample are obtained. Unfortunately, this method takes time and is awkward to operate, particularly when a large size sample is required. To overcome these difficulties random numbers are used.

Some calculators and most computers will have a random number generating function available to them, but if not, random number tables can be used. Such a table is shown in Table 2.1. It consists of double figure numbers in columns and rows. Although the columns and rows have been numbered in the illustration this would not be done in a real table, and they have only been included here for explanatory purposes. Read the notes below the table now.

Table 2.1 Random number table

Rows \ Columns	1 2	3 4	5 6	7 8	9 10	11 12	13 14
1	57	07	28	69	65	95	38
2	69	47	76	34	32	48	14
3	11	34	27	78	72	35	94
4	29	76	14	05	48	47	85
5	85	62	66	87	45	25	54
6	48	24	84	56	15	74	07
		etc., etc.					

Notes

1 Suppose our company has 800 customers and we wish to contact a sample of 50 customers chosen at random. Each customer is given a reference number of 1 to 800.
2 Using the table, we pick a column number (using random selection by drawing from a hat containing pieces of paper numbered 1–14).
3 As there are three digits in the number 800, we shall need to use three columns, so if our starting point results in the fourth column being the starting column, our first number selected will be from columns 4, 5 and 6.
4 We now need a starting row. Our illustration shows only six rows but there would in fact be more than six. Selecting a starting row by random methods we might arrive at the third row as the starting point.
5 Our chosen sample will therefore start at column 4 in row 3. The first customer is therefore 427 (using the figures in columns 4, 5 and 6). Continuing by reading down the columns gives us 614 as the second customer's number, 266 as the next, 484 the next, and so on.
6 Any number greater than 800 will be ignored, as will be any repetition of a number, since we obviously could not ask the same customer twice.

Both simple random sampling and random number table sampling avoid bias in the selection process and both are independent of human judgement. This will provide the necessary conditions for the application of probability statements to sample results. Unfortunately random sampling is time-consuming and expensive to operate, and consequently it may be an advantage to use a second type of sampling.

Systematic sampling

In this method, sometimes known as quasi-random sampling, the starting point is chosen at random, with each subsequent sample member set at some predetermined interval. Let us look at the procedure to be followed in order to obtain a sample of 50 out of 800 customers, as in our previous example:

1   Divide the population number by the sample number i.e. $\dfrac{800}{50} = 16$.

2   Choose at random some number from 1 to 16 (say 12) which will give us the first sample number.

3   The remaining sample numbers will be obtained by adding 16 to the previous sample number.

Therefore the first sample number will be 12, the second will be $12 + 16 = 28$, the third $28 + 16 = 44$ and so on. This procedure is easy and convenient, and in some cases is an improvement over simple random sampling because the sample is spread evenly throughout the whole population. Even so, systematic sampling does not completely satisfy our definition of a random sample, because it does not give every member of the population an equal chance of selection. Nevertheless, a systematic sample can be treated as if it were a random sample, providing that the population list is in a random order or in some order which is unrelated to the subject under investigation. For example, an inspection of every sixteenth car manufactured in a factory with eight assembly lines could not be considered random because every car examined would come from the same production line. It would be preferable to examine every fifteenth car or cars chosen completely at random.

Is the sample representative of the population?

So far we have discussed procedures in simple random sampling and in systematic sampling which will give us an unbiased selection of sample members, but this will not necessarily give us a representative sample. It will do so if the population is homogeneous (made up of similar units) but not if it is heterogeneous. For instance, are car drivers homogeneous or heterogenous as a group? Clearly the term car driver is homogeneous, but within the car-driving fraternity there will be many subdivisions, such as age, experience, type of car driven, etc. and in that sense they will be heterogeneous. If our investigation is such that the various subdivisions must be represented in our sample, then we will have to take steps to ensure that this happens. This can be achieved if we use the next method.

Stratified sampling

This method aims to link a knowledge of the population to the principle of random selection in order to increase the precision and representativeness of the sample. The population is divided up into its various elements (strata) according to the nature of the investigation, and a random sample is chosen from each strata according to its size in relation to the total population. Care must be taken to see that, in dividing up the population into these subpopulations, no bias is introduced.

A simple example will make the procedure clear. Suppose we wish to investigate the response of our labour force to a proposed change in working conditions, and we decide to use a satatified sample based on age. The groups might be as follows: under 20 years, 20 to under 30 years, 30 to under 40 years, 40 to under 50 years, 50 to under 60 years, 60 years and over. If the total labour force is 5 000 and there are 100 workers under 20 years, this will give a fraction of $\frac{1}{50}$ i.e. 2 per cent for this age group. Consequently 2 per cent of the sample will also be chosen from this group, using one of the random selection procedures already discussed – and similarly for all age groups until the total sample is obtained.

Of course the stratification can be taken further in that these age groupings could be subdivided into male and female, skilled or unskilled, factory or office staff, and so on. The increasing complexity of the strata will also tend to increase the need for human judgement, thereby providing the means for introducing bias into the results. Even in the simple case outlined above it might be argued that there is not much homogeneity in an age group of 10 years, and that it ought to be 5 years, or maybe 3, or less. Someone has to decide, and that decision could mean biased results.

Other sampling methods

The theory of sampling is largely dependent on random selection, but there are times when schemes which only use part-random selection procedures have to be considered. These occasions arise, firstly, because random sampling is, in the main, very costly and may be prohibitive for many investigations; secondly, there may not be a suitable, comprehensive list of the population from which to take a random selection; or thirdly, it may be considered that the sample is unlikely to give a true representation of the population. Estimates based on these other sampling designs are generally not as reliable as estimates based on random samples of a similar size, *but when costs are taken into account, they may be more reliable per unit of cost* – a factor of great importance to market and opinion researchers.

1   *Cluster sampling*   Let us suppose that we wish to choose a sample of 1 000 from the adult population of Great Britain. A complete (very nearly) list of this population is available and so we could extract a random sample from it. From a theoretical point of view, this may be ideal, but in practice the cost and difficulty of contacting such a sample spread thinly over the whole country would be enormous. It is more likely that we would attempt to limit costs and difficulties by restricting the area or areas in which we would make the survey. For instance, four preliminary constituencies could be chosen at random or as representatiives of the whole country, and from them a randomly selected sample of 1 000 could be taken.

This would be an example of cluster sampling by area. But any criteria could be used to define the cluster, provided that it was appropriate to the investigation.

2   *Multi-stage sampling*   This is a development of the previous method, in that clusters are taken, not at one stage only, but at several stages. Continuing the previous example, from the cluster of four constituencies a random sample of five polling districts might be taken, and from them the 1 000 members of the sample drawn by means of some selection process. This would be a two-stage sampling design, but three, four, or more stages could be utilized in order to minimize costs and other difficulties. For example, it is easier to question members from a few polling districts than from a whole constituency, but it is even easier to question people from a single street within each polling district, so long as the street has been chosen randomly, and is likely to be representative of the whole district.

3   *Quota sampling*   This method differs fundamentally from all others in that personal judgement enters into many aspects of the work, and, in particular, into the actual choice ot the sample members. In all previous designs the final selection is made at random, but in quota sampling it is left to the interviewer to make the choice from among previously designated members of the population. For example, if the quota is thirty interviews, the interviewer might be instructed to include fifteen men and fifteen women, in a specified age group, from named social classes, in particular occupations. Within the constraints imposed, the interviewer will be free to make his/her own selections, and obviously his/her personal preferences will play a large part in the choice. There is considerable scope for disagreement in the interpretation of social classes and job groupings, and although attempts have been made to define them in objective

terms, a great deal will depend on the integrity, skill and background of the interviewer if a representative sample is to be obtained.

2.4 The sampling frame

No matter which sampling system is chosen, it will be necessary to have a complete (if possible) list of the population from which the sample is to be taken. Such a list is known as the **sample frame**. If a large company wishes to ascertain the reaction of its employees to a proposal to introduce a profit-sharing scheme, it may well decide to use a sample survey. The list of all its employees would be the sample frame.

Any sample frame must be chosen with great care, because of its influence on the validity of the sample results. Some of the factors which must be taken into account when selecting the frame are:

1 It must be adequate for the purpose of the investigation.
2 It must be complete.
3 There must be no duplication.
4 It must be up-to-date.
5 It must be accurate.

The main national sampling frame is the Register of Electors which is compiled each October and published in the following year. Investigations into its accuracy and completeness have on the whole been reassuring, but of course the register is already about 4 months out of date at the time of publication, and this will extend to 16 months before its replacement. People will have died, or moved in, or moved away, during this time.

2.5 Methods of data collection

It does not matter whether we are using a sample or the population in a statistical investigation the actual collection of the data must be carefully planned and organized. The three chief methods of data collection are observation; the use of forms (often called 'returns' because they have to be returned to head office by stated dates so that control can be exercised over branches and depots if the figures given are unsatisfactory in any way); and questionaires, which may be used as a basis for conducting an interview or as a means of obtaining responses to a postal enquiry.

Each of these methods needs detailed examination.

Observation

Observation has been the traditional method of obtaining and recording data, but as the complexity and size of investigations have increased, so has the difficulty of using observation methods. Even with fairly small surveys the task of getting objective information has become a problem. The mere sight of a pencil and form is usually enough to inhibit a continuous natural response by the subject under scrutiny,

Traffic census   Christchurch Estate
                                                      Bournemouth –
                                                      Christchurch Road

Date _____   Time: 8 a.m.–9 a.m.

(Cars and vans)	(Heavy goods vehicles)
ﬀﬀ ﬀﬀ ﬀﬀ ﬀﬀ ﬀﬀ ﬀﬀ ﬀﬀ ﬀﬀ ﬀﬀ ﬀﬀ ﬀﬀ ﬀﬀ III (63)	ﬀﬀ ﬀﬀ ﬀﬀ ﬀﬀ ﬀﬀ ﬀﬀ ﬀﬀ ﬀﬀ ﬀﬀ ﬀﬀ ﬀﬀ (55)

(Buses and coaches)	(Motorcycles)	(Cycles)
ﬀﬀ ﬀﬀ (10)	ﬀﬀ ﬀﬀ ﬀﬀ ﬀﬀ ﬀﬀ ﬀﬀ ﬀﬀ ﬀﬀ ﬀﬀ ﬀﬀ ﬀﬀ III (58)	ﬀﬀ ﬀﬀ ﬀﬀ ﬀﬀ II (22)

Figure 2.1   A traffic census

Notes:
1   The precise purpose of the inquiry is to find out exactly what traffic uses the road through the estate. Residents complain about the volume of heavy goods traffic and the public service through-traffic run by tour operators and excursion organizers. Is there real cause for complaint, or not?
2   We decide to define heavy goods vehicles as 'large goods vehicles carrying containers, or enclosed vehicles such as removal vans or large distribution vans destined for depots and warehouses'. Small vans and hire-drive vans, caravanettes, etc., will all be treated as 'cars and vans'. Buses and coaches are to be recorded as such only if they have thirteen seats or more. Minibuses with twelve seats only are to be classed as 'cars and vans'. The term 'motorcycles' includes scooters and mopeds.
3   It seems best to conduct the survey over a full working day, from 6 a.m. to midnight. An hour at a time is considered enough for a stint as 'census-taker'. A rota is prepared to cover each census period, and staff are trained to use the 'five-barred gate' system.

whether it be the worker under the eye of the time and motion engineer, the learner driver and the examiner, or the family and the social researcher.

On the other hand, direct observation eliminates the necessity of relying on someone's memory and on information embellished by vanity, prejudice and exaggeration. It will give a first-hand picture of the situation which should be accurate if the view is totally objective (viewed from the viewpoint of a disinterested outsider) and not solely in the eye of the beholder.

A simple example of observation is a **traffic census**, where observers placed at strategic points record traffic movements along a particular road. The term **census** is used when the entire population of an enquiry is recorded. In a traffic census every vehicle passing the observation point will be included in the data collected. An advantage of this type of census is that it will report upon and reflect the true traffic situation, since vehicles cannot alter their pattern of behaviour when they discover they are being observed. Figure 2.1 shows the use of the five-barred-gate method of recording. The first four vehicles of a particular type are recorded by a vertical line, and the fifth vehicle is recorded as a diagonal line to make a five-barred gate. This system makes for easy counting. At the end of the observation period (in this case 1 hour) the totals can be inserted, and later collated with the observations made for the rest of the day.

There are many situations when direct observation is either too costly in relation to the probable returns or not practical, and in such cases we must look to alternative methods – usually forms for eliciting the information on a regular basis, or the use of questionnaires in a one-off inquiry.

Collecting data by means of forms

Today a great deal of routine data is generated by computer, so that the term 'form' has to be taken to cover 'printouts' of data generated in this way. Practically all businesses and organizations such as local and central government bodies require regular records of such matters as sales, returns, output figures, attendances at schools and colleges, expenditures incurred against budgets, credit granted to customers, etc. If these statistics can be obtained by capturing data as events occur – for example EFTPOS (Electronic Funds Transfer at the Point Of Sale) transactions in retail trade or library issues on computerized library programs – it is obviously desirable and effortless (once the programs have been written and validated). Management can call for a printout at any time, or, more likely, at known regular intervals.

Where computerization is not in use, the same information can be provided more laboriously by the design of a good form which has to be completed by the responsible official and returned to Head Office or some similar control point on a regular basis. Daily reports, weekly returns or monthly returns may be called for and the data will then be reviewed so that remedial action can be taken, e.g. a congratulatory letter or a 'rocket' from Head Office, or a visit by the area manager to sort out a problem. A Chief Education Officer may need to implement official policies by closing evening classes which fail to meet attendance criteria laid down by the education authority, though there will usually be 'discretion within a policy' which he/she can exercise. Figure 2.2 shows a typical return, showing classes of three types, A, B and C, with different criteria. Study Figure 2.2 and the notes below it and decide which classes are due for closure.

The design of forms is closely related to the design of questionnaires, which is discussed fully in the next section.

Questionnaires

A questionnaire is a systematic series of questions designed to elucidate from a respondent information which will throw light upon the subject under investigation, whatever it may be. Although there are no scientific principles to guide us in the design of a questionnaire, certain points should be taken into consideration so that we can obtain accurate data and a satisfactory response rate:

1 The purpose of the inquiry should be clearly stated at the head of the form, together with the name of the body conducting it.
2 There should be the minimum number of questions consistent with attaining the objective of the investigation.
3 The layout should be as attractive as possible.
4 The design should make it easy for the respondent to answer.
5 The questions should follow each other in a logical fashion.
6 The respondent should not be required to identify himself/herself on the form unless absolutely necessary. This will help to create a situation within which questions can be honestly answered and opinions freely given.
7 The layout should take into account the analytical procedure to be used.
8 If the completion of the questionnaire is a statutory duty, this should be made clear, and the penalty for non-compliance should be stated.
9 If the completion is not compulsory, it may be advisable to offer some incentive to the respondent. This could take the form of a cash reward, a voucher, a sample of a product, or the chance to compete in a draw.

Centre: Thriving adult centre   **Month:** March 19. .

Course	Type	Week 1	Week 2	Week 3	Week 4	Week 5
				*Attendances*		
A-level law	A	17	16	13	16	16
Export incentives	A	19	17	16	13	12
Accountancy	A	23	21	14	24	19
Secretarial studies	B	42	41	24	23	28
Keyboard skills	B	18	17	12	16	17
Computer studies	B	28	24	19	24	26
Book-keeping	B	23	16	14	13	12
How to run a small business	B	27	23	17	22	21
French	B	19	18	15	18	17
Italian	B	22	17	8	11	9
Fencing	C	23	24	9	16	7
Ladies' keep fit	C	32	30	16	19	28
Basketball	C	22	21	16	24	23
Swimming	C	39	33	16	27	26

Figure 2.2   Educational returns from the Thriving Adult Centre

Notes:
1   Type A classes are high-quality educational classes at an advanced level which require a minimum of ten students only.
   Type B classes are lower level courses with a minimum attendance of fifteen students (since there are always more students on lower level courses).
   Type C classes are recreational classes where the minimum is twenty students.
   Classes which fall below the minimum on 3 consecutive weeks are to be closed unless discretion can be exercised (usually because of bad weather, transport disruption or some similar external influence).
2   What is the position with the following classes?

   (a) A-level law
   (b) Keyboard skills
   (c) Book-keeping
   (d) Italian
   (e) Fencing
   (f) Ladies' keep fit

3   What can you say about the attendance in Week 3?

With regard to the wording of the actual questions, the following criteria will be found appropriate:

(*a*)   Questions should be concise and unambiguous.
(*b*)   They should be capable of being answered either Yes/No or by ringing or ticking a set of predetermined answers, e.g. excellent, good, fair, poor, very bad.
(*c*)   They should not be framed in such a manner that they indicate the answer required (this will introduce bias).
(*d*)   They should not contain provocative words.

These general guidelines must be considered against the background of the particular investigation, and the actual design of the questionnaire will be primarily dictated by it. Suppose we have been instructed to find out details of traffic movements and parking requirements in a local town. We might design a questionnaire as shown in Figure 2.3.

Such a questionnaire may be presented to all vehicle drivers or riders on a given day, or at selected hours of a given day, according to the size of the sample required. Clearly the choice of such a sample could take many factors into account, e.g. the chosen day may be unrepresentative because of abnormal weather conditions. Whatever the sample decided upon, the questionnaire must now be presented to our chosen sample for completion. There are two main methods employed: (*a*) personal interviews, and (*b*) postal inquiries.

First we must consider **pilot surveys**.

Pilot surveys

It is useful to carry out a small-scale trial run of the investigation before the survey proper. This pilot survey can provide information on:

1   The effectiveness of the questionnaire.
2   The adequacy of the sampling frame.
3   The costs of the survey.
4   The percentage of replies which can be expected.
5   In addition, it can test both the method used to collect the data and its subsequent analysis.

The pilot survey can also provide a means of training staff who are to be used in the full enquiry. For example, if the questionnaire is to be filled in by an interviewer, the pilot survey gives prospective interviewers a chance to encounter the problems that will be met, and to discuss them with the investigator. This may lead to the refining of definitions that have proved inadequate, as where certain respondents could not be classified in any of the ways suggested – we might need an extra category (other types) to be added to our questionnaire.

Town Centre Motorized Traffic Enquiry
Howard District Council

The Council is investigating traffic problems in the Town Centre area, since it wishes to improve conditions for shoppers, workers and business people, both pedestrians and drivers. Your help is needed. Please complete this form and hand it in at any Council office, or at a car park. It may also be given to any Traffic Warden.

1 Where did you start this journey?

Home ☐   Factory ☐   Office ☐   Other ☐

Address: Street ....
               Town ....

2 Give your destination:

Home ☐   Factory ☐   Office ☐   Other ☐

Address: Street ....
               Town ....

3 What is the main purpose of your visit to the town centre?

Shopping	☐	Delivery of goods	☐
Leisure	☐	Business call	☐
Passing through	☐	Other	☐

4 When did you start this journey?   ☐ a.m.   ☐ p.m.

5 When will you finish this journey?   ☐ a.m.   ☐ p.m.

6 How many people were in or on your vehicle when you received this form?

1 ☐   2 ☐   3 ☐   4 ☐   5 or more ☐

7 What type of vehicle were you driving (or riding)?

Car ☐   Light commercial ☐   Heavy commercial ☐   Other ☐

8 Where did you park your vehicle in the town centre?

1	Market CP	☐	5	Multi-storey CP	☐
2	College CP	☐	6	Parking Meter	☐
3	Wye CP	☐	7	Private	☐
4	Bull Ring CP	☐	8	Not applicable	☐

9 If you could effect **one** improvement in the Town Centre traffic arrangements, what would it be? ....
....
....

10 If you wish to give your name you may do so here, with your home address if not already given above.

Name .... Address ....
.... Post Code ....

Thank you for your cooperation.

Figure 2.3   A questionnaire about town-centre problems

Personal interviews

The most favoured method of using a questionnaire is for some specially trained person to present it to the respondent in a face-to-face interview. There are certain advantages in doing it this way:

1 There is usually a high response rate.
2 Any queries about the questionnaire can be answered at once by the interviewer, so that mistaken responses are avoided.
3 The interviewer is able to probe further into answers given, if necessary, and form some opinion of the accuracy of the information provided.
4 A less formal type of questionnaire can be used, in that the interviewer is given certain key points around which to build the interview.

Unfortunately this procedure is fairly costly and raises a major problem of interviewer bias. This arises because the mere presence of an interviewer will almost inevitably have some effect on the respondents, and their replies may, as a consequence, adversely affect the validity of the survey. For example, the interviewer may lay stress on a particular word or phrase which may alter the meaning of the question. Well meaning attempts to clarify answers given may lead to a wrong interpretation of the answer and merely reflect the interviewer's own ideas. However, the major area for abuse lies in the actual choice by the interviewer of the person to be interviewed. Details of the sample to be selected may have been given, but the interviewer may be tempted to make substitutions because the original member may be difficult to contact or not easy to interview.

One recent area of development has been in the use of interviews conducted by telephone. It has many of the advantages of the face-to-face interview, as well as being considerably less expensive, but has some additional limitations. Not everyone is on the telephone, many will be suspicious of telephone inquiries, it is very easy to refuse or terminate the interview by replacing the telephone, and there will be inevitably some time restriction on the length of the interview.

Postal questionnaires

The second main method employed is to send out questionnaires through the post. The main benefits of using this procedure are:

1 It may be cheaper, particularly when using random samples.
2 It may be quicker.
3 It may bring forth a more accurate response to questions of a personal nature.

4   It will give time for a considered reply.
5   It avoids any possibility of influence by the interviewer.

The first three advantages must be qualified, because the opposite may well apply in some circumstances. For example, if very few returns are received so that no valid results are obtained, the postal method has been expensive, no matter what the cost. It could be that there is a considerable lapse of time between the despatch and the return of the questionnaire, and this time lag would also permit the deliberate presentation of a biased answer. But two rather more specific drawbacks can be highlighted:

(*a*)   The percentage of returns, i.e. **the response rate**, is usually very low and often biased,
(*b*)   It is difficult to conduct any investigation in depth.

It is the problem of non-response which constitutes the main difficulty in mail surveys. If the respondents are well educated and/or highly motivated, then a good response rate might be expected, but in the main it is vary rare to have anything approaching a satisfactory response. For instance, a questionnaire sent through the post to residents of a particular area could well elicit a high response rate if it was about local finance, but a low response if it was about national economic problems. It would not be too much of a problem if those who did bother to reply were representative of the population, but it is more likely that they will form a biased minority, e.g. a survey amongst car owners about a particular make of vehicle will probably produce a very high response from dissatisfied customers but a lesser response from satisfied ones.

One way of increasing the response rate is to offer a good incentive to encourage the return of questionnaires.

2.6   More about errors and approximations

Something has already been said (see Section 1.8) about errors and approximations, but it cannot be over-emphasized how important it is to collect accurate and relevant data so that any conclusions drawn will be valid and not misleading. Statistical error can arise either through the method employed to collect the data or in the actual recording of it.

Errors caused by the survey method employed

These can be listed as follows:

1   The purpose and scope of any investigation must be clearly stated so that only relevant information will be obtained. Other data must

be disregarded, otherwise it may lead to error in the presentation of results.

2   Most statistical investigations use samples, and any predictions we make about the population from which the samples are drawn may be in error to some extent unless the samples are completely representative. We usually cannot be absolutely sure of this representativeness, but we are able to estimate sampling errors and present them in probability terms, provided a random sample has been used.

3   Error may be introduced by the interviewer, who may be guilty of not complying with the sample selection profile as regards age, occupation, sex, etc. Substitution of the suggested interviewee by some more accessible respondent will lead to bias and error.

4   Another possible source of error could be in the design of the questionnaire. Questions may be ambiguous, provocative and indicate the answer required.

Errors in recording data

These may occur in the following circumstances:

1   During the recording of observations.
2   In copying data from other documents.
3   Incorrect recording of answers given by the respondent to the interviewer.
4   Respondents giving inaccurate information or approximate data. Suppose you were asked to give your age, you may well reply 18 or 20 or whatever, depending on your particular age, but this is unlikely to be your correct age. In exact terms you may be, say, 18 years 3 months 2 weeks 4 days 10 hours etc., and your reply was therefore only approximate.

Approximations

The reason why you only gave your approximate age was probably based on your estimation of the degree of accuracy required for that question, and on the amount of time you were prepared to spend in order to give an accurate answer. Therefore some questions by their very nature will only bring forth an approximate reply, and consequently some error will be present.

In fact there are many situations in which it is a positive disadvantage to present a precise set of data. The managing director of a large company could be sent the information about sales in the company shown in Table 2.2.

Table 2.2   Monthly sales

Product	January	February	March	April
SOAKIT	1 440 420	1 421 243	1 521 196	1 533 247
WASHIT	930 129	910 683	963 964	966 021
RINSIT	763 293	663 429	821 186	802 433
SPINIT	1 102 639	1 097 723	1 015 769	1 106 224
DRYIT	1 189 221	1 142 375	1 203 522	1 263 576
AIRIT	876 242	893 349	862 467	879 765
IRONIT	1 568 892	1 682 129	1 829 561	1 976 621

On the other hand, the data could be rounded to the nearest thousand and presented as in Table 2.3.

Table 2.3   Monthly sales (to the nearest 000)

Product	January	February	March	April
SOAKIT	1 440	1 421	1 521	1 533
WASHIT	930	911	964	966
RINSIT	763	663	821	802
SPINIT	1 103	1 098	1 016	1 106
DRYIT	1 189	1 142	1 204	1 264
AIRIT	876	893	862	880
IRONIT	1 569	1 682	1 830	1 977

The second table is superior to the first, because it is much easier to comprehend, takes much less time to read, indicates the important points more clearly, and is accurate enough for most purposes.

The rounding of data implies the adjusting of the original data to some degree and for some purpose. Frequently numbers are rounded to a certain number of **decimal places**, e.g. 16.636 rounded to two decimal places is 16.64 because 16.636 is nearer to 16.64 than to 16.63. Similary, if rounded to one decimal place, it is 16.6 and if rounded to the nearest whole number it is 17. There is some problem with 16.635 because it is equidistant from 16.64 and 16.63, but in practice you can either round up or down, unless there are many numbers of this type. In these circumstances it is advisable to employ some method which will alternate the rounding so that the cumulative rounding error is minimized, e.g. always round so that the digit preceding the 5 is even, i.e. 16.365 is rounded up to 16.36, 16.345 becomes 16.34, being rounded down to the even number, and so on.

Some of the measurements we obtain will depend for their precision on the accuracy of the measuring instrument available. If we use a device which measures the depth of tread of a tyre to the nearest millimetre, a reading of 3mm indicates that the true depth is somewhere between 3.5mm and 2.5mm.

Sometimes the degree of accuracy of data is shown by the use of significant figures, e.g. the value of 162.736 will be 162.74 rounded to five significant figures; 162.7 to four significant figures; 163 to three significant figures; 160 to two significant figures and 200 to one significant figure. Consequently, there will be some error in approximating data. In Chapter 1 reference was made to absolute and relative errors. Recapitulating these we may say:

1   *Absolute error*   This is the difference between the true value and the rounded figure, e.g. actual sales of SOAKIT in January were 1 440 420. Approximated sales to the nearest '000 were 1 440. The absolute error will therefore to be $1\,440\,420 - 1\,440\,000 = 420$.

2   *Relative error*   Error values given in absolute terms are of limited use. If you had made an error of £5 in totalling some receipts, it would be relatively unimportant if the total was in hundreds of thousands of pounds, but very important if the total was £9. Relative error is the absolute error expressed as a ratio of the true value. In this case it is $\frac{420}{1440420}$ or $\frac{7}{24007}$ or an error of 0.0002919 of the true value. Clearly this is a small error.

3   *Percentage error*   The relative error may be expressed as a fraction or a decimal but both forms are rather cumbersome. The error amount becomes more meaningful if given in percentage terms, as follows:

$$\text{Percentage eror} = \frac{7}{24\,007} \times \frac{100}{1} = 0.03\,\%$$

If there are a number of rounded figures to be totalled, the errors tend to cancel out one another, i.e. compensating errors, but sometimes the absolute error lies in one particular direction. For example, people underestimate their consumption of cigarettes and alcohol, and overestimate their expenditure on food. Such an error is known as a biased or systematic error.

2.7   Questions on Chapter 2

1   What are primary data? What are the advantages of this type of data? Are there any disadvantages?

2   Statistics collected by the Inland Revenue for tax purposes are often used for other purposes by investigators studying various

aspects of the economy. What criticisms could you make of this practice?

3   You are investigating sinistrality (left-handedness) in industrial workers. Would you investigate the population or a sample? What would be the chief problems in such an investigation?

4   Write short explanations (5–8 lines) of each of the following:

   (*a*)   population
   (*b*)   sample
   (*c*)   random selection
   (*d*)   observation
   (*e*)   census
   (*f*)   questionnaire

5   Why do statisticians believe in random sampling? How may a random sample be selected? When we have a random sample, will it necessarily be representative of the population under investigation?

6   Write short notes (15–20 lines) on (*a*) multi-stage sampling and (*b*) quota sampling.

7   Draw up a list of points to be borne in mind when designing a questionnaire.

8   A manufacturer proposes to conduct a survey into the demand for a new product – a perfume in the higher price bracket. The present proposal is to market it in a gift pack to men for presentation by each to the lady of his choice. Draw up a list of the points that might be worth enquiring about, (*a*) in an enquiry directed at men, (*b*) in an enquiry directed at the female recipients. Design the questionnaire for either (*a*) or (*b*).

9   'Opinion polls are inaccurate and therefore misleading.' Discuss this statement, illustrating your answer with examples.

10   A company plans a move from the South of England to a new location in the Midlands. The company considers that it is important to take as many of its existing staff as possible should the move take place. You have been asked to find out the reactions of the staff to the move – how many are prepared to go, what demand will there be for housing, schools, etc. (*a*) How could you conduct the survey? (*b*) Design an appropriate questionnaire for use in this survey.

11   In response to the government's desire to widen share ownership, a company wishes to introduce an employee share bonus scheme. The company wishes to know the reactions of the staff to the idea, and to this end you have been asked to conduct a sample survey among the 2 300 staff employed.

   (*a*)   Indicate the type of sample design you would use, giving reasons for your choice.
   (*b*)   Design an appropriate questionnaire.

(c)   Briefly describe how you would conduct the survey.
12   What qualities are required by an interviewer who has to take respondents through a fairly lengthy series of questions in a questionnaire?

2.8   Summary of Chapter 2

1   Primary data are data collected within an organization, or by the investigators for a particular enquiry. Such data tend to be more relevant and more accurate than secondary data collected by outsiders, often for some quite different purpose. On the other hand, primary data can be more expensive and time-consuming.
2   The difficulty with secondary data is that the figures have usually been collected for some quite different purpose, using terms and units of measurement which may be inappropriate for our enquiry. Many official statistics are collected by the completion of forms circulated by the department concerned, and conscientious attention to the accuracy of replies may not always be paid by the respondents.
3   Although data collected from the complete population under investigation gives the most accurate information, we generally have to use a representative sample, because the cost and effort of surveying the whole population would be prohibitive.
4   A sample should be a random sample, which means that every member of the population has an equal chance of being selected. However, a random sample may not necessarily be representative of the whole population (it could be that too many similar individuals turn up in the random sample). The essential feature of a sample is that it should be a good predictor of the results that would have been achieved from a survey of the whole population.
5   Two methods of random sampling are simple random sampling (drawing from a hat or from a random number table) and systematic sampling (where we choose a starting point by random selection and then take our selected items by a predetermined interval from that point – say ever fiftieth item).
6   We can frequently secure a representative sample by stratified sampling.
7   Costs can be reduced by using cluster sampling, multi-stage sampling and quota sampling.
8   The chief methods of collecting data are (a) observation, (b) the completion of forms which constitute a record of relevant data, as with sales figures, output figures, attendance records, examination grades, etc., (c) the completion of a questionnaire by a skilled interviewer, and (d) the completion of a postal questionnaire on a compulsory or voluntary basis.

9 Rules for designing a questionnaire include the following: (*a*) state the purpose of the enquiry, (*b*) notify the respondent of the penalty for failure to complete it if it is a compulsory questionnaire, (*c*) develop the questions in logical sequence, (*d*) make each question simple and easy to answer with a 'yes' or a 'no' or a choice from a range of answers, (*e*) design the questionnaire in such a way that it is easy to mark and record the results, (*f*) keep it as brief as possible, consistent with the objectives of the enquiry, and (*g*) make sure questions do not indicate what the answer should be, and are not provocative.

10 A pilot survey is useful to (*a*) test out the questionnaire, (*b*) train interviewers and investigators (*c*) discover the likely response rate, (*d*) discover the likely cost of the full inquiry, and (*e*) test out the analytical processes to be used in the full enquiry.

11 The advantages of using interviewers to complete questionnaires with chosen respondents are that the response rate is high, the chance of misunderstanding is reduced because the interviewer can clarify any points that are not understood, an interviewer soon gets to know the form and the chances of error are reduced, and the interviewer can usually jolly the respondent along to answer a rather longer list of questions that would otherwise be possible. The disadvantages are that the interviewer may introduce bias either accidentally or deliberately, and, if the choice is left to the interviewer, he/she may select inappropriate people for interview, e.g. a set of cronies in the local public bar.

3
Presentation of data: tables

3.1 Making sense of raw data

The collection of statistics can be justified by the need to produce a clear picture of some activity. That clear picture, it is hoped, will be given by the figures amassed about it. For example, it is difficult to make any accurate pronouncement about the fishing industry until we have collected some data about the catches made from various ports.

Suppose that figures were collected every day for every boat, from every port involved in fishing. There would soon be so many sheets of statistics, that, rather than clarify the situation, they would further confuse it. This is certainly a problem with most statistical enquiries – the raw data in their unprocessed form are too bulky to do anything but create confusion. An attempt therefore has to be made to arrange the figures collected in such a fashion that they yield up the information they contain more easily, and the figures are in a more suitable form for further processing.

This processing might involve the extraction from the data of certain **derived statistics**: averages, percentages, etc. With the advent of computers a whole range of data processing can take place once the raw data have been assembled into some manageable form. This chapter deals with the ways in which some clarification can be brought to a mass of figures. There are two problems:

1   To reduce the amount of detail.
2   To bring the data into a form where significant features stand out prominently.

The first problem is solved by classifying the data into groups of similar or related items. The second may be solved in several ways. In this chapter **tabulation** – the drawing up of tables – is explained as a means of displaying information. Later chapters deal with other methods of presentation.

3.2 The classification of data

Classification involves bringing together those items of information which have something in common. For example, we might find in our fishing enquiry that, of the fish landed, some were haddock some cod, some mackerel, some herring, etc. It is useful to know how much of each type of fish has been caught. Therefore it would be in order to classify, i.e. group together, the species of figh caught. This also reduces the number of classes. Instead of each fish being an individual, there are only half-a-dozen or so classes for all the millions of fishes caught. This makes the handling of the information much easier.

When attempting to classify data, much will depend upon the nature of the data themselves and upon the purposes of the enquiry. There is no clear cut 'correct' way of classifying and presenting all data. For example, though a census every 10 years is sufficient to discover changes in the size of the United Kingdom population, such a time-scale is not a suitable classification for the measure of the United Kingdom rainfall, statistics for which are collected daily. The reader would do well to remember, then, that the nature of the enquiry is important in determining the classification.

This is not to say that there are no general rules available to guide students when they come to construct their own tables, or when they are required to interpret published statistics. There are such rules and the following are among the most important:

Categories must be comprehensive

The classes or categories chosen must be comprehensive, i.e. all the possible responses must be taken into account. The statistics relating to fish landed in the United Kingdom are incomplete if only the categories, cod, herring, haddock, plaice and mackerel are included. There are many other varieties of fish and at least one additional category, 'Other', is required to make the classes complete.

Categories must not overlap

Though the classes must be comprehensive they must not overlap, since this then allows them to be ambiguous. If we are measuring ages and we have classes of 10–20 years, 20–30 years, etc. we clearly have some element of overlap. The observations of 'age 20 years' could fit into both. A more satisfactory and unambiguous classification would be 10 and under 20; 20 and under 30; etc.

Classes should be few in number

The classes chosen should be sufficiently few in number to allow comparison with each other. Nothing is worse than spending a great deal of time classifying information, only to find that there are so many classes available that no conclusions can be arrived at, or comparisons made. A few large classes will damp out fluctuations in the statistics which are irrelevant to the enquiry in hand. Thus it may be of biological interest that there is one subspecies within the general grouping 'haddock', but for a summary of landings of fish in the United Kingdom it is sufficient to consider all haddock as the same species; subdivisions in this instance could confuse and not clarify.

At the same time the number of classes must be large enough to give an impression of the range of information that has been collected. Between six and eleven classes are generally considered most suitable for tables and frequency distributions (see Table 3.1).

Classes should be homogeneous

Where possible, the items included within a class should all have the same characteristics. They should be homogeneous (or alike). If a class contains items which are vastly different from each other, then few general conclusions can be drawn from it. The statements made about it will tend to be unrepresentative of the items within the group.

3.3   The tabulation of data

Once the statistician has decided upon the classification to be used, the problem of presentation has to be faced. The **table** has been found to be a most useful method of presentation. Often information may be presented as a written report, but if possible it should be arranged into tabular form, i.e. under vertical columns and horizontal rows. Consider the following report written by the sales director of an industrial company to the managing director:

Total sales of the company increased from £3.85 millions in Year 1 to £6.27 millions in Year 2. Product A provided 24 per cent of the total sales in Year 2 at £1.49 millions but only 15 per cent at £0.56 millions in Year 1, whereas the contribution of product C fell from £1.21 millions in Year 1 to £1.09 millions in Year 2. Product B and the combined group of other products increased their sales over the period. Product B from £0.47 millions to £0.76 millions and 'other products' from £1.61 millions to £2.93 millions.

This same information could have been presented in tabular form as in Table 3.1.

Table 3.1 Sales by product group (£ million)

Product	Year 1 £m (%)	Year 2 £m (%)
A	0.56 (15)	1.49 (24)
B	0.47 (12)	0.76 (12)
C	1.21 (31)	1.09 (17)
Other	1.61 (42)	2.93 (47)
Total	3.85 (100)	6.27 (100)

It can be seen that tabulation has these advantages:

1 A large amount of data can be presented in a compact form.
2 It is easy to understand.
3 The main features of the data are indicated.

Constructing a table

Tables are, by their very nature, varied and flexible, and it is up to us to exercise judgement about how to tabulate the data so that it is presented in a clear, concise and attractive form. Nevertheless, there are certain points which should be borne in mind when constructing a table:

1 Give the table a title which will briefly but explicitly describe the contents of the table.
2 Give the source and date of the data.
3 Give the units of measurement used.
4 All column and row headings should be given.
5 Where appropriate use column and row totals and sub-totals.
6 Do not make a table too detailed. It is better to use two simple tables rather than one complex table.
7 Where columns of figures are to be totalled, place the totals at the bottom of the table, unless particular attention is to be drawn to the totals, when they may be placed at the top.
8 Use rulings to break up the table. Horizontal lines called eye-lines assist the reader's comprehension of the table. Every fifth line should be followed by an eye-line, or in a short table of, say, eight lines one eye-line inserted halfway down is sufficient.
9 If a table is to be printed, italics can be used to pick out important points.

A general plan for the layout of tables is given in Figure 3.1, and described in the notes below it.

1   TITLE

2 Class description	3 Column headings	etc.	etc.		
4 Row headings	5 Data in these columns				
____ etc.					
6 Totals					

7 Footnotes

8 Source notes

Figure 3.1   A general plan for tabular presentation

Notes:
1 A table should always have a clear title, which states exactly what the information within the table sets out to show. If units are used they should be clearly stated.
2 Unless it is obvious, the left-hand column heading will describe what is listed in the column below. For example, a table of industrial production might indicate at the top 'Type of Industry', and below this heading the various industries would be listed.
3 The columns of statistics under scrutiny should have clear column headings indicating what the columns represent.
4 Row headings for the collected data should be listed in the left-hand column.
5 The data themselves, ordered according to the information which it is desired to extract.
6 Any totals necessary should be presented.
7 Footnotes, which explain variations or points of importance, should be given immediately below the table.
8 Sources should be given where the origin of the table is some other set of published statistics, and acknowledgements should be made if necessary.

3.4   Simple tables

The rules of tabulation and classification outlined in Section 3.3 above are easily applied to some sets of data, since by their nature they are uncomplicated and easy to handle. For example, the tabulation of the following catches of fish in a United Kingdom port for 1–7 October does not present any difficulties: Sunday, 187 kg; Monday, 2008 kg; Tuesday, 2775 kg; Wednesday, 1090 kg; Thursday, 2050 kg; Friday, 1720 kg: Saturday, 1928 kg. Table 3.2 is a simple way of presenting this information more effectively.

Table 3.2   Catches of fish, 1–7 October

Day	Weight caught (kg)
Sunday	187
Monday	2008
Tuesday	2775
Wednesday	1090
Thursday	2050
Friday	1720
Saturday	1928
Total	11758

Rounding

As already explained (see Section 2.6), a table can be simplified considerably, and yet convey the same information, if the figures are 'rounded off'. For example, the figures for catches in Table 3.2 could be rounded off to the nearest 100 kg without the loss of detail affecting to any serious extent the accuracy of the information conveyed.

When rounding, it is usual to round up or round down to the accuracy required. Thus Sunday's catch of 187 kg would be rounded up to 200 kg since 87 kg is much more than half a hundred kilograms and therefore is closer to 200 kg than 100 kg. Monday's catch of 2008 kg would be rounded down to 2000 kg and so on. Where the figures to be dropped are exactly halfway, as in 2050, the convention is to round in such a way as to leave the retained part an even number. So 2050 kg would be rounded down to 2000 kg, while a catch of 2150 would be rounded up to 2200 kg, since 2100 kg would be an odd number of hundreds.

Having rounded off the figures in Table 3.2 to the nearest 100 kg, we now arrive at Table 3.3. The reader should note that a tiny inaccuracy has crept into the figures, for if the total of Table 3.2 was rounded up, it would come to 118 lots of 100 kg. The rounding process in Table 3.3 has produced an error, but it is insignificant. The general impression gathered from the two tables is the same, and the figures in the table which has been rounded are simpler to understand. Such errors are known as 'rounding errors' and they may be disregarded.

Table 3.3   Catches of fish, 1–7 October

Day	Weight caught (100 kg)
Sunday	2
Monday	20
Tuesday	28
Wednesday	11
Thursday	20
Friday	17
Saturday	19
Total	117

3.5   Exercises: simple tabulation

1   Gas consumption in millions of therms is given as follows in a report of a nationalized body: 1st quarter, 4 197; 2nd quarter, 2 611; 3rd quarter, 1 872; 4th quarter, 3 630. Present this information in tabular form to bring out the total annual consumption.

2   The following information from an agricultural research project refers to: (*a*) cows and heifers in milk; (*b*) cows in calf but not in milk; (*c*) heifers in calf with first calf; (*d*) bulls for service; (*e*) all other cattle and calves. Present the data, given in thousands, to show the information in tabular form, and the total of this type of livestock. The figures are: (*a*) 2 627; (*b*) 691; (*c*) 455; (*d*) 90; (*e*) 7 951.

3   A trade journal gives the following figures for sales of floorcoverings – (*a*) refers to carpets and rugs and (*b*) to linoleum and plastics. Your are asked to round off the figures in each case to thousands of square metres, and present them in a table showing the sales of each type, the total quarterly sales and the total annual sales. The figures are: 1st quarter, (*a*) 38 174 353 square metres, (*b*) 19 264 852 square metres; 2nd quarter, (*a*) 37 291 453 square metres, (*b*) 16 458 391 square metres; 3rd quarter, (*a*) 41 284 723 square metres, (*b*) 14 586 948 square metres; 4th quarter, (*a*) 38 516 849 square metres, (*b*) 21 326 724 square metres.

4   Exports are listed in five categories. These are: (*a*) foods, beverages and tobacco; (*b*) fuels; (*c*) industrial materials; (*d*) finished manufactures; (*e*) other transactions. You are asked to round the figures off to the nearest £m and present them in tabular form for Year 1 and Year 2 to bring out the annual totals. The figures are: (*a*) Year 1 £3 094 276 153, Year 2 £4 993 463 218; (*b*) Year 1 £1 724 858 300, Year 2 £5 652 721 494; (*c*) Year 1 £6 239 434 721, Year 2 £8 738 346 829; (*d*) Year 1 £4 174 059 628, Year 2 £6 386 995 240; (*e*) Year 1 £424 736 284, Year 2 £595 106 386.

3.6 Time series

A time series is a particular type of table which shows how data changes over a period of time. For example, Table 3.4 shows a simple time series about the profits of a company.

Table 3.4 Profits of XYZ Ltd (£'000s)

Year 1	Year 2	Year 3	Year 4	Year 5
188	266	382	394	456

This type of time series is the subject of careful analysis in Chapter 12, where we attempt to discover the **trend** over time. It will not be discussed further at this point.

3.7 Frequency distributions

Where the information is less simple than that outlined in Section 3.4, it may be necessary to construct a **frequency distribution**, which is merely a table that has values repeated a number of times, and these are grouped together according to how often (or how frequently) they occur. The frequency distribution is a common and important way of arranging data. Its effectiveness can be seen in considering Example 3.1 below, which consists of **raw**, or unprocessed, **data**.

Example 3.1(a)
The following were the earnings in pounds (£) of 100 fishermen for 1 day in October:

28	64	73	64	37	29	39	70	73	37
56	62	48	39	37	37	70	39	28	37
48	73	39	37	37	70	37	37	64	37
32	39	29	62	73	28	48	62	73	70
73	28	64	56	70	32	32	56	64	70
39	70	56	64	39	29	48	64	37	39
37	70	62	56	29	37	32	56	29	28
70	32	37	39	37	46	70	39	39	37
28	48	39	46	64	48	70	46	70	37
32	37	37	28	73	28	28	28	73	64

The random presentation of this mass of data is most confusing. It conveys little in the way of information. However, it is possible to make the understanding of such data a little easier by displaying it in the form of an **array**, which is a collection of figures listed in order of size, i.e. they run from the smallest to the largest.

Example 3.1(b)

28	29	32	37	39	39	48	62	70	70
28	29	37	37	39	39	56	64	70	70
28	29	37	37	39	46	56	64	70	73
28	29	37	37	39	46	56	64	70	73
28	29	37	37	39	46	56	64	70	73
28	32	37	37	39	48	56	64	70	73
28	32	37	37	39	48	56	64	70	73
28	32	37	37	39	48	62	64	70	73
28	32	37	37	39	48	62	64	70	73
28	32	37	37	39	48	62	64	70	73

Even this array is rather formidable and the student will notice that some items occur many times over. Further simplification, therefore, can be achieved by **listing the number of times an item occurs** (the frequency of its occurrence) instead of including it in the table in full each time it appears. Such a summary results in the frequency distribution Table 3.5.

Table 3.5   The earnings of 100 fishermen for one day in October

Earnings (£)	Frequency (*number of men*)
28	10
29	5
32	6
37	19
39	12
46	3
48	6
56	6
62	4
64	9
70	12
73	8
Total	100

Table 3.5 is an ungrouped one, i.e. the frequencies for different values are kept separate, they are not grouped together. Every observation of

value £28 appears in a class with other values of £28, and not with, say, values of £29. But it will be noticed that the frequency distribution is rather lengthy, having twelve classes. Real-life surveys of earnings would have even more classes. Therefore it is convenient to convert this type of ungrouped frequency distribution into a grouped one. This is done by widening the class limits, so that observations of differing (but not random) values can be included. This process is demonstrated in Example 3.2.

Example 3.2

Table 3.6 Grouped frequency distribution of earnings of 100 fishermen for one day in October

Earnings (£)	Frequency (number of men)
20 and under 30	15
30 and under 40	37
40 and under 50	9
50 and under 60	6
60 and under 70	13
70 and under 80	20
Total	100

The student will appreciate how much more concise Table 3.6's form of presentation is, and how it makes the information more comprehensible. Some important points may be listed as follows:

1 Class intervals must be chosen to give a representative view of the information collected. As mentioned in Section 3.2 above, 6–11 groups are usually adequate. The class limits should be unambiguous. A selection of typical methods of expressing class intervals is given in Table 3.7.

2 A frequency distribution must have a total, and the total of frequencies must correspond with the total number of observations – in Example 3.2 this was 100 fishermen.

3 Where the class intervals chosen for some reason do not embrace all the observations, a final class interval must be added to conform with the rule in Section 3.2 calling for comprehensiveness. In frequency distributions this will usually have a description like '30 and over' (in Table 3.7B for example).

Table 3.7 Methods of expressing class intervals

A	B	C
		(Correct to nearest whole number)
Under 5	0–	0–4
5 and under 10	5–	5–9
10 and under 15	10–	10–14
15 and under 20	15–	15–19
20 and under 25	20–	20–24
25 and under 30	25–	25–29
30 and under 35	30–	30–34

Notes

(a) In A the class intervals are unambiguous, and in accordance with the rules of classification in Section 3.2, that they should not overlap.

(b) In B the class intervals are exactly the same as in A. 0– means under 5, 5– means 5 and under 10, etc. When used to refer to ages this method indicates that a child exactly 5 years old would be included in the second group, not the first. The final interval, 30–, is open-ended.

(c) When figures are specified as correct to the nearest whole number, as in C, a slight difficulty arises. Because of the rules for 'correcting up' and 'correcting down' (which hold that when a number ends in 5 we correct to the nearest even number), 0–4 means that the items in that group might be as large as 4.5, while the 5–9 group includes items greater than 4.5 and up to 9.499, for 9.5 would be rounded up to 10 (the nearest even number).

A further example will illustrate the procedure for drawing up a frequency distribution table.

Example 3.3

A recent survey was undertaken to find out the speed of vehicles on a certain section of road which had a speed limit of 30 mph. They were timed to the nearest tenth of a mile per hour. The raw data was as follows:

Speeds (mph)

29.4	30.2	20.8	36.0	44.6
35.1	32.8	41.3	33.7	28.7
29.8	40.2	25.9	22.6	39.8
36.3	42.2	37.6	26.4	29.9
30.9	28.8	38.8	27.5	22.7
32.8	46.4	29.4	23.5	33.1
30.6	38.6	28.8	28.0	42.9
36.4	37.9	24.4	47.6	36.0
32.6	38.4	43.7	40.8	37.8
37.8	30.4	35.2	36.8	32.4

34.2	43.6	39.8	39.4	32.2
43.6	31.6	37.9	33.0	29.0
33.8	28.3	40.9	29.6	32.8
42.4	51.2	27.3	35.8	25.3
45.6	33.4	28.7	32.6	33.4
29.8	40.9	35.6	38.6	38.6
26.4	24.2	42.8	29.6	37.6
43.8	40.6	38.4	33.4	22.8
29.7	28.9	32.5	23.8	32.2
30.3	35.8	34.8	33.9	34.8

The student who arranges these in an array will find that the lowest speed is 20.8 mph and the highest is 51.2 mph. This has not been done here, to save space, but students should practise their ability to draw up arrays by doing it now.

Clearly there are almost as many classes as there are variables, and so it is necessary to group classes together to form a **grouped frequency distribution.** In choosing the number of groups required, we must bear in mind that too many groups will give a lengthy table, whereas too few groups will lose much of the precision of the original data. In examinations the amount of data given will of necessity be limited and will probably not exceed 100 variables, requiring the use of about ten groups. Outside the examination room, several hundred variables are normally collected, which may require ten to twenty groups.

To form the grouped table, follow this procedure:

1 Arrange the raw data into an array, in ascending order of magnitude.
2 Subtract the lowest value of the raw data from the highest to obtain the **range**. In our example the range $= 51.2 - 20.8 = 30.4$.
3 Decide the number of groups that seems desirable. In some cases, as with this set of data, an obvious size for a group suggest itself, e.g. groups increasing by 5mph would be easy to understand and would require six groups to cover the range of 20mph up to 50mph. There is one speed of 51.2mph, which could be accommodated by having the last group open-ended. In other cases where such an easy group size was not so obvious we might decide on a number of groups, say ten. If we divide the range (in this case 30.4) by 10 we get 3.04. Taking 3 as the nearest whole number this would give a group interval of 3mph. This is called the class interval. In our particular case we will take six groups as best, with a class interval of 5mph, the last being open-ended.
4 We now work out the groups, starting in this case at 20 since the slowest speed we have to record is 20.8. The groups are therefore 20 and under 25; 25 and under 30, etc. We now allocate the variables

to their appropriate groups, using the tally method of counting by five-barred gates. This means that you take each variable in turn and place a tally mark against the group into which it falls. Total the tally marks for each group to give the frequency. The result is shown in Figure 3.2.

Class (speed in mph)	Tally marks	Frequency (number of vehicles)
20 and under 25	~~IIII~~ III	8
25 and under 30	~~IIII~~ ~~IIII~~ ~~IIII~~ ~~IIII~~ II	22
30 and under 35	~~IIII~~ ~~IIII~~ ~~IIII~~ ~~IIII~~ ~~IIII~~ I	26
35 and under 40	~~IIII~~ ~~IIII~~ ~~IIII~~ ~~IIII~~ ~~IIII~~	25
40 and under 45	~~IIII~~ ~~IIII~~ ~~IIII~~	15
45 and over	IIII	4
		100

Figure 3.2 Recording data as a frequency distribution

3.8 Cumulative frequency tables

It may be useful to present our data in such a manner that we can show the frequency with which a variable falls above (or below) a certain value, e.g. how many motor vehicles actually observed the 30mph speed limit according to our data. The table presents the same data as before, but in addition has cumulative frequency columns added to it. The accumulation can start from the smallest figure and build up to the highest, or vice versa, as shown in Table 3.8, which uses the data given in Figure 3.2.

Table 3.8 Cumulative frequency tables

Class (speed in mph)	*Frequency (no. of vehicles)*	*Cumulative frequency (ascending order)*	*Cumulative frequency (descending order)*
20 and under 25	8	8	100
25 and under 30	22	30	92
30 and under 35	26	56	70
35 and under 40	25	81	44
40 and under 45	15	96	19
45 and over	4	100	4
	100		

We can see that 30 vehicles observed the speed limit of 30mph, whereas 70 exceeded the speed limit.

3.9   Bi-variate tables

Sometimes we wish to show more than one variable in a table, and to do so we must subdivide either the rows or the vertical columns. Usually it is simpler to subdivide the vertical columns, the eye taking in the subdivisions more easily in columnar form. An example is given in Figure 3.3. It shows a table with variables in both the horizontal rows and the vertical columns. The students of given ages are analysed into departmental enrolments, and also by sex. Cross-totting the columns to get total enrolments in each year by sex can be confusing – only every other row has to be included. The total figures thus arrived at give a very clear idea of the composition of the student body (see page 54).

3.10   Exercises: frequency distributions

1   A traffic inquiry investigating the use of private motor vehicles collects raw data from traffic queueing at traffic lights as follows:

Number of persons per car

```
1,  3,  1,  2,  1,  1,  1,  4,  1,  2,
1,  1,  2,  1,  4,  2,  5,  2,  2,  1,
2,  3,  1,  2,  1,  1,  3,  1,  4,  2,
1,  2,  2,  1,  2,  3,  1,  2,  2,  3.
```

Rearrange the data in the form of an array, in increasing order of magnitude, and hence draw up a frequency distribution in 5 groups.

2   Little-but-good Ltd has thirty employees whose weekly wages are given below. Arrange these in a frequency distribution, choosing appropriate class intervals:

Wages: Machine shop: £256, £262, £184, £148 (earned by four employees), £82 (earned by six apprentices).
Office: £156, £168, £120.

3   Weekly turnover for 40 shops in a pedestrian precinct is found to be as follows. Arrange these in a frequency table with suitable class intervals:

Number of students

Age on 1 Sept 19..	General education		Business studies		Science		Tourism and catering		Engineering		Totals by sexes		Total enrolments
	M	F	M	F	M	F	M	F	M	F	M	F	
Under 17	126	242	145	172	85	95	48	92	172	28	576	629	1205
17	96	84	68	89	46	39	26	51	74	11	310	274	584
18	77	81	56	76	42	45	13	46	68	19	256	267	523
19	86	59	69	29	41	55	14	42	55	5	265	190	455
20	56	72	74	55	36	19	10	26	54	18	230	190	420
21+	34	73	19	26	11	21	3	17	41	13	108	150	258
Totals by Sexes	475	611	431	447	261	274	114	274	464	94	1745	1700	3445
Total enrolments	1086		878		535		388		558		3445		3445

Figure 3.3   A bi-variate table – enrolments at a technical college

£240	£346	£721	£658	£989	£1,100
£1,370	£1,475	£1,800	£1,250	£5,500	£1,975
£1,650	£1,800	£1,980	£7,500	£5,900	£1,950
£1,880	£1,860	£13,500	£1,350	£1,925	£1,290
£1,450	£1,940	£8,500	£1,820	£1,375	£1,700
£1,224	£25,000	£4,950	£1,840	£32,000	£1,775
£1,960	£1,700	£1,416	£1,790		

4   The wages (in £s) paid to fifty men in a factory in a particular week are given as follows:

£	£	£	£	£
141	142	152	144	172
157	156	148	145	146
169	138	172	149	147
151	128	150	156	144
148	155	144	182	145
149	173	146	174	128
154	148	147	148	172
148	152	149	136	175
166	155	169	152	146
169	153	184	160	156

Group the data into seven classes and present the results in tabular form. Why would it be wrong to specify classes as £120–£130, £130–£140, etc.?

5   An earnings survey reveals that earnings per week in a certain works were as follows. You are asked to present the information as a table grouped into eight classes. Include in your table a cumulative frequency column. The figures are in £ sterling:

154	73	91	169	100
72	84	93	95	100
162	158	174	167	120
99	81	96	102	120
164	74	99	120	76
86	94	165	75	166
77	82	102	106	130
88	105	124	124	106
79	106	78	130	79
97	106	89	107	89

6   A quality control sample of nails is taken fifty-six times in one week
from a machine which makes them automatically. There are twenty
nails in each sample. The number of failures in each batch is given
out of twenty, as follows:

4,	6,	5,	13,	7,	9,	16,
2,	9,	2,	3,	5,	3,	1,
1,	17,	0,	11,	12,	16,	11,
13,	5,	3,	12,	10,	14,	5,
5,	10,	14,	9,	2,	5,	11,
6,	3,	17,	5,	11,	16,	7,
19,	7,	14,	4,	18,	0,	9,
0,	2,	11,	15,	5,	4,	3.

(a) Rearrange these items as an array.
(b) Display the data as a grouped frequency distribution in seven
groups, in the form 0–2 failures, 3–5 failures, etc.
(c) Insert an extra column to show the cumulative frequency.
(d) What percentage of the samples had less than six failures?
(Answers correct to 1 decimal place.)

3.11   Summary of Chapter 3

1   Data normally become available as a mass of evidence from forms,
questionnaires, etc., and in this form are known as raw data. To
present them as part of a report we need to clarify them by
classification and then present them in an attractive way, as a
table, pictogram, graph or in some other diagrammatic form.
2   In the classification of data, the categories used should be few in
number, as homogeneous as possible, not overlapping and comprehensive (i.e. including all the data collected). For example, we may
need a class headed 'other items' to cover anything unusual.
3   A good table should have (a) a clear title, (b) units, if used, clearly
indicated, (c) headed columns, with rows clearly labelled, (d) clearly
stated data in neat columns, (e) totals and sub-totals if these are
helpful, (f) clear indications of sources of statistics, and (g) any
necessary extra information as footnotes.
4   In many cases the raw data may be most easily represented as a
frequency distribution. The data are first arranged as an array, in
ascending order of magnitude, and then the frequency of items will
become apparent.
5   If the number of classes is too great, it is usual to draw up a grouped
frequency distribution, with groups selected in such a way as to

display the data most effectively. We can have an open-ended class either at the start of a table or at the end, or both, to group together extreme items. Thus salaries might be shown in the form – under £100 per week, £101–125, £126–150, etc. up to an open-ended class: over £300.

6 A cumulative frequency column is one where the frequencies listed in the main table are accumulated from group to group. This can be done in ascending or descending order. (See Table 3.8 to revise this point).

7 Bi-variate tables are tables which have variables in both the horizontal rows and the vertical columns. They give a more detailed picture of the data under consideration.

4

Pictorial representation of statistical data 1: pictograms and other diagrams

4.1 Introduction

Often when data have been arranged in a table, frequency distribution or time series, the information which the statistics carry becomes clear, especially to those who use figures regularly. However, many people who could benefit from the knowledge contained in a statistical series are unlikely to absorb such knowledge unless it can be presented in a simple visual form.

It is generally accepted that pictures, diagrams, and graphs are convenient methods of conveying simple ideas of a statistical nature, even to those who are largely uninterested in statistics as a science. Frequent use of pictures, diagrams and graph is made on television, in the press and in magazines to pass on information relating to the cost of living, the level of unemployment, the cost of building society mortgages, etc.

This chapter deals with some of the more regularly used pictures and diagrams, whilst the slightly more complicated matter of graphs forms the subject of Chapter 5. It should be stressed here that neither of these chapters claims to be exhaustive – they are intended as a guide, not a complete account.

The purpose of both graphs and diagrams is to present data in a clear and vivid manner so that it is easy to read and understand. There are a few general rules to be observed when drawing a diagram

1   The diagram should have a title.
2   All units of measurement should be given.
3   Any axes should be labelled.
4   The source of the data should be shown.
5   If shading or colouring is used, a key may be necessary.

The most common diagrams are (a) pictograms, (b) bar charts, c) histograms, (d) Gantt charts, (e) pie charts and (f) frequency polygons.

4.2   Pictograms

These are the simplest pictorial representations. Simple outline figures
are used to represent quantities or values. For example, if the statistics
relate to the changing level of unemployment over 10 years, the
pictogram could be drawn as a number of human outlines, each one
representing a given level of registered unemployed. Similarly, Figure
4.1 illustrates the population of developing countries by income groups,
with each human figure representing 100 million people.

	Total population (in millions)
Low-income countries *Less than US$ 265 per capita*	1,132
Lower middle-income countries *US$ 265–520 per capita*	292
Intermediate middle-income countries *US$ 521–1,075 per capita*	386
Upper middle-income countries *US$ 1,076–2,000 per capita*	121

Figure 4.1   Developing countries: population by income groups (*Reproduced
by courtesy of Finance and Development*)

A more complex pictogram, which includes both pictures and
numerical data, is shown in Figure 4.2.

Care must be taken when designing pictograms that a false impression
is not created. For example, where the height of an illustration is used
to depict increasing quantities, the area of the diagram also changes,
but not in the same proportion. An unscrupulous presenter might take
advantage of this to convey a false impression. Figure 4.3 illustrates
the difficulty, the basket for year 4 appearing to be much more than
twice as large as the basket for year 1.

The tendency of diagrams and graphs to mislead is a problem to
which we shall constantly be referring.

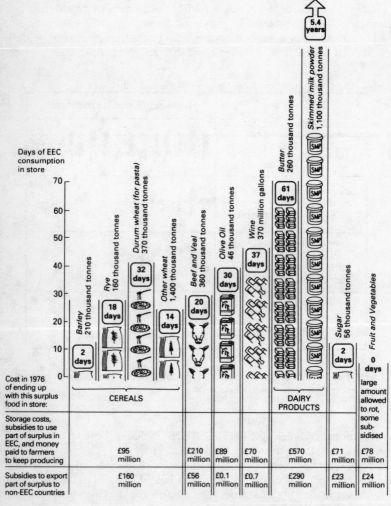

Total storage costs and subsidies for all mountains and lakes in the diagram = £1,736.8 million

Figure 4.2   Food mountains and wine lakes under the Common Agricultural Policy (Courtesy of *Which?* magazine)

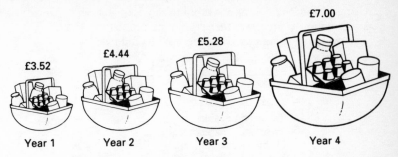

Figure 4.3 False impressions of the cost of a standard basket of goods; years 1–4

4.3 Exercises on pictograms

1 The following data have to be displayed in pictorial form. Choose an appropriate symbol and draw a pictogram.

Colour television sets in use in United Kingdom (thousands)	
1966	0
1970	500
1974	6 800
1978	10 800
1982	12 500
1986	16 600
1990	17 500

2 The volume of traffic can be measured by discovering the number of vehicles per mile of roads. A comparison of traffic densities in a number of countries produced the following results:

Country	Number of vehicles per road-mile
United Kingdom	61
West Germany	51
Netherlands	51
Italy	49
Belgium	36
France	26
Sweden	20

Using a motor vehicle as a symbol to represent every ten cars, draw a pictogram to illustrate the set of statistics.

3   The profits of a famous bank are used as follows:

	£m
Taxation payable	96
Preference shareholders	4
Ordinary shareholders	28
Kept in reserves	140
	£268

Using piles of pennies as your symbol, illustrate how many pence in each £1 of the profits are used for each of these purposes.

4   Measured in billion passenger miles, bus and coach passenger mileages changed as follows:

1952	123
1962	90
1972	64
1982	50

Using a suitable symbol illustrate this decline with a pictogram.

4.4   Bar charts

Bar charts seek to relate information to the horizontal or vertical length of a bar or thick line. They are of two main types: those which compare statistics for a given period of time and those which compare them over a succession of periods of time.

For example, in Figure 4.4 an ice cream firm has investigated the popularity of different flavours of ice cream by collecting statistics about the value of sales in a given week in one particular seaside resort. The statistics collected and presented in a bar chart in this way might lead to a decision to reduce the variety of flavours offered, or to an advertising campaign to promote less popular flavours.

1   *Scale*   The scale chosen must enable the graphics designer to represent the data clearly on the size of paper to be used.
2   *Length of bar*   The length of the bar in each case must be calculated to represent the correct fraction of the full scale chosen. Thus the

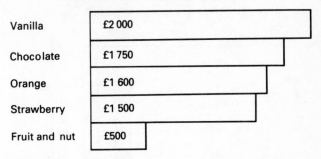

Figure 4.4   A bar chart

£1 750 bar in the diagram must be $\dfrac{1\,750}{2\,000} = \tfrac{7}{8}$ of the length of the longest bar.

3   *Shading, colour, etc.*   In some bar charts it might be desirable to pick out the bars in particular cross-hatchings or colours to present a clearer picture.

4   *Title, source details, etc.*   A suitable title, explanation of source material and date or dates (if required) should be added to the diagram, and the lettering and layout should be stylish and well presented.

5   *Three-dimensional effects*   Many published sets of data are illustrated with bar charts where the bar has been given a three-dimensional solid appearence. In some cases this makes it difficult to see exactly where the bar ends, and may detract from the presentation. Even more important, students sitting examinations are likely to waste time drawing in the three-dimensional effect, and trying to get it looking correct, when they should be getting on with the next question.

Where comparisons are being made over a series of time periods, the periods should be of equal length. The fact that some years are leap years, and have an extra day, may make an insigificant difference to statistics collected on a yearly basis, but the differing lengths of months can make a significant difference to monthly sales figures. It is quite common for sales figures to be collected in a 4-weekly basis, each 'lunar' month thus having 28 days. There will then be 13 months in the year, and a problem of designation arises. What period is actually meant by the seventh 4-week period in the year? It requires a calendar to sort out the answer.

In Figure 4.5 the vertical bar chart shown gives a clear indication of the number of vehicles in use in Great Britain over the given time range.

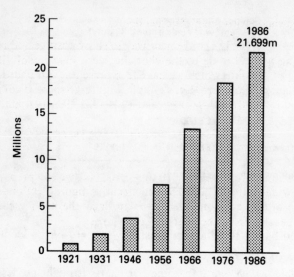

Figure 4.5 A vertical bar chart. Vehicles in use in Great Britain 1921–86 (*Source: Transport Statistics*)

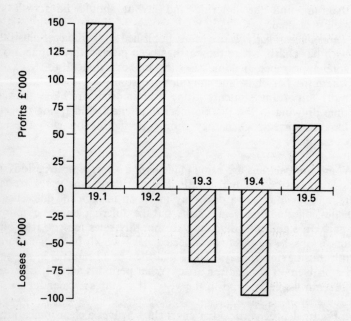

Figure 4.6 Positive and negative figures on a bar chart

Charts showing positive and negative figures

The simple bar chart is a convenient way to show positive and negative figures. The vertical scale of the chart has zero conveniently located (according to the data which we have to represent), with figures above zero and figures below zero. For example, Figure 4.6 shows a company's profits and losses over 5 recent years, 19.1, 19.2, 19.3, 19.4 and 19.5:

Profits: year 1, £150,000; year 2, £120,000; year 5, £60,000
Losses: year 3, £65,000; year 4, £95,000

Selecting a range from + £150,000 to − £100,000, we can prepare a bar chart showing both the positive and negative figures. By choosing a wide scale on the horizontal axis we can draw the bar for each year clearly separated from the years adjacent to it.

Multiple bar charts

Multiple bar charts bring out comparisons between sets of figures, because they show a number of bars adjacent to one another. They can be drawn in different ways to bring out the comparisons more clearly, according to the purpose of the diagram. For example, suppose a company is predicting the likely trends in its labour force over the years ahead and as part of this study has drawn up age profiles for the years 19.8 and 19.9:

Ages of employees	19.8	19.9
Under 30 years	40	24
30–39 years	80	56
40–49 years	36	72
50 and over	24	48
	180	200

These statistics might be presented in alternative ways as shown in Figure 4.7.

Component bar charts

A component bar chart can be used to display the various components that make up a whole set of data. For example, a recent census of the United Kingdom population gives figures as shown on page 66.

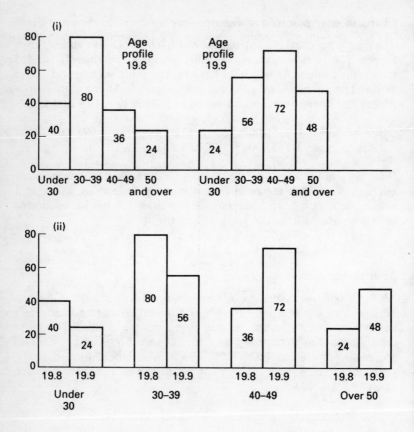

Figure 4.7   Multiple bar charts for comparison purposes

Notes:
1   Figure 4.7(i) emphasizes the distribution of the age groups within the 2 years.
2   Figure 4.7(ii) compares the age groups between the two years, bringing out the changing structure of the labour force over the period under consideration.

UK population (millions), 19.1

England	46.1
Scotland	5.1
Wales	2.8
Northern Ireland	1.8
Total	55.8

This can be represented as a component bar chart, as shown in Figure 4.8. Of course the bar could be shown as a horizontal bar, rather than a vertical one.

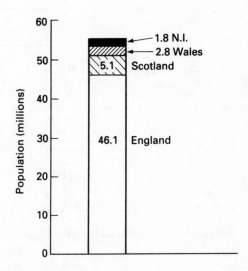

Figure 4.8 A component bar chart of population

Percentage bar charts

A percentage bar chart is similar to a component bar chart. It is one in which the total body of statistics collected (100 per cent) is divided up into its component parts to show each part as a percentage of the whole. This is most useful where the total set of statistics has some special significance. This special method of presentation is often used in profit statements to show how the profits made have been allocated. For example, taking each £1 of profit it might be that 35 pence went in Corporation Tax, 22 pence to Ordinary Shareholders, 8 pence to Preference Shareholders, 5 pence to Special Reserves and 30 pence into General Reserves. Such a set of statistics could be easily displayed using a percentage bar chart.

In Figure 4.9 the annual expenditure of an average household is broken down into its percentage component elements of expenditure. The calculations of the percentages are shown in a box alongside the bar chart.

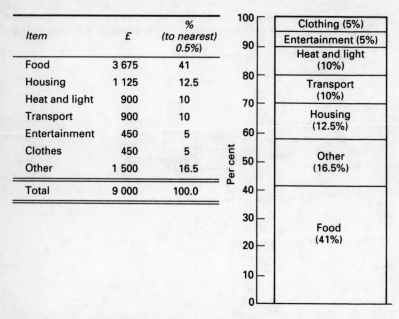

Item	£	% (to nearest) 0.5%)
Food	3 675	41
Housing	1 125	12.5
Heat and light	900	10
Transport	900	10
Entertainment	450	5
Clothes	450	5
Other	1 500	16.5
Total	9 000	100.0

Figure 4.9   A percentage bar chart: annual expenditure of an average household

4.5   Exercises on bar charts

1   Sales of a department store were as follows:

Department	£ '000
Furniture	5 800
Soft furnishings	2 300
Ladies' fashions	12 750
Menswear	8 250
Household items	3 700
Jewellery and fine art	3 250
	£36 050

Draw a horizontal bar chart to illustrate these sales, using a scale of 1cm = £1 million.

2   Immunization injections administered in a certain health area were as follows in the year 19.1

Measles, etc.	10 580
Whooping cough	5 400
Influenza	9 600
Yellow fever	2 500
Anti-tetanus	9 600

Draw a vertical bar chart to illustrate this set of data, using 1cm for each 1 000 injections.

3   Cars per 1 000 of the population were as follows in the 2 years shown below:

	1979	*1989*
European Community	280	360
Other Europe	150	220
Japan	160	250
USA	480	560

Draw a multiple bar chart to show the changing situation in the four areas over the 10-year period, using a scale of 1cm = 100 cars.

4   Improvements in pupil–teacher ratios are shown in the following table. Draw a bar chart to illustrate the changes:

Pupils per teacher in primary schools
(England and Wales only)

Year	*Number of pupils per teacher*
1921	48
1931	43.5
1951	39
1961	36
1971	31.5
1981	27.5

Note: The War was on in 1941 – no data available

5   Figures for 1 year's world fibre output in millions of tonnes were as follows:

Country or bloc	Natural fibre	Man-made fibre
United Kingdom	0.5	1.0
Other West Europe	1.5	2.0
USA	1.5	3.5
Communist Bloc	2.0	5.0
Third World	3.5	4.5

Draw a bar chart to illustrate these outputs. Use shading or colours to distinguish natural and man-made fibres.

6 In four years the investment funds used by United Kingdom companies were obtained from the following sources:

	Profits ploughed back (£m)	Bank borrowing (£m)	Overseas borrowing (£m)	Other (£m)
Year 1	4 000	1 000	1 000	500
Year 2	5 000	3 000	2 000	500
Year 3	7 000	5 000	3 000	1 000
Year 4	8 000	4 000	3 500	2 000

Draw a component bar diagram to illustrate the figures, and show the total invested in each of the 4 years.

7 Powered vehicles using roll-on, roll-off ferries from the UK to Europe were recorded as follows in the years shown. Figures are in thousands.

Country of destination	1975	1980	1985	1990
Belgium	85	110	130	150
France	100	140	180	200
Netherlands	30	50	60	80
Others	5	15	25	40

Draw a component bar chart for each year, showing the figures for the four destinations, using shading to distinguish between them. Choose a suitable scale.

8 The income of the United Kingdom Government in 19.8 was drawn from the following sources:

	£(000 million)
Taxes on income	61.4
Taxes on expenditure	56.6
Social security contributions	31.8
Other sources	13.2
	163.0

Draw up a percentage bar chart showing clearly what percentage of Government expenditure comes from each source.

9 Central Government public expenditure in 19.8 was as shown below. Draw up a percentage bar chart to show what percentage of expenditure went on each item:

	£ million
Defence	19 800
Education	1 200
Health	21 800
Social security	22 600
Other consumption	10 300
Local authorities	23 300
Interest on National Debt	17 000
Other	44 000
	160 000

4.6 Histograms

These are diagrams which display frequency distributions. Here a vertical block is drawn to represent each class interval. The greater the frequency of the group, the higher the block. Where class intervals are equal, as in Figure 4.10, the width of the block is immaterial and may be chosen to suit the space available. The rules for drawing a histogram with uniform class intervals are as follows:

1   Select a width of class interval which is appropriate for the size of paper to be used and the number of rectangles (class intervals) to be drawn. The class intervals will be marked along the horizontal axis and the frequencies up the vertical axis.

2   At the midpoint of each class interval mark in a height above the horizontal axis which is proportional to the frequency of that particular class interval. Draw a horizontal line at this height equal to the width of the class interval.

3   Now draw in the sides of the rectangles by joining up the ends of these lines to the horizontal axis. The result is a series of adjacent rectangles. The heights of the rectangles are proportional to the frequencies of their respective classes, and the total earnings are represented by the total area of the histogram.

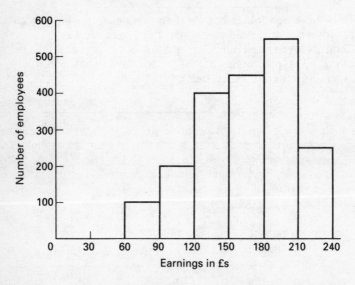

Figure 4.10   A histogram: weekly earnings of engineering apprentices and craftsmen

Histograms with unequal class intervals

If the class intervals are unequal (which frequently happens when the final class interval is an 'other items' class), the area of the rectangle becomes the important factor, and must be kept proportional to the class interval multiplied by the frequency of the class. Thus a class of twice the size of a normal class interval would be halved in height, providing that the number of frequencies was identical in both cases.

To illustrate this point consider the following data about the number of passengers on buses entering a certain town:

Number of passengers	Number of buses
0–4	4
5–9	6
10–14	15
15–19	21
20–24	28
25–29	16
30–39	14
	104

The unequal group here is the final group, which includes those buses with 30–39 passengers on board. The regular class interval is 5 passengers (though in the first group buses with no passengers feature in the data provided). The last group has an interval of ten. The width of the bar will be drawn to show the class interval, and must be twice as wide as the other groups. Care must be taken to ensure that the area of the unequal group is proportional to the areas of the other groups, and as it is twice as wide, it will not need to be so high. The height required is pretty obvious here – it will only need to be half if it is twice as wide. The general formula for finding the correct height is: divide the frequency of the unequal group by its class interval and multiply by the regular class interval.

In this case we have:

$$\text{Height} = \frac{14}{10} \times 5 = 7$$

This gives us a histogram as shown in Figure 4.11 overleaf.

Histograms and frequency polygons

Frequencies can also be illustrated by frequency polygons. One way of drawing a frequency polygon is to draw up a histogram first and then draw in the polygon by joining up the midpoints of the tops of the blocks, in the manner shown in Figure 4.12, where the frequency polygon has been drawn in around the histogram shown in Figure 4.10.

An alternative way to draw a frequency polygon is to use graphical methods, plotting the frequencies as if they occurred at the midpoints

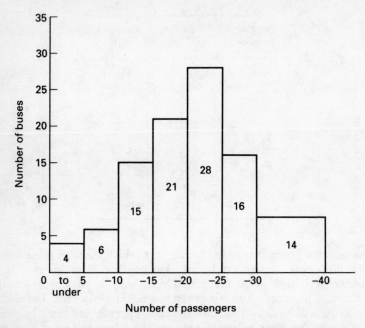

Figure 4.11 A histogram with one class interval larger then the others

Notes:

1 The data is a grouped frequency distribution of continuous data, and therefore the limits of the data are printed at the limits of the bars.
2 The class interval is up to five passengers in each case, except the last interval which is up to ten extra passengers.
3 It is advisable where there is an unusual class interval to write the frequency into each bar so that the frequency in the unequal group is clearly understood (in this case not 7, but 14).
4 Where a distribution has an open-ended designation, either at the beginning or the end it is usual to give it the same class interval as the following group, or the preceding group, thus keeping the class intervals uniform throughout. In Figure 4.11 this would not be done as the class interval was clearly designated as double the normal class interval.

of the class intervals. Once again, this is only possible if the class intervals are uniform in size. Examples of such polygons are given in Chapter 5, Section 5.13.

4.7 Exercises on histograms

1 Employees' wages in the New Town area are shown below for the first week in June. Draw a histogram to illustrate the data. You may assume that no New Town resident earns less than £25 or more than £225 per week.

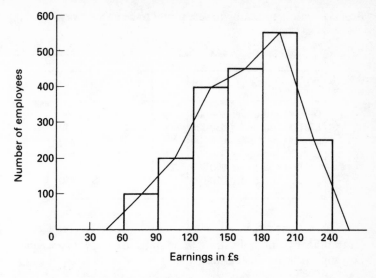

Figure 4.12 A frequency polygon drawn on to a histogram

Notes:
1 The polygon is drawn by joining up the midpoint of the top of each block to the midpoint of the next one.
2 The area of the polygon is exactly the same as the area of the histogram, since in each case where the two points are joined up they create two congruent triangles; one triangle is left out of the polygon, to be replaced with an equal triangle, now included in the polygon, which was not part of the histogram.
3 However, we can only draw in a polygon in this way if the class intervals are uniform. The procedure does not give a correct result if one or more intervals is greater. We could therefore not draw in such a polygon around the histogram in Fig 4.11.

Class range	Percentage of population with earnings in the group
Under £50	4.5
£50 and under £75	7.5
£75 and under £100	15.5
£100 and under £125	20.0
£125 and under £150	34.0
£150 and under £175	12.0
£175 and under £200	5.0
£200 and under £225	1.5
	100.0

2   Property values in Seatown were found to be as follows in a survey:

Price range	Number in class
£40 000 and under £50 000	1 250
£50 000 and under £60 000	3 750
£60 000 and under £70 000	4 500
£70 000 and under £80 000	5 500
£80 000 and under £90 000	4 500
£90 000 and under £100 000	3 750

Draw a histogram to illustrate these statistics. Draw in a frequency polygon on to the histogram.

3   Monthly take-home pay is revealed by a census of bank employees to give the following range of earnings:

£ Sterling	Number of pay packets
£0 – £99	None
£100 – £199	7
£200 – £299	27
£300 – £399	42
£400 – £499	50
£500 – £599	44
£600 – £699	36
£700 – £799	12
£800 – £899	10
£900 – £999	8

Draw a histogram to illustrate the data and draw in a frequency polygon upon it.

4   Shareholders in a public limited company are found to be grouped as follows:

Number of shareholders

Number of shares held	Number of shareholders in the group
Less than 500 shares	1,000
500 – 749	2,000
750 – 999	1,500
1 000 – 1 249	1,000
1 250 – 1 499	750
1 500 – 1 749	500
1 750 – 1 999	400
2 000 – 3 000	250
3 000 – 4 000	100

Draw a histogram to present this set of data.

5 Commercial properties in Suburbia are rented out at the following rates, according to a survey conducted by the local authority. Draw a histogram to present this data.

Annual rental (£)	Number of properties
Under £2 500	60
£2 500 – £4 999	84
£5 000 – £7 499	72
£7 500 – £9 999	48
£10 000 – £14 999	36
£15 000 – £19 999	24

4.8 Gantt charts

The object of the Gantt chart is to relate actual performance to planned or anticipated performance. The procedure is to mark on the chart a series of equal divisions, say weekly or monthly, each of which represents the planned performance for that period. Against these divisions the actual performance can be plotted in as a thin bar. If the target output, or target sales, is fully achieved, the bar will cross from one side of the division to the other. If the target is not fully achieved, a gap will be left, while if the target is exceeded, a second bar can be started to show the excess. The useful feature of this layout is that, although the divisions are equal, the targets to be achieved are not the same each month. It

is therefore possible for seasonal variations to be taken into account.
A salesman in a slack August period might be set a target of £1 000.
In the pre-Christmas rush the October target might be raised to £15 000.
Since the 'actual achievement' bar illustrates the salesman's percentage
success in reaching the target, there is no problem in accounting for
seasonal variations.

Week	Planned	Actual
1	3 600	3 360
2	3 750	3 540
3	3 900	4 500
4	4 050	4 830
5	4 200	5 460
6	4 350	5 850

(a)

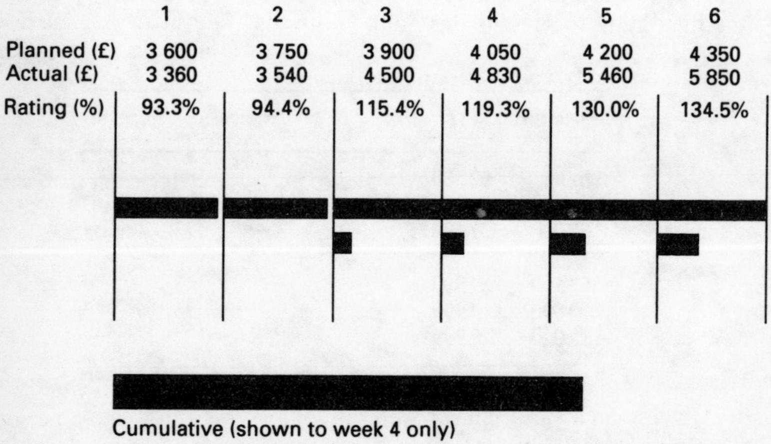

	1	2	3	4	5	6
Planned (£)	3 600	3 750	3 900	4 050	4 200	4 350
Actual (£)	3 360	3 540	4 500	4 830	5 460	5 850
Rating (%)	93.3%	94.4%	115.4%	119.3%	130.0%	134.5%

Cumulative (shown to week 4 only)

(b)

Figure 4.13   (*a*) Sales – planned and actual. (*b*) A Gantt chart.

Figure 4.13 illustrates a sales manager's targets for one of his
salesmen, over a 6-week period. Figure 4.13(*a*) shows the planned and
actual sales in tabular form. These data are shown in the form of a
Gantt chart in Figure 4.13(*b*). Here each division (denoted 1, 2, 3, etc.)
represents the target performance for one week. The divisions are of
equal size, *even though the sales targets are not*. A target is shown as

being reached exactly when the horizontal bar *just* fills the division. If it falls short of the division then actual performance is less than planned. If it more than fills the division (shown by the addition of a second bar), then actual performance exceeds that planned. For clarity the actual and planned figures and a percentage success rating can be written in on the chart.

It is also possible to add a further bar below the 'percentage performance' bar which is cumulative, and shows the extent to which targets have been met over a longer period. To illustrate the method this second bar in Figure 4.13(*b*) has only been marked in for the first 4 weeks. At the end of this 4-week period the cumulative target sales were £15,300 but actual sales were £16,230. This means that £930 of the fifth week's target of £4 200 has already been achieved. This is about 22 per cent of the fifth week's target and the cumulative line at the end of the fourth week therefore goes on to mark in 22 per cent of that division.

4.9   Exercises on Gantt charts

1   A salesman's sales figures were as follows for the 4-week period commencing 5 April. Draw a Gantt chart to illustrate the data, on both a weekly and a cumulative basis.

Week commencing	Target sales (£)	Actual sales (£)
5 April	£2 500	£1 150
12 April	£3 000	£2 450
19 April	£4 000	£3 000
26 April	£5 000	£6 250

2   A salesman's sales figures were as follows for the 4-week period commencing 10 July. Draw a Gantt chart to illustrate the data, on both a weekly and a cumulative basis.

Week commencing	Target sales (£)	Actual sales (£)
10 July	5 000	4 720
17 July	8 000	6 550
24 July	10 000	8 750
31 July	6 000	9 750

3   A salesman's sales figures were as follows for the 4-week period
    commencing 1 October. Draw a Gantt chart to illustrate the data,
    on both a weekly and a cumulative basis.

Week commencing	Target sales (£)	Actual sales (£)
1 October	15 000	24 250
8 October	17 500	25 500
15 October	20 000	23 850
22 October	25 000	22 950

4.10   Pie charts

One of the simplest methods to represent the way in which a whole
statistical collection breaks down into its component parts is to use the
'pie' diagram. A pie is a circular culinary delicacy, and we are familiar
from childhood with the advantages to be enjoyed by securing a larger
slice of pie than other members of the family. The pie chart depicts the
component parts of any set of statistical data as slices of pie.

The complete circle represents the whole set of data. Any subdivisions
within the set are then shown by subdividing the circle in proportion.
In Figure 4.14, for example, the 'one-person pensioner index gives a
weighting of 442 parts in 1 000 to food. The general index, by contrast,
gives food a weighting of 278 parts in 1 000, since food does not form
as large a proportion of total expenditure in general households. What
share of the pie diagram should be given to 'food' in these two pie
charts? There are 360° in a circle, and therefore the calculations are as
follows:

$$\text{Pension index:} \qquad \text{Food} = \frac{442}{1000} \times 360°$$

$$= 159.1°$$

$$\text{General index:} \qquad \text{Food} = \frac{278}{1000} \times 360°$$

$$= 100.1°$$

When drawing the pie chart having calculated the sector of the circle
to be allocated to each part of the data, you will find it helpful to show

the actual data on the chart. It is common practice to colour or shade the sectors to distinguish them from one another.

In order to draw the pie chart you need a compass and protractor, and you should be prepared to take them to an examination because they are rarely provided by the examiners. The diameter you should use for your circle depends on the number of component parts of the data – the more parts the larger the circle. In examinations a radius of 3cm or $1\frac{1}{4}$in. would be satisfactory, and it will be to your advantage to colour the sectors in order to provide a striking diagram, provided that time permits.

When comparing sets of information in this way, two methods are possible. In Figure 4.14 we see that the circles are the same size, and the comparisons drawn bring out the different proportions of total income spent on a particular item of expense. For example, we can see that whereas food forms a large part of the expenditure of pensioners, transport and vehicle expenses form a much smaller part.

Suppose that our data included a further piece of information – that the average annual income of pensioners is £3,000, whereas the average annual income of the whole population is £12,000. Clearly, even though the pie chart is comparing the weights, and there are 1 000 in each case, the two equal-sized circles give a misleading impression. It would be better to have the circles reflecting the comparative totals of expenditure, which are in the ratio of 4 to 1. Since the area of a circle is πr^2, it would be appropriate to have the radii of our circles in proportion to the square roots of 4 and 1, i.e. 2 to 1. Using a radius of 3cm for the pensioners' circle, this would mean a radius of 6cm for the general index circle. The student might care to redraw these pie charts to see the difference in the presentation.

We may conclude that the pie chart is a good method of presentation if we wish to show the relative size of the various components making up a set of data. It is not a good method if we wish to:

1 Compare totals of varying size.
2 Present data which has many component parts within the total, particularly when some parts are very small in relation to the total. Thus to show the quantities of stock in a warehouse with many different lines would mean too many subdivisions of the circle, with awkward calculations.

In Chapter 3, and again in this chapter, reference has been made to the dangers that statistics may be distorted either deliberately or inadvertently. Diagrams, charts and graphs are among the easiest of statistical tools to use dishonestly, and since they are more easily understood than other presentations, they may therefore delude a larger number of people. Deliberate distortion aside, an enthusiastic individual, with a point of view to express which is believed to be in the public

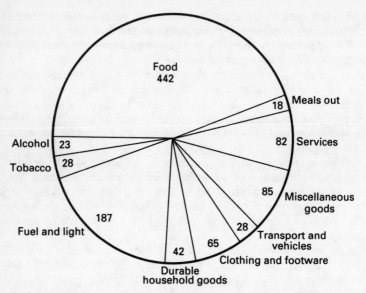

(a) Index for one-person pensioner households (Total weights = 1 000)

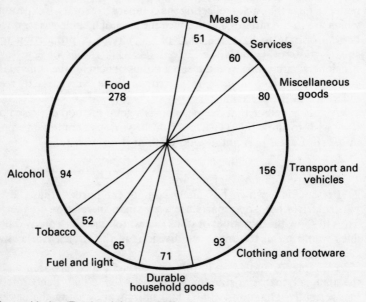

(b) General index (Total weights = 1 000)

Figure 4.14   Pie charts showing the weights used in retail price indices (Source: *Economic Progress Report*)

interest, may unwittingly bring biased, incorrectly presented data forward in the genuine belief that it is correct. Students should appriase all their own work critically, and also the presentations put before them by others, to detect shortcomings.

4.11   Exercises on pie charts

1   Draw a pie chart to illustrate the following set of statistics, which is taken from *Social Trends*:

Families in Great Britain, 19..

	Percentages
All families	100
Families with no dependent children	51.9
1 child	20.5
2 children	16.5
3 children	6.9
4 or more children	4.2

2   Consumers' expenditure in 19.. is given as follows, in £ million:

Food	12 500
Drink and tobacco	7 500
Housing, fuel and light	8 300
Clothing	5 100
Cars and motor cycles	6 500
Durable household goods	3 600
Other goods	4 500
Other services	3 000
	51 000

Draw a pie diagram to illustrate the figures provided.

3   United Kingdom local authority income for 19.8 was made up as follows:

	£ million
Grant from Central Government	23 000
Rates	18 000
Interest	1 000
Rent	3 000
Trading surpluses	3 000
	£48 000

Draw a pie chart to illustrate this data.

4   Banking records show that trading activities on the London financial markets in 1986 and 1989 were carried out as follows:

Manner of trading	% of trades 1986	% of trades 1989
Between two UK principals	11	13
Between one UK and one foreign principal	34	34
Through brokers	43	38
Direct with customers	9	15
For 'other market participants'	3	–
	100%	100%

Draw two pie charts to illustrate these figures.

5   UK exports and imports by country of destination and origin were as follows in 19.7. Draw two pie charts to show the pattern of exports and imports, based on these figures, given in £m.

Area	Exports	Imports
European Community	39 021	48 031
Other Western European	7 788	12 327
North America	12 992	10 140
Other developed countries	4 085	6 892
Oil-exporting countries	5 280	1 606
Rest of the world	10 256	10 588
Totals	79 422	89 584

4.12   Summary of Chapter 4

1   Data are difficult to appreciate even when well tabulated, and in many situations some sort of pictorial representation enhances understanding.

2   All diagrams should have a title, should show the sources of the data where possible, should give any units of measurement, and should be as fully labelled as space permits. If shading or colouring is used, a key may be necessary.

3   Pictograms use a small drawing to represent the data being illustrated. Thus population may be represented by matchstick men, traffic by motor cars, accident statistics by red triangle warning signs, etc.

4   Bar charts represent data by horizontal or vertical bars. Multiple bar charts show related sets of data, perhaps with various types of shading to distinguish them. Component bar charts show on a single bar the various elements of which a total is made up. Percentage bar charts are similar, the total coming to 100 per cent.

5   Histograms are ways of representing frequency distributions as parallel blocks, each block representing a class interval. Some sets of open-ended data may have blocks which represent more than one class interval. Frequency distributions can also be represented by frequency polygons.

6   Gantt charts enable planned performances to be compared with actual performances. The planned performance is given a bar of fixed width, even if the performance required is different from week to week. Actual performance is filled in as a band which, if the plan is exactly achieved, crosses the full width of the bar provided. Under-performance means the bar is not crossed fully, while over-performance means a second band has to be started to cross the bar.

7   Pie charts are circular diagrams, the component parts appearing as slices of the pie. The size of the circle can be varied if the total 'pie' to be shared up grows or diminishes.

5
Pictorial representation of statistical data 2: graphs

5.1 Introduction to graphs

We have used tabulation in order to present data in a compact and manageable form, and a number of pictorial methods of representation to illustrate data in more interesting ways, which might appeal to any in our audiences who are not particularly numerate and find tables of data rather difficult to understand. There are many occasions when it will be advantageous to use graphical methods to complement or replace tables of data.

Essentially a graph is a diagram which shows the relationship between two variable quantities each measured along one of a pair of axes, at right-angles to one another. Graphs are frequently drawn on squared paper, which assists the 'plotting' of the observed data as a number of points, which may then be joined up by a line. In any pair of variables – say, sales during the months of the year – one variable is usually dependent upon the other. Thus the sales vary as the months follow one another. The months may therefore be said to be the **independent variable** and the sales in the various months are the **dependent variable.** The sale of Easter bonnets depends upon the closeness of the month to Easter, while the sale of fireworks varies with the approach of various festivals as the year passes.

Most graphs are drawn on arithmetic (or natural scale) graph paper, in which both the horizontal scale and the vertical scale are ruled up in the same 'natural' measurements, e.g. centimetres and millimetres. We shall see that another type of graph paper, logarithmic paper, is ruled rather differently, but this need not concern us yet.

Since both the horizontal and vertical scales are ruled up in the same way, we finish up with a neat graticule of squares, and the term 'squared paper' is often used.

Figure 5.1 shows how points are plotted on graph. The following matters are important:

1 Two lines, known as axes, are drawn in at right-angles to one another, meeting at the point O, which is called the origin of the graph. The horizontal axis, the X axis, is scaled in units of the **independent** variable, whereas the vertical axis, the Y axis, is scaled in units of the **dependent** variable, i.e. Y depends on X. For example, the sales of umbrellas in the United Kingdom is closely linked to the time of year, and therefore the sales (Y) depend on the month (X) to a considerable extent.

2 Every graph should be self-explanatory, and therefore there must be a title to the graph, the source of the data must be given, and all axes must be fully labelled. Where more than one curve is marked on the graph, it may be necessary to insert a key, to let the audience know what the different lines mean, e.g. one line might be dotted and another marked with a series of dashes. Different colours may be used if a colour presentation is possible, and the key will indicate what the various colours represent. Alternatively, the curves may be labelled. The headings, sources, keys, etc. may be positioned on the graph in a convenient way so as not to interfere with the visual impression created.

3 A scale must be chosen for each axis which not only enables the data to be plotted over the full range, but also displays the information in the best way possible. Thus the same vertical axis could be made to show up to 100, 1 000 or even 1 million umbrellas, but the scale chosen would need to be different. The scale should present the data as large as possible, using the full width of the page, so that it is easy to plot the points and to 'interpolate' as necessary. The meaning of 'interpolate' and 'extrapolate' is explained later (see page 99). The axes should be clearly labelled, both with the name of the variable (for example, 'sales') and with the units in which the variable is measured (for example, 'thousands' or 'millions').

4 **Points are plotted** on the graph by using the values given in the table supplied, or found in the statistical enquiry which is being carried out. Each pair of related facts, such as the fact that 68 000 umbrellas were sold in February, gives a unique point on the graph. The point may be marked by a tiny dot, but preferably by a small cross made by two short lines intersecting at the exact spot. In such graphs the points are clearly picked out, and the curves joining up the points may be discontinuous to give greater emphasis.

The data represented in Figure 5.1 come from the Umbrella Trades Federation, UK, and are as follows:

Month	Sales
January	75
February	68
March	57
April	84
May	36
June	19
July	18
August	27
September	36
October	58
November	56
December	67

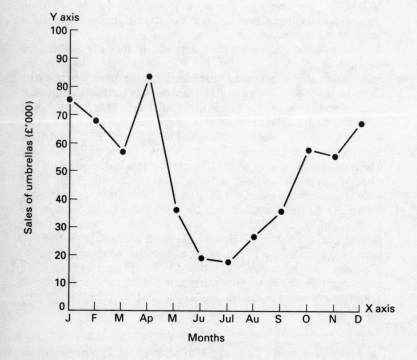

Figure 5.1   Plotting data on a simple graph

5.2 Exercises: simple graphs

1 The following information relates to the total sales (value) of a
 supermarket chain over a 12-month period. Using a suitable scale,
 record the information in the form of a graph.

Month	Sales (£)
1	270 000
2	200 000
3	240 000
4	300 000
5	320 000
6	400 000
7	410 000
8	400 000
9	420 000
10	440 000
11	410 000
12	500 000

2 The following sales for the year were achieved by the two departments
 of a two-centre store. Plot these on a graph, using a suitable scale.

Sales of Supertraders Plc

	Groceries (£)	Greengroceries (£)
Jan.	28 250	12 750
Feb.	24 250	11 500
Mar.	36 500	16 500
Apr.	33 750	14 750
May	34 500	15 500
Jun.	37 250	18 000
Jul.	25 000	13 250
Aug.	28 750	14 500
Sep.	34 000	18 500
Oct.	42 500	20 250
Nov.	43 500	21 000
Dec.	56 000	23 500

3 Mechanical Parts Ltd makes two models of a particular machine, the 'Junior' model and the 'Senior' model. Sales during the year are given below. You are asked to record these figures. *and total sales*, on a graph, labelling all parts of the graph as necessary.

Mechanical Parts Ltd: sales during year 19..

	Jan. (£)	Feb. (£)	Mar. (£)	Apr. (£)	May (£)	Jun. (£)
Junior	5 000	5 500	7 000	8 000	8 500	9 000
Senior	14 000	13 500	12 000	13 000	11 000	8 000

	Jul. (£)	Aug. (£)	Sept. (£)	Oct. (£)	Nov. (£)	Dec. (£)
Junior	8 500	7 000	9 500	10 000	10 500	12 000
Senior	8 500	3 500	4 000	4 500	4 000	5 000

5.3 Breaking the axis on a simple graph

Although we always use the available space on a graph as fully as possible, and we always start the vertical axis at zero, it often happens that the range of data we are trying to illustrate only occupies a small part of the full range. In this situation it clarifies the picture if the vertical scale is broken at a point slightly above the zero point, and the scale then only shows the more limited range within which the data falls. For example, in Figure 5.2 (*a*) and (*b*) we are illustrating some data about company sales as follows:

Sales of XYZ Co Ltd (19.1–19.5)

	Sales (£'000)
19.1	600
19.2	640
19.3	670
19.4	710
19.5	730
19.6	780
19.7	820

The sales represented on an unbroken vertical scale (Figure 5.2(*a*)) are exactly the same as those illustrated in Figure 5.2(*b*), where the breaking of the scale has enabled us to use a much larger scale over the very limited range of the data. Instead of being compacted in a small area

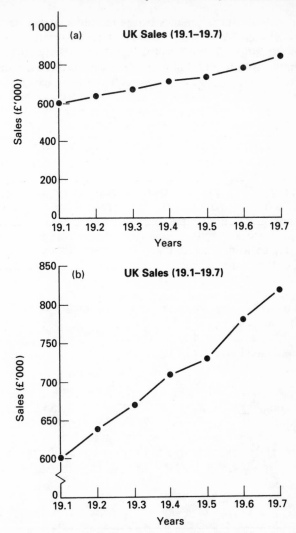

Figure 5.2 Improved clarity achieved by breaking the vertical scale

Notes:
1 In graph (*a*) the data are shown on a normal scale. As all the data occur between sales of £600,000 and £820,000 much of the scale is wasted (from £0 – £600,000 and from £820,000–£1 million).
2 In graph (*b*) the scale is broken above the zero mark. The detailed scale above the break is much larger than in graph (*a*) and consequently the change in profits can be more easily assimilated.
3 This use of the broken vertical scale is particularly useful where comparisons between two sets of figures are being studied (so long as both lie in the restricted range shown by the enlarged scale).

of the paper, the data is presented over the full space available, and relative to a much larger scale. The zigzag break in the vertical scale draws our attention to the fact that the scale from zero up to the break-point is not properly represented – we have taken a liberty with the scale to make the actual change in profits easier to see on the graph. It is very important to exercise discretion when using a broken scale in this way, and to draw the attention of the reader to the break in the scale, so that a wrong impression is not created.

5.4   Z graphs

A Z graph or Z chart is a diagram which can be used in various departments within a company because it shows data in several forms on the same graph, and is particularly useful for comparing actual results with forecast results. It is a type of time series graph and its name is derived from the fact that the completed diagram is shaped like a Z. The three separate lines which make up the letter Z are obtained as follows:

1   Monthly values for one year (very occasionally weekly or daily intervals are used).
2   Monthly cumulative values for the year.
3   Moving annual totals (MATs).

These ideas can best be followed from an actual example. We will use some company sales figures to illustrate the method. Since one of the statistics to be plotted on the Z chart is a moving annual total (MAT), we must have at least 12 months' figures already available. The sales figures given cover 2 years and the Z chart we will draw will cover year 2 (we need the year 1 figures to find the Moving Annual Total (MAT).

Company sales (£'000)

Month	Year 1 sales	Year 2 sales	Cumulative sales (year 2)	MAT (year 2)
January	22	27	27	427
February	20	24	51	431
March	25	28	79	434
April	35	40	119	439
May	40	42	161	441
June	41	44	205	444

July	32	33	238	445
August	30	35	273	450
September	40	46	319	456
October	45	48	367	459
November	46	50	417	463
December	46	51	468	468

A moving annual total is found by adding up all the monthly sales for the previous 12 months. In year 1 the total sales were £422,000, so that the MAT for December in year 1 was £422,000. As we move into January, we add on the January year 2 sales and drop off the January year 1 figure. So the MAT in January year 2 was £427,000 (£422 000 − £22 000 + £27 000 = £427,000).

The reader will note that by the time we reach December in year 2 we have dropped off all the Year 1 figures and picked up all the year 2 figures, so that the cumulative monthly total and the 'moving annual'

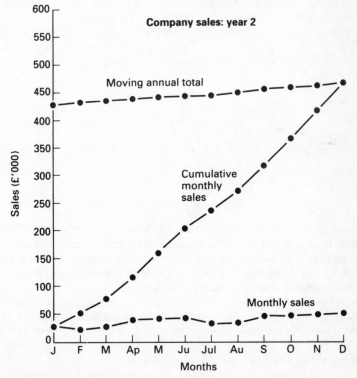

Figure 5.3   Z chart of business sales

total are the same. This is why the figure must finish up as a Z chart, because the last cumulative figure plotted completes the Z.

You will sometimes find a Z chart drawn with more than one scale on the vertical axis in order to better accommodate the wide range of values to be plotted. Unfortunately it can lead to a somewhat confusing diagram, and therefore, unless it is important to show small changes from month to month, it is better to use one scale only.

What do we learn from the Z chart shown in Figure 5.3? First, the lowest line of the Z shows us the sales achieved, month by month, and although these are fairly steady towards the end of the year, they do grow fairly erratically early in the year. The diagonal line of the Z shows us the accumulating total as the year proceeds. The MAT has an interesting effect. It smooths out some of the monthly fluctuations, giving a trend which reveals that sales are moving in a general upward direction throughout the year. The increase is not spectacular but it is steady, and this is encouraging. You will often find that Z charts are plotted continuously from year to year in order to form a graphical record over a substantial period of time. Such a long-term record is very helpful in showing the growth of a company, e.g. in making a presentation to a bank when seeking funds for expansion.

Our next example will illustrate the use of a Z chart as a management device for comparing actual performance with targets. Suppose your company has budgeted maintenance costs as follows for the year just commencing:

Months	J	F	M	A	M	J	Ju	Au	S	O	N	D
Estimated costs (£'000s)	4	6	6	5	3	3	8	10	6	4	6	6
Previous year's (£'000s)	4	5	5	4	4	3	5	5	5	4	4	3

The previous years' figures show that by December last year the moving annual total was £51 000. We can draw a budgeted cost chart for the current year at a start of the year as soon as the budget is agreed, and it will appear as shown in Figure 5.4, calculating the cumulative and the MAT figures from the data given above.

What we now wish to do is to monitor the actual maintenance costs as the various parts of the maintenance programme proceed in the current year, to see how closely the actual figures are linked to the budgeted figures. Clearly we cannot expect an exact correspondence between the two sets of figures (breakdowns can occur at any time) but we need to know what is happening. The table required to produce the two Z charts is given below. What is not given in the Table is the

Month	Budgeted costs		Actual costs		This year's budgeted totals cumulative MAT
	Last year	This year	Last year	This year	
J	4	4	5		4
F	5	6	6		10
M	5	6	6		16
A	4	5	4		21
May	4	3	4		24
J	3	3	3		27
Jul	5	8	5		35
Au	5	10	4		45
S	5	6	4		51
O	4	4	5		55
N	4	6	2		61
D	3	6	2		67

actual figures for this year, which we are waiting to discover. Eventually we find these are:

J	F	M	A	May	J	Jul	A	S	O	N	D
5	6	7	7	4	5	7	8	5	4	5	5

This gives us the dotted Z chart shown in Figure 5.4.

You can see from the chart that costs were greater than those budgeted for in the first 6 months of the year. But clearly some corrective action was taken, because actual costs moved below budget in the second half of the year, bringing the overall figures very close to the target by the end.

5.5   Exercises on Z graphs

1   From the following information prepare a Z chart of the sales performance of Alpha Ltd for the present year and comment on the year's results as revealed by the diagram:

Sales (£ '000)

	Last year	This year
Jan.	56	75
Feb.	54	78
Mar.	58	82
Apr.	62	85

May	66	91
Jun.	66	93
Jul.	71	96
Aug.	73	98
Sep.	75	105
Oct.	78	108
Nov.	80	112
Dec.	81	115

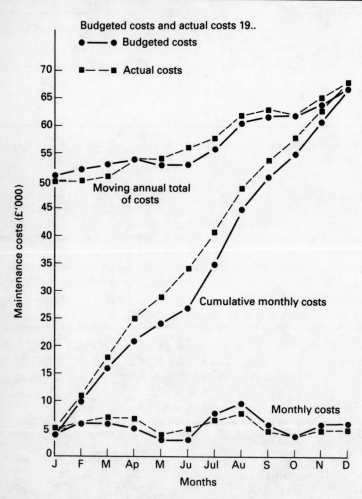

Figure 5.4   Budgeted costs and actual costs compared

2 From the following figures for output by the Heavy Components Co. Ltd draw up a Z chart showing the present year's production achievements, and comment on the diagram:

Output in units

	Last year	This year
Jan.	27	45
Feb.	24	43
Mar.	28	27
Apr.	40	15
May	42	0
Jun.	44	0
Jul.	33	0
Aug.	35	38
Sep.	46	58
Oct.	48	64
Nov.	50	72
Dec.	51	74

3 An agricultural machinery supplier has budgeted its cost for this year as shown in column 2 below. All figures are in £'000s. Its previous year's budgeted and actual costs are shown in columns 1 and 3. This year's actual costs are not yet known of course. You are asked to draw up figures on a sheet of paper for columns 5 and 6, and hence draw a Z chart of this year's budgeted costs.

Month	Budgeted costs		Actual costs		This year's budgeted totals	
	Last year col. 1	This year col. 2	Last year col. 3	This year col. 4	Cumulative col. 5	MAT col. 6
J	8	9	7	–	?	?
F	8	9	7	–	?	?
M	7	6	8	–	?	?
A	4	4	7	–	?	?
May	4	3	7	–	?	?
J	2	3	4	–	?	?
Jul	2	3	4	–	?	?
Au	2	1	1	–	?	?
S	2	1	1	–	?	?

O	3	3	1	–	?	?
N	5	7	4	–	?	?
D	8	10	4	–	?	?

You are then asked to draw in on the same graph a Z chart of this year's actual costs (the column 4 figures), which turn out to be as follows: January £10 000, February £12 000, March £7 000, April £7 000, May £4 000, June £3 000, July £1 000, August £1 000, September £1 000, October £2 000, November £3 000, and December £8 000.

4   A hospital has budgeted its maintenance costs for this year as shown in column 2 below. All figures are in £'000s. Its budgeted and actual costs for last year are shown in columns 1 and 3. This year's actual costs are not of course known yet (column 4). By working out the figures for columns 5 and 6, you are asked to draw a Z chart for this year's budgeted costs.

| Month | Budgeted costs | | Actual costs | | This year's budgeted totals | |
	Last year col. 1	This year col. 2	Last year col. 3	This year col. 4	Cumulative col. 5	MAT col. 6
J	10	12	13	–	?	?
F	12	12	13	–	?	?
M	15	16	16	–	?	?
A	18	20	16	–	?	?
May	15	16	18	–	?	?
J	15	16	18	–	?	?
Jul	8	10	10	–	?	?
Au	8	10	10	–	?	?
S	12	10	8	–	?	?
O	14	12	10	–	?	?
N	15	14	10	–	?	?
D	15	14	15	–	?	?

You are now asked to draw on the same graph a Z chart of the actual costs for this year, which turn out to be January £14 000, February £14 000, March £14 000, April £19 000, May £16 000, June £18 000, July £12 000, August £6 000, September £6 000, October £14 000, November £15 000 and December £14 000.

5.6 Straight-line graphs

The simple graph of sales in Figure 5.1 rose and fell in line with quantity sold – it was a zigzag line. However, some graphs, where the data are in a special relationship, consist of straight lines. Such a graph arises where one set of data varies directly with changes in the other set of data.

For example, in Figure 5.5 the cost of a particular product is plotted against the number of units required, up to a total of 50. Each unit is £12, and there is a direct relation between the cost of a particular order and the number of units ordered. The result is a straight-line graph passing through the origin (since when no units are ordered there is nothing to pay).

A straight-line graph of this sort was once widely used as a ready reckoner. This particular straight-line graph can be used to read off the total cost of any number of units from 1 to 50. To do this we draw a horizontal line across from the number of units required (32 in the diagram) until it intercepts the graph. We then drop a perpendicular from that point on to the price axis, where we find that 32 units cost £384 altogether.

Reading off values in this way is called **interpolation** – finding the intermediate terms in the known range of a series from the values

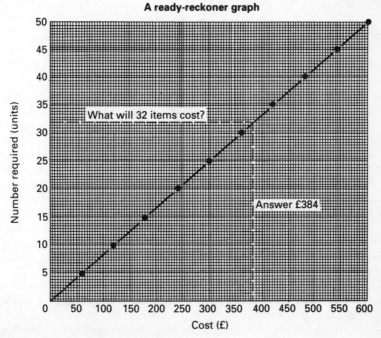

Figure 5.5   A straight line graph

already known. If we were to extend the straight line and find values outside the range already given, it would be called **extrapolation**.

Today the electronic calculator has made such ready reckoners largely unnecessary.

Many straight-line graphs pass through the origin, where both variables are zero. For example in Figure 5.5 the cost of no units was £0, as we would expect. This is not always the case, and a straight-line graph may intercept one of the axes at some point. In the break-even chart in Figure 5.6 certain fixed costs of an output of a certain product are incurred before any output can be produced at all. This might include costs of jigs and tools to be used in manufacture, or design costs incurred before even a prototype product is produced. The cost of manufacture will therefore start with these fixed costs (50 000 in the graph) and the other variable costs which vary directly with output must be borne in addition as output commences. The cost line therefore does not pass through the origin but intercepts the price axis at the £50 000 mark. By contrast, the proceeds from the sale of the output do start at the origin. Since selling price is fixed at a sufficiently high level to achieve a profit eventually, the 'sales proceeds' line is steeper than the cost line. The two lines therefore intersect at the break-even point. At this point the total costs incurred are covered, and every unit sold after this point will yield a profit.

5.7   Break-even charts

In Figure 5.6 every unit costs £10 of variable cost (in addition to its share of the fixed costs). If these costs are added to fixed costs, we have a total cost line cutting the Y axis at the £50 000 point on the axis. Each unit is sold for £25, and is therefore making a £15 **contribution** (over and above repaying its variable cost). What is this £15 contributing to? To begin with (before we reach the break-even point) the £15 is contributing to the recovery of the fixed costs of production. At £15 contribution per unit it will take sales of $3333\frac{1}{3}$ units to recover the £50 000 fixed costs. At this point – the break-even point – the sales proceeds are $3,333\frac{1}{3} \times £25 = £83\,333.33$. This is £50 000 fixed costs and £33 333.33 variable costs (at £10 per unit). We have recovered all our fixed costs and from the break-even point on the £15 on each unit begins to contribute to profit. The student might like to ponder the effects of the following changes (redraw the diagram if you like, to study the effects):

1   The management decides to raise the price to £35 per unit, without any change in costs.
2   The variable costs rise to £15 per unit, and because of competition it is deemed impossible to raise the price to the public.

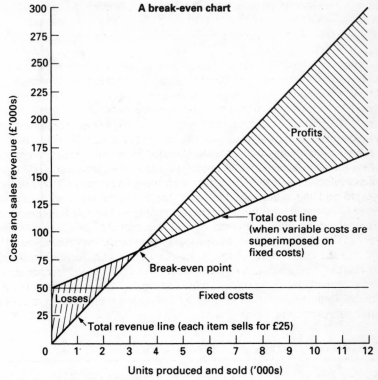

Figure 5.6 A break-even chart

3 The variable costs rise to £15 per unit and the price is raised to £30 per unit.

What will be the break-even point in each case? (See answers at the end of the chapter, p. 128.)

We can draw a break-even chart in a different way, as shown in Figure 5.7. The variable costs are drawn first and the fixed costs appear as a parallel band above the variable costs. The sales revenue is drawn in as before. The advantage of this presentation is that a vertical line drawn from the X axis to touch the Sales revenue line shows the recovery of the variable – cost and the contribution above it. Any sale recovers the variable cost – even a sale of a single unit recovers the £10 variable cost and provides £15 towards the £50 000 fixed costs. At sales of 1 000 units we see the variable costs recovered and some contribution to fixed costs. At the break-even point we see the recovery of the variable costs and the recovery of all the fixed costs, to break even. At sales of 9 000 units we see the recovery of all the costs and a useful contribution to profits of £85 000.

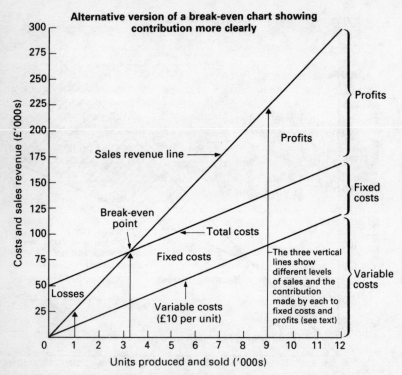

Figure 5.7   A break-even chart, showing the contribution made at any level of output by fixed costs and profits (if any)

5.8   Exercises on break-even charts

1   A business has fixed costs amounting to £60 000 and a single product which costs £15 per unit and sells for £40. Draw the break-even chart for this product, the total output of which cannot exceed 10 000 units because of limited capacity.

   From your diagram read off the following figures:

   (a) The profit at full capacity if the entire output is sold.
   (b) The profit at an output of 8 000 units.
   (c) The loss at an output of 1 000 units only.

2   An engineering business has fixed costs amounting to £120 000 and a single product which costs £20 per unit and sells for £60. Draw the break-even chart for this product, the total output of which cannot exceed 30 000 units because of limited capacity.

   From your diagram read off the following figures:

(*a*) The profit at full capacity if the entire output is sold.
(*b*) The profit at an output of 20 000 units
(*c*) The break-even output.

3   A clothing business has fixed costs amounting to £100 000 and a single product which costs £8 per unit and sells for £35. Draw the break-even chart for this product, the total output of which cannot exceed 15 000 units because of limited capacity.
From your diagram read off the following figures:

(*a*) The profit at full capacity if the entire output is sold.
(*b*) The profit at an output of 10 000 units.
(*c*) The loss at an output of 3000 units only.

4   The costs of a project are £1 000 fixed costs and then £20 per unit produced. The proceeds from the sale of the units are £50 per unit. Draw a graph for costs and another for sales on the same diagram, using 0, 5, 10, 15, 20, 25, 30, 35 and 40 units of output, and thus determine which unit of production will bring the project past the break-even point.

5   (*a*) From the following information, calculate by means of a graph the sales value and volume at break-even point and comment on its significance:

Total receipts (sales)	£1 200 000
Fixed costs	£800 000
Variable cost	£150 000
Volume	300 000 units

(*b*) What would be the effect on the break-even point if the fixed cost was reduced by 10 per cent? Indicate your conclusions on the graph and comment fully on their significance.

6   (*a*) From the following information calculate by means of a graph the sales value and volume at break-even point and comment on its significance.

Total receipts (sales)	£800 000
Fixed costs	£250 000
Variable cost	£240 000
Volume	960 000 units

(*b*) What would be the effect on the break-even point if the fixed cost was reduced by 20 per cent? Indicate your conclusions on the graph and comment fully on their significance.

5.9   Scatter diagrams

A scatter diagram is a technique for comparing the relation between
two variables. One of the variables is assigned to the horizontal axis,
the other to the vertical axis. Observed relations between the two
variables are then plotted as points on the scatter diagram. In any
business we frequently have to compare one set of data with another
in order to establish whether there is any relation between them. For
example, does the amount spent on advertising have any effect on sales?
Does the wearing of seat belts decrease the number of serious injuries
caused in car accidents? A scatter diagram provides a visual representation
of any relation which may exist and helps us to decide whether this
relation is close or not.

In a scatter diagram we plot the information we have collected, with
the independent variable plotted against the horizontal (X) axis and
the dependent variable plotted against the vertical (Y) axis. Each pair
of data gives us a single point on the graph. These points are not joined
together, because we are looking for patterns of relationship. Sometimes
we may find all the points in the scatter diagram compacted together
at the top of the graph, or over to one side of the graph. In such a case
it may be appropriate to use a broken scale. In Figure 5.2, we had a
broken scale on the vertical axis, but with scatter graphs we can employ
a broken scale on either axis. As before, a broken scale will enable us
to plot more accurately, because we can use a larger scale; but it may
also distort the visual relationship. Therefore, unless the plots are
compacted at the top of the graph paper or at one side of the horizontal
scale, do not use a broken scale.

Scatter diagrams showing linear relationships

For our example of a scatter diagram we shall compare the output of
a particular component with its unit cost of production.

Output (in units)	Cost per unit (£)
50	4
100	3.7
150	3.4
200	3.1
250	2.8
300	2.5
350	2.2
400	1.9

When each of these pairs of data is plotted as a small point on the scatter diagram, we have a result as shown in Figure 5.8. It is clear that the 'scatter' is non-existent – in fact we have a perfect relation between the two sets of data. This is perhaps rather unlikely in most production situations, since it seems that similar increases in output produce exactly similar economies in production to cut the unit cost of the component.

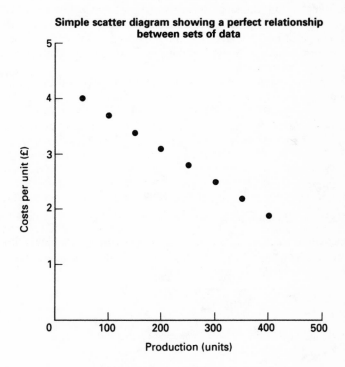

Figure 5.8   A simple scatter diagram

Notes:
1   The scatter diagram has been drawn with production on the *X* axis and unit costs on the *Y* axis because the unit costs depend upon the volume of output.
2   All the plots lie on a straight line which indicates there is a perfect relation between the two sets of data.
3   As production increases by 50 units the cost per unit falls by £0.3 (i.e. 30 pence).
4   The relation is said to be inverse, because as production rises, unit cost falls.

Taking a second component we have the following data:

Output (in units)	Cost per unit (£)
5	10
10	9.5
15	9.3
20	8.5
25	8.0
30	7.7
35	7.0
40	6.4
45	6.0
50	5.6
55	5.3
60	5.0

The scatter diagram is as shown in Figure 5.9.

A scatter diagram showing a curvilinear relationship

Consider the data shown below, which compares sales achieved by a department store with its advertising expenditure.

Advertising (£'000s)	Sales (£'000s)
10	200
12	230
14	255
16	267
18	275
20	280
22	284
24	284

The scattergraph is as shown in Figure 5.10. It appears that the relation between sales and advertising is not linear (in a straight-line) but curvilinear. The number of people who can be persuaded to buy the product appears to reach exhaustion at an expenditure of about £22 000, and further advertising becomes pointless.

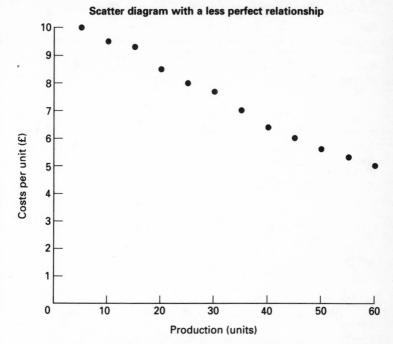

Figure 5.9 Economies in production with increasing output

Notes:
1 Again the relation is said to be inverse, with costs falling as output rises.
2 The relation between the two sets of data is more erratic than in Figure 5.8, but it is still fairly close.
3 We could imagine a straight line drawn through the middle of the data, with some items of the scatter on one side and some on the other.
4 A good way for students to work out such a line is to take a length of cotton and stretch it tightly between the two hands. Then hold it over the scatter diagram to find the line of best fit. More detailed lines of best fit are discussed later in this book (see Section 10.3).

A scattergraph with wide scatter

A finance house collects data on the returns earned on its loans and also on the risks envisaged by the branch managers at the time the loan was made. Interest earned varies between 5 per cent at the lowest point and 40 per cent at the highest point. Risks are required to be assessed on a scale from 0 per cent to 60 per cent (any risk considered to be greater than 60 per cent aborts the request for a loan). Twenty-five loans were investigated as a random sample and gave the following results:

Risk v interest on a sample of twenty-five loans

% risk	0	0	5	5	5
% interest	12	30	15	36	20

% risk	5	10	10	10	10
% interest	24	28	25	6	12

% risk	15	15	15	20	20
% interest	14	29	10	15	30

% risk	25	25	30	30	30
% interest	28	30	20	14	24

% risk	35	35	40	40	50
% interest	18	29	16	32	12

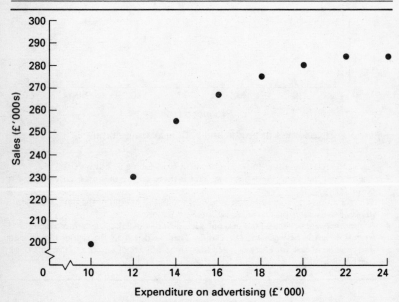

Figure 5.10   A curvilinear scatter

Notes:
1 Notice that the graph has been drawn with broken scales on both axes so that the effective scatter is well positioned in the middle of the diagram rather than off centre with some sectors of the diagram unused.
2 The cluster indicates that there is some link between the two sets of data, but it is not as direct as in the linear relations already considered.
3 The relation is **positive** – as advertising increases so do sales.
4 The relation is curvilinear, the sales increasing to a smaller and smaller extent as advertising rises. Our advertising budget policy would obviously reflect the fact that the increased yield per £1 of advertising expenditure falls away.

Average risk $= \dfrac{485}{25} = 19.4$ per cent

Average earnings $= \dfrac{529}{25} = 21.2$ per cent

The scatter diagram is shown in Figure 5.11.

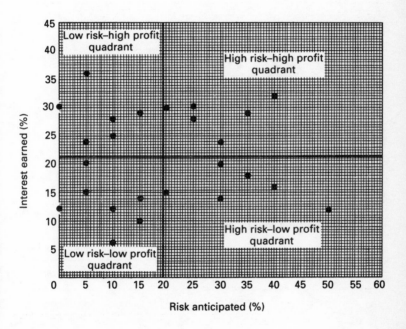

Figure 5.11 Risk and yield on finance house loans

Notes:
1 The scatter is wide and shows no particularly close relationship between the risk run and the yield earned, except that the loans with the smaller degrees of risk do generally speaking have lower yields – in other words in view of the low risk, the finance company kept the rate charged low.
2 The display of the average risk and the average earnings divides the scatter into four quadrants which might make useful training material for staff managers – the need to relate rates to risk is shown up rather well by the four quadrants.

5.10   Exercises on scatter diagrams

1   Twelve students were given an assessed mark by their tutor. They
then sat the end of the year examinations. The marks gained were:

Person	Assessed	Exam
1	92	85
2	70	72
3	64	70
4	62	50
5	52	62
6	47	70
7	52	77
8	69	92
9	70	62
10	61	60
11	70	47
12	62	60

Construct a scatter diagram of these data and draw the line of best fit.

2   The following is the result of a survey into family expenditures on
food and clothing in Commuterville in 1 year:

Families	Expenditure on food (£)	Expenditure on clothing (£)
A	2 000	1 000
B	2 080	840
C	2 360	800
D	1 680	2 240
E	2 600	960
F	4 200	2 800
G	8 000	3 280
H	3 680	4 004
I	2 160	1 280
J	2 080	1 200
K	2 240	840
L	2 040	880

Construct a scatter diagram of these data and draw the line of best fit. What do your findings indicate?

3   The following figures relate to income and expenditure on alcohol of a number of salesmen in the year 19..

	Income (£)	Expenditure on alcohol (£)
Mr A	7 200	2 500
Mr B	12 700	2 600
Mr C	24 000	1 270
Mr D	27 500	1 300
Mr E	29 000	1 000
Mr F	45 200	2 500
Mr G	60 000	2 270
Mr H	61 500	1 250
Mr J	50 000	4 200
Mr K	60 000	7 200

Construct a scatter diagram and draw the line of best fit. What conclusions does the graph suggest?

4   The heights of fathers and their eldest sons, in inches, are tabulated below:

Height of father	63	68	70	64	66	72	67	71	68	62
Height of son	65	66	72	66	69	74	69	73	65	66

Draw the data as a scatter diagram and comment on the results.

5   The weights of fathers and their eldest sons, in kilograms, are tabulated below:

Weight of father	63	77	76	84	69	73	67	91	68	62
Weight of sons	65	75	70	78	67	76	69	83	65	59

Represent the data on a scatter diagram and comment on the results.

6   An investigation into twenty small firms reveals the following:

	Capital invested at start of year £	Profits achieved £		Capital invested at start of year £	Profits achieved £
A	5 000	8 250	K	12 000	3 250
B	8 000	7 750	L	17 000	8 250
C	10 000	6 500	M	9 000	10 000
D	20 000	26 750	N	16 000	12 500
E	500	12 000	O	18 000	15 500
F	1 500	9 250	P	14 000	6 500
G	18 000	4 750	Q	32 000	12 500
H	60 000	9 500	R	27 000	13 250
I	48 000	11 500	S	60 000	47 500
J	52 000	26 000	T	48 000	46 000

Draw a scatter diagram and comment on the results, to bring out whether the amount of capital available is an important influence on profitability or a relatively insignificant factor.

5.11   Logarithmic (or ratio) graphs

Consider the company sales figures presented in the graph in Figure 5.12. The sales of Company A are based on the following set of data.

Sales of Company A

	£
Year 1	100 000
Year 2	200 000
Year 3	300 000
Year 4	400 000
Year 5	500 000

When plotted on an arithmetic scale, as in Figure 5.12, they give a straight-line increase in sales from year to year (£100 000 increase each year).

However, consider the same set of figures not from an arithmetic viewpoint but from the point of view of a ratio. How do the figures look as a ratio, or a percentage increase, from year to year?

In year 2 the increase was $\dfrac{£100\,000}{£100\,000} = 100\%$ increase.

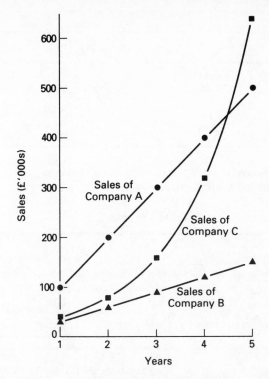

Figure 5.12   Sales increases viewed arithmetically

In year 3 the increase was $\dfrac{£100\,000}{£200\,000} = 50\%$ increase.

In year 4 we have $\dfrac{£100\,000}{£300\,000} = 33\frac{1}{3}\%$ increase.

and in year 5 we have $\dfrac{£100\,000}{£400\,000} = 25\%$ increase

This puts a different complexion on the increases being achieved. The rate of increase is actually slowing down each year, and would probably cause management some concern.

Now consider the sales figures for Company B. Sales in the first year are £30 000, and increase each year by £30 000. Because the arithmetical increase in terms of actual sales is smaller, the gradient on the graph is much less and the impression created is that Company B is not doing so well as Company A – yet in fact it is growing at the same rate, as the figures overleaf show:

Sales of Company B

	£	% growth rate
Year 1	30 000	–
Year 2	60 000	100 (£30 000 increase on £30 000)
Year 3	90 000	50
Year 4	120 000	$33\frac{1}{3}$
Year 5	150 000	25

If we now consider Company C, whose sales double every year, we have sales and growth rate as shown below:

Sales of Company C

	£	% growth rate
Year 1	40 000	–
Year 2	80 000	100
Year 3	160 000	100
Year 4	320 000	100
Year 5	640 000	100

Plotted on the arithmetic scales of Figure 5.12 we see that this gives a curve which shows the sales rising by an increasing amount every year, because each doubling of the sales is larger than the previous year in arithmetical terms.

From these diagrams it seems that graphs drawn on arithmetic scales can tell us the truth in one way but give a misleading impression in another, from the point of view of the rate of change. So often in business it is the relative performances we are interested in. Is one department relatively more profitable than another? Is one company making better progress than another? We can get a more truthful picture of the relative performance of these companies if we use semi-logarithmic graph paper (sometimes called semi-logarithmic ratio paper).

Logarithmic paper

It is perhaps unfortunate that the names logarithmic paper and semi-logarithmic paper are applied to these special graph rulings, since to use them one does not need to know anything about logarithms. All that has happened on logarithmic papers is that either one of the scales (semi-logarithmic paper) or both the scales (logarithmic paper) are ruled to give equal amounts of space to equal *relative* changes. Since this is a relatively simple textbook, we shall only refer here to semi-logarithmic paper, which has an ordinary arithmetic horizontal scale but a logarithmic vertical scale. This is illustrated in Figure 5.13. The essential point to realize about it is that, because of the special vertical scale, changes that appear to have equal dimensions to the eye represent equal percentage changes, i.e. equal ratios. So the move by the eye from 20 to 40 (double the value) is the same distance as when the eye moves from 40 to 80 (double the value).

The other strange thing is that when the paper gets to 9 it reverts to 1 again, but it is understood that the next cycle of rulings is ten times as great as the cycle below it, and if we go on above the second cycle to a third cycle, the third cycle is ten times as great as the second cycle, and 100 times as great as the first cycle.

You can buy semi-logarithmic paper at any good stationer's shop, but the illustration in Figure 5.13 may be sufficient explanation. It shows the sets of data for Companies A, B and C plotted to bring out the relative changes, not the absolute changes shown in Fig. 5.12.

There is one other special point to note about logarithmic paper. Unlike a natural scale, where you almost always start your graph at 0 on the vertical axis, there is no logarithm for 0. A logarithm is a power of 10 (in other words an index number) and the logarithm 0 is the value 1. Therefore your scale will start at some power of 10. It could be 1 or 10 or 100, or it could be 0.1 or 0.01, etc.

Your semi-logarithmic graph paper will normally be pre-printed with a basic pattern of 1, 2, 3 .... 1, 2, 3 .... 1, and so on, usually on the right vertical axis. You must decide whether this scale is to represent 1–10, or 10–100, or 0.1–1. You could go from 100 to 1 000, 1 000 to 10 000, etc. Your decision will depend upon the data to be plotted. In Figure 5.13, since the smallest figure is 30 000, we made the scale start at 10, 20, 30, etc. (the scale being labelled in £'000s). If you decide to label the first scale 1–10, the second scale will be 10–100, and if it is three-cycle paper the third cycle would be 100–1 000. As we have only used two-cycle paper and have labelled the lowest cycle 10–100 the second cycle is 100–1 000.

Study Figure 5.13 closely now and compare the result with Figure 5.12.

Advantages of using the semi-logarithmic graph

1   It shows the rate of change and it is the slope of the lines which are important. The steeper the slope, the greater the rate of change. A straight line indicates a constant rate of change.
2   We are able to compare two or more sets of data with different units on the same graph, because the graph only compares rates of change. For example, we could plot the sales (*continues on page 117*)

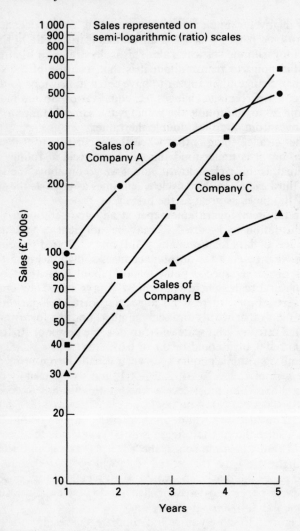

Figure 5.13   Two-cycle semi-logarithmic (ratio) paper showing the relative performances of three companies

Notes:
1 We see that the sales of Company A and Company B now have the same curve, because the curve now shows the rate of change of the sales, and the two companies sales are growing at the same rate, even though they are at different levels. One starts at £30 000 and the other at £100 000.
2 By contrast, what was (in Figure 5.12) a curved graph of sales for Company C is now a straight line, because the rate of growth of Company C's sales was steady – they doubled every year. The straight-line graph shows that this growth performance is much the best of the three companies.

in tonnes of a cement company, the number of staff it employs and the revenue earned all on the same semi-logarithmic graph.

3 A wide range of data can be plotted clearly on a logarithmic scale without the smaller values being obscured.

5.12 Exercises on semi-logarithmic graphs

1 A business has a 10-year profit record as follows:

	£m		£m
Year 1	2.1	Year 6	11.5
Year 2	2.7	Year 7	13.0
Year 3	3.8	Year 8	27.0
Year 4	4.6	Year 9	46.0
Year 5	5.9	Year 10	95.5

Plot this series on semi-log paper.

2 The tables below show the profit records of two companies over a 6-year period. Plot them on a semi-logarithmic graph and hence comment on their relative performances.

	Company A (£'000s)	Company B (£'000s)
Year 1	100	80
Year 2	200	120
Year 3	300	180
Year 4	400	270
Year 5	500	400
Year 6	600	610

3 Here are the profits figures of three companies A, B and C. Plot them:

(a) On ordinary graph paper to show the growth in profits of each company.

(b) On semi-logarithmic graph paper to show the *rate of growth of profits* of each company.

	Company A (£'000)	Company B (£'000)	Company C (£'000)
Year 1	92.1	23.9	15.0
Year 2	160.0	44.9	31.5
Year 3	226.4	67.0	63.4
Year 4	284.1	89.0	130.0
Year 5	348.7	117.9	258.0

(c) An investment trust specializes in investing in growing companies. Which of the three would you recommend as the best growth investment?

5.13   Frequency distribution graphs

In Chapter 4 we saw that frequency distributions can be represented as histograms, each class of data appearing as a rectangular block alongside other rectangular blocks representing adjacent class intervals. We also showed that the same information can be displayed by a frequency polygon drawn around the histogram (see Figure 4.12, page 75). It is possible to present the data of a frequency distribution in graphical form, as a polygon without the histogram. The classes are plotted on the horizontal axis and the frequencies on the vertical axis. The frequencies for each group are plotted at the midpoint of the group and joined together with straight lines. Figure 5.14 shows such a polygon drawn on the basis of the data shown in the table alongside the diagram.

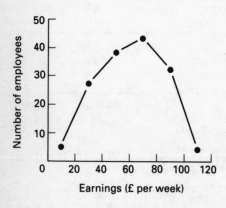

Earnings (£)	Number of employees
0 and under 20	5
20 and under 40	27
40 and under 60	38
60 and under 80	43
80 and under 100	32
100 and under 120	4

Figure 5.14   A frequency polygon

Unfortunately the effect is to have a polygon which appears to be suspended in mid-air because it does not reach the horizontal axis. The practice is to include one extra class interval at either end of the polygon with zero data, so that our polygon can be joined to the midpoint of this class at the horizontal axis at both ends of the diagram. Such a frequency polygon is shown in Figure 5.15. based upon the following data. The grouped frequency distribution below shows the earnings of 100 engineering craftsmen and apprentices for the week commencing 14 April 19..

Earnings (£)	Frequency (number of staff)
50– 99	16
100–149	26
150–199	19
200–249	17
250–299	16
300–349	6
Total	100

The frequency polygon drawn from this information is shown in Figure 5.15.

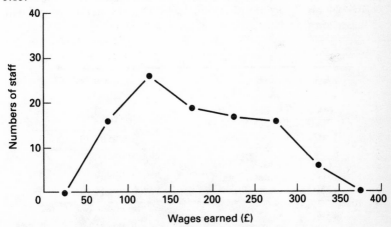

Figure 5.15   A frequency polygon with extra class intervals

Notes:
1   The frequencies are plotted at the midpoints of the class intervals.
2   To make sure the polygon is complete we have an extra class interval at the beginning and at the end of the data, with zero frequencies so that the polygon stands on the horizontal axis of the graph.

5.14   Exercises on frequency polygons

1   The grouped frequency distribution shown below gives the monthly earnings of 1 000 staff in the brick industry. Draw a frequency polygon based on this data.

Earnings (£)	Frequency (number of staff)
200– 399	6
400– 599	44
600– 799	185
800– 999	346
1 000–1 199	165
1 200– 1 399	166
1 400– 1 599	42
1 600– 1 799	34
1 800– 1 999	12
Total	1 000

2   The grouped frequency distribution shown below gives the profits of 120 small businesses in Suburbia. Draw a frequency polygon based on this data.

Profits earned (£)	Frequency (number of staff)
5 000 and under 7 500	4
7 500 and under 10 000	7
10 000 and under 12 500	18
12 500 and under 15 000	29
15 000 and under 17 500	45
17 500 and under 20 000	17
Total	120

3   The grouped frequency distribution below shows the monthly salaries of staff in an advertising agency. Draw a frequency polygon based on this data.

Earnings (£)	Frequency (number of staff)
200 and under 400	6
400 and under 600	44
600 and under 800	185
800 and under 1 000	346
1 000 and under 1 200	165
1 200 and under 1 400	166
1 400 and under 1 600	42
1 600 and under 1 800	34
1 800 and under 2 000	12
Total	1 000

4 Houses in Laburnumville are priced as shown in the grouped frequency distribution below. Draw a frequency polygon to show this data.

House prices (£)	Number of properties
30 000 and below 50 000	23
50 000 and below 70 000	35
70 000 and below 90 000	108
90 000 and below 110 000	125
110 000 and below 130 000	49
130 000 and below 150 000	45
150 000 and below 170 000	19
170 000 and below 190 000	16
Total	420

5.15 The Lorenz curve

It is well known to economists and statisticians that an unequal relation exists between such items as wealth and population, size of manufacturing plant and percentage of total output, etc. For example, if we were to regard total population in the United Kingdom as 100 per cent, we would not expect to find that *each* 1 per cent owned 1 per cent of the total wealth. Instead we would expect, say, the first 50 per cent of the population to own only 10 per cent of the wealth, and the most prosperous 5 per cent of the population to own, say, 50 per cent of the wealth.

Such relationships involving disparity of proportions can be expressed in a **Lorenz curve**.

To illustrate the Lorenz curve the figures given in Table 5.1, and developed in Table 5.2, may be used. These figures show the incomes earned by the nationals of an imaginary nation, Country A. There are a great many people in the first three low income groups and as the incomes rise, the number in successive groups falls. When each income group is worked out as a percentage of the total population, and its income is worked out as a percentage of total national income, these two percentage figures can be plotted against one another to give the Lorenz curve. It is important to note that Lorenz curves compare the **percentage** distribution of one variable with the **percentage** distribution of the other.

Table 5.1   The income of Country A

Personal income (£)	Number of individuals	Total income (£m)
Less than 5 000	3 000 000	7 500
5 000– 7 499	8 000 000	50 000
7 500– 9 999	12 500 000	109 375
10 000–19 999	1 310 000	19 650
20 000–39 999	120 000	3 600
40 000–99 999	60 000	4 200
100 000–499 999	9 000	2 700
500 000–999 999	750	562
1 000 000 and over	250	2 413
Totals	25 000 000	200 000

Table 5.2   Percentages of income earned by various groups

Number of individuals			Total income (£m)		
Actual	%	Cumulative %	Actual	%	Cumulative %
3 000 000	12	12	7 500	3.75	3.75
8 000 000	32	44	50 000	25.00	28.75
12 500 000	50	94	109 375	54.69	83.44
1 310 000	5.24	99.24	19 650	9.82	93.26
120 000	.48	99.72	3 600	1.8	95.06
60 000	.24	99.96	4 200	2.1	97.16

9 000	0.036	99.996		2 700	1.35	98.51
750	0.003	99.999		562	0.28	98.79
250	0.001	100.0		2 413	1.21	100.0
25 000 000	100.0	100.0		200 000	100.0	100.0

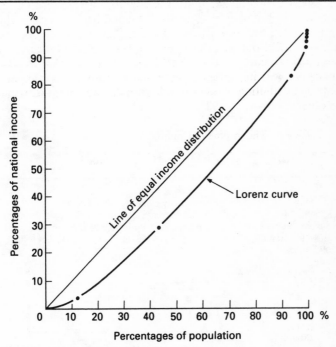

Figure 5.16   The Lorenz curve

Notes:

A Lorenz curve is composed of two parts:

1 The line of equal distribution, which shows a 'per cent for per cent' relationship and serves to act as a guide from which to measure the degree of non-proportionality. This per cent for per cent line will be at 45° on the graph and shows therefore the curve that would be plotted if 10 per cent of the population had 10 per cent of the income, 20 per cent had 20 per cent of the income, 30 per cent had 30 per cent of the income, etc.

2 The second line, by contrast, shows the true state of affairs, with the large low-income groups first. Thus we can see that the first quarter of the population (25 per cent) had only 12 per cent of the income and the first half of the nation had only 35 per cent of the income. The bottom three quarters of the nation had only about 60 per cent of the income while the top quarter had 40 per cent of the income.

3 These figures were based very roughly on the United Kingdom income and we can see the inequalities were not too severe. In many less developed countries the inequalities would be truly scandalous, with the bottom 75 per cent of the nation having only about 10 per cent of the income and the top 5 per cent of the nation having 50 per cent of the wealth. Such a Lorenz curve is shown in Figure 5.17, based on the data from Table 5.3.

Table 5.3 Percentages of income earned by various groups

Number of individuals			Total income (£m)		
Actual	%	Cumulative %	Actual	%	Cumulative %
3 000	32.6	32.6	3 000	2.1	2.1
2 000	21.7	54.3	4 000	2.7	4.8
1 500	16.3	70.6	7 500	5.2	10.0
1 000	10.9	81.5	10 000	6.9	16.9
800	8.7	90.2	16 000	11.0	27.9
500	5.4	95.6	25 000	17.2	45.1
300	3.3	98.9	30 000	20.6	65.7
100	1.1	100.0	50 000	34.4	100.1
Total 9 200	100.0		145 500	100.1	

Notes

(a) Due to rounding, totals do not necessarily come to 100 per cent.

(b) Each 'actual' figure is calculated as a percentage of its column total. A cumulative percentage column can then be constructed. Cumulative percentages are then taken in pairs – for example, 32.6 and 2.1; 54.3 and 4.8, etc – and entered upon the graph, to build up the Lorenz curve.

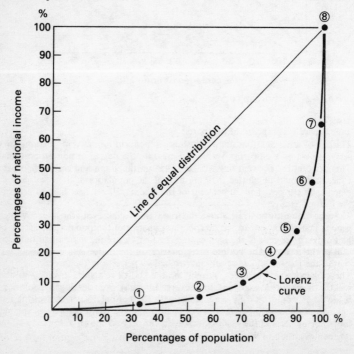

5.16 Exercises on Lorenz curves

1 From the following table draw up a Lorenz curve to illustrate the inequalities of wealth in the United Kingdom.

United Kingdom distribution of wealth in 19..

Percentage of population	Percentage of wealth owned
Poorest 50	8.6
Next 25	18.8
Next 15	21.7
Next 5	12.1
Next 3	11.1
Next 1	5.9
Next 1	21.8

2 The following figures come from the returns of Agro Incorporated, a body which surveys developments in agriculture. They are for the year 19..

Agricultural units	Net output (£ '000)
46	1 300
40	2 160
36	3 500
20	2 750
24	3 000
14	4 900
21	18 600
201	36 210

Analyse the table by means of a Lorenz curve.

Figure 5.17 The Lorenz curve of an underdeveloped country's national income (*see figure on page 124*)

Notes:
1 The disparity of incomes is very great, with the bottom 80 per cent of the population only having about 17 per cent of the wealth.
2 By contrast the top 5 per cent of the population have 55 per cent of the wealth.

3　Incomes in Inegalitaria are divided amongst the population as follows in the year 19..

Number of people (millions)	Income enjoyed (£ millions)
26	1 800
16	2 100
9	3 200
4	4 100
0.1	6 100
55.1	17 300

Analyse the table by means of a Lorenz curve.

4　The population of a country is divided into ten social groups. The following data are available, showing the before-tax and after-tax incomes of these groups. Draw two Lorenz curves, on the same graph, to show the affect of tax on the distribution of wealth.

Group	% of population	Cumulative %	% of income before tax	Cumulative % before tax	% of income after tax	Cumulative % after tax
A	1	100	40	100	20	100
B	3	99	16	60	10	80
C	3	96	5	44	6	70
D	4	93	5	39	6	64
E	7	89	8	34	9	58
F	8	82	4	26	6	49
G	9	74	4	22	6	43
H	10	65	4	18	6	37
I	25	55	8	14	16	31
J	30	30	6	6	15	15

5.17　Summary of Chapter 5

1　A graph is a diagram which shows the relation between two variable quantities, one measured against a horizontal axis (the X axis) and the other against a vertical axis (the Y axis)

2　The independent variable is usually recorded on the horizontal axis and the dependent variable on the vertical axis. These axes will be labelled appropriately.

3   The squared pattern resulting from the ruling of the divisions along the axes is called the graticule, and the paper is called squared paper. However, this only applies to arithmetical subdivisions; logarithmic paper has different rulings which do not result in a squared graticule.

4   We can mark up the axes in any way we choose to accommodate the data we wish to display. This is called the scale of the graph.

5   Sometimes we break the axis of a graph to omit some area of the graph where there are no data to illustrate, and this gives us a larger scale further along the graph. The larger the scale, the easier it is to plot the data.

6   The words graph, chart, scatter diagram, etc. are interchangeable and often used indiscriminately by examiners.

7   A simple graph (such as a temperature chart used in hospitals) joins up the points plotted by straight lines to show the pattern of changes.

8   A Z chart is a chart which plots monthly figures, cumulative monthly figures and a moving annual total all on the same chart. The figures result in a Z shape because they are all related figures, and as the monthly figures build into an annual total, they must connect with the moving annual total on the last day of the year, when the moving annual total comes to apply to this year alone.

9   A straight-line graph is one where the relation is constant between the data being plotted, such as the relation between units sold at a given price and the total sales revenue. Such a group can be used as a ready reckoner, though in these days of electronic calculating they are rarely used.

10   A break-even chart plots fixed costs, variable costs and sales revenue to find out the point where a particular product will break even, i.e. recover all the costs incurred and start to make a profit. The amount by which the selling price (say £15) exceeds the variable costs of the article (say £10) is called the **contribution**. This is the contribution the article makes (*a*) to recover fixed costs and (*b*) after all the fixed costs have been recovered, to profit.

11   A scatter diagram is a plotting of many points of collected data, to see if we can detect any relation between them. We may find a positive linear relation, with one item increasing in line with another. We may find a negative linear relation, or a curvilinear relation. A wider scatter implies little relation between the two sets of data.

12   Logarithmic graphs and semi-logarithmic graphs bring out the rate of change of data, rather than the actual data themselves. Thus an equal arithmetical increase year by year in sales will give a straight-line graph on arithmetic paper, but in fact the rate of increase in sales is declining every year (because the same increase

is based upon an increased starting point each year). On a semi-logarithmic graph the rate of change will give a curved line as the rate of increase falls away year by year.

13   A frequency polygon shows the distribution of data, in a grouped frequency table, in graphical form. In order to complete the polygon on the horizontal axis we must draw in an imaginary group at each end of the polygon with zero data.

14   A Lorenz curve is one which shows the percentages of one set of data plotted against the percentages of another set of data. Thus if we plot percentages of population against the percentages of national income, we can see how 'fair' a society is. In a completely egalitarian society each 10 per cent of the population would enjoy 10 per cent of the national income, and we should have a line of equal income distribution at 45° across the graph – a straight-line graph. Income is rarely distributed in this fair way, and if we plot the actual shares enjoyed by various income groups, the distance of the curve that results from the 'ideal' 45° line is the measure of the inequalities in society.

Answers to text problems in Section 5.7

1   The contribution rises to £25 per unit. We shall now break even at the point where 2 000 units have been sold (2 000 × £25 = £50 000 fixed costs). Total takings at sales of 2 000 units will be £70 000, i.e. £20 000 variable costs (2 000 × £10) and £50 000 fixed costs recovered.

2   The contribution will fall to £10 per unit. We shall have to sell 5 000 units to recover £50 000 fixed costs. At sales of 5 000 units receipts will be £125 000, and we shall break even as we recover £75 000 variable costs (5 000 × £15) and £50 000 fixed costs.

3   The contribution is still £15 per unit. Break-even point will be at $3\,333\frac{1}{3}$ units, when we receive $3\,333\frac{1}{3}$ × £30 = £100 000. This recovers $3\,333\frac{1}{3}$ × £15 variable costs (£50 000) and £50 000 fixed costs ($3\,333\frac{1}{3}$ units at £15 contribution).

6

Averages: measures of central tendency

6.1 The use of averages in statistics

Any statistical enquiry results in a mass of data. While each piece of information is of interest, its relation to the whole set of data is more important. Thus, in examining electric light bulbs to see how long they last, the fact that one of them out of 3 000 went 'pop' the moment it was put into the lampholder is interesting, but is it very significant? If the other 2 999 each burnt for more than 500 hours it would seem that this particular bulb was not typical of the whole group. A particular statistic therefore may prove to be of no significance. Similarly, the orderly arrangements of data presented in Chapters 3–5 while they have many uses, do not summarize the statistics. A more convenient, less detailed form of presentation is sometimes required. It is important, however, that the summary should still be capable of illustrating those points for which the data were initially collected. Hence there are several methods of summarizing data, and the one chosen will depend upon the objectives of the enquiry.

The most common methods of summary are those which seek to find an average statistic which represents the whole group reasonably well. Since any averaging activity tends to reduce the significance of extreme values and stress the 'middle' ones, the various averages are often referred to as **measures of central tendency**. In everyday life phrases like 'average attendance' or 'average score' are commonly used, and they do give a quick, clear impression of a particular situation. Thus the information that a batsman scored 1, 94, 72, 68, 13, 8, 5, 7, 149, 186, 22 and 145 runs in matches played in the first 2 months of the cricket season is of great interest, but rather confusing. To say that his average score over 2 months was 64.17 gives a clearer picture of his ability.

Treating data in this fashion can be extremely useful. Where comparison has to be made between different sets of figures, it is more convenient to take a single (representative) figure from each set as the basis of comparison than to utilize every figure available. For example, a comparison of wage rates among the four largest United Kingdom car manufacturers would be exceptionally difficult if each worker's wage was included in the presentation. Instead, for comparison, a figure representative of each plant, trade or firm is taken.

The three most commonly used measures of central tendency are:

1 The arithmetic mean.
2 The median.
3 The mode.

Two other averages which are sometimes used are the geometric mean and the harmonic mean.

6.2 The arithmetic mean

This is the average measure most commonly used in everyday life. Sometimes referred to simply as the **mean** or the **average**, it is what most people would understand when the word 'average' is mentioned. It is found by adding up the values of the variable (the scores in the cricketing example mentioned earlier) and dividing by the number of items (the innings played). A further instance is given in Example 6.1 below. It refers to the earnings of an insurance broker for the first 10 weeks of the financial year. The arithmetic mean is found by adding the set of earnings and dividing by the number in the set.

Example 6.1 Earnings of an insurance broker:

19.. Week		£
Apr.	7	420
	14	400
	21	90
	28	460
May	5	240
	17	400
	19	310
	26	430
June	2	260
	9	410
Number of weeks	10	Total £3420

Clearly the mean earnings are £3420 ÷ 10 = £342 per week.

Information of this sort is called 'ungrouped data' to distinguish it from information which has been sorted out into a slightly more coherent form, in groups. Where data has been arranged in groups, it presents a slightly more difficult problem in finding the arithmetic mean.

In business statistics it is usual to use the sign $\bar{x}$ to represent the arithmetic mean. This is simply the letter x with a bar over the top.

For ungrouped data a formula for the arithmetic mean would be

$$\bar{x} = \frac{\Sigma x}{n}$$

where $\bar{x}$ (pronounced x bar) is the arithmetic mean, x is each of the measurements or values of the variable, n is the number of measurements or values, and Σ (sigma) means 'the sum of'. (*Note*: by using Σ the notation $x_1 + x_2 + x_3 + x_4/n$ is avoided.)

Using this notation for Example 6.1 we have

$$\bar{x} = \frac{\Sigma x}{n}$$

$$= \frac{£3420}{10}$$

$$= £342 \text{ per week.}$$

Some students worry when presented with a formula. Remember a formula is only a shorthand way of remembering how to do a calculation. Familiarity breeds contempt. If you are worried about formulae, do a lot of exercises using them. You start by writing down the formula, and then substitute in on the general formula the particular data for the calculation you are doing. Then simply obey the normal rules of arithmetic. In this book the chapter summaries at the end of each chapter contain all the formulae you should know.

6.3   Exercises: arithmetic means of a simple series

Using the formula given in Section 6.2 above find the arithmetic mean of the following sets of statistics:

1   Electricity consumed during the quarter in a certain factory was as follows:

Jan.	27 284 units
Feb.	35 266 units
Mar.	41 928 units

Find the mean monthly consumption.

2 The ages of students attending an evening course, to the nearest year, are as follows: 17, 18, 18, 18, 19, 19, 22, 24, 25, 27, 27, 28, 38, 54 and 63. What is the mean age?

3 A library issues books as follows: Monday 742 books, Tuesday 1 529 books, Wednesday 2 472 books, Thursday 495 books and Friday 1 246 books. Only 237 books were issued on Saturday. What is the mean issue per working day? (Answer correct to one decimal place.)

4 Five mills produce the following outputs of cloth in a particular week: 72 856 metres; 49 263 metres; 17 256 metres; 29 254 metres and 86 276 metres. What is the mean output?

5 An experimental crop of wheat from seven plots of land produces the following outputs:

(a) 224 kg	(e) 495 kg
(b) 330 kg	(f) 532 kg
(c) 75 kg	(g) 184 kg
(d) 176 kg	

What was the mean output?

6.4 The arithmetic mean from a frequency distribution

In a simple series the individual items may occur only once, and the frequency is therefore one. In a mass production world many business statistics involve frequencies greater than one. Thus a garage might sell seven 'Apollo' cars, fifteen 'Hermes' traveller models and twenty-three 'St Christopher' touring vehicles. With such a frequency distribution the arithmetic mean must take into account not only the value of an item, but also the number of times that item occurs.

The formula must now become

$$\bar{x} = \frac{\Sigma fx}{\Sigma f}$$

where $\bar{x}$ is the arithmetic mean, x the values of the individual items, f the number of cases of each value, fx is the product of the frequency of an item and the value of the item and Σ 'the sum of'. This is illustrated in Example 6.2.

Example 6.2 What is the mean value of the policies sold by the XYZ agency, whose sales are given in the frequency distribution below (answer to nearest penny)?

Value of policy (£) (x)	Number of policies sold (f)	Product (f × x)
1 000	165	165 000
5 000	290	1 450 000
10 000	105	1 050 000
50 000	92	4 600 000
	$\Sigma f = 652$	$\Sigma fx = 7\,265\,000$

$$\bar{x} = \frac{\Sigma fx}{\Sigma f}$$

$$= \frac{£7\,265\,000}{652}$$

$$= £11\,142.64$$

6.5   Exercises: the arithmetic mean from a frequency distribution

1   A fish farm has 120 ponds. Find the mean surface area of the ponds from the following frequency distribution (answer correct to one decimal place).

Surface area (square metres)	Number of ponds
65	25
70	40
75	28
80	14
85	13

2   The following table illustrates the annual bonus to be paid by a firm to a number of its employees. What is the mean value of the bonus paid?

Bonus £	Number of Employees
3 900	7
2 800	15
1 600	28

3   The weight of timber taken from 48 trees is as shown below. Arrange the information in a frequency distribution and calculate the mean weight of timber (answer to the nearest kg).

Weight of timber (kg)

1 000	1 200	1 000	1 100	1 400	1 300
1 200	1 000	1 000	1 100	1 100	1 000
1 100	1 200	1 100	1 400	1 300	1 100
1 200	1 300	1 400	1 500	1 000	1 400
1 400	1 100	1 200	1 300	1 400	1 200
1 300	1 200	1 400	1 300	1 100	1 100
1 200	1 300	1 200	1 200	1 100	1 200
1 100	1 200	1 200	1 300	1 300	1 000

4   Below are listed the sums taken at a box office for tickets sold one morning. From the information draw up a frequency distribution and from it find the mean price per ticket sold (correct to the nearest penny).

£11.60	£5.50	£9.50	£6.50
£ 9.50	£7.60	£6.50	£9.50
£ 9.50	£9.50	£7.60	£6.00
£ 6.00	£6.00	£5.50	£9.50
£11.60	£5.50	£5.50	£6.50

6.6   The arithmetic mean from grouped data

Where data have been grouped, so that data of similar value are put together, the absolute accuracy which is available when every value is known is naturally lost. Thus, if twenty-seven second-hand cars are sold in the £900–£1 000 range, we cannot know precisely what the sale price of each car was. It is then necessary to take an assumed value for the group and the midpoint of the group is the most obvious point to choose. This midpoint is often called the class value, or the class mark.

The assumption then is that all the items within each group when taken together will have a mean value represented by this midpoint. This method may give rise to some inaccuracy, but this inaccuracy will be minimized if the number of frequencies is large. Example 6.3 shows how the arithmetic mean is derived from grouped data. The formula is still

$$\bar{x} = \frac{\Sigma fm}{\Sigma f}$$

where $\bar{x}$ is the arithmetic mean, f the number of cases within the class interval, m the midpoint of each class and Σ 'the sum of'.

Example 6.3 Earnings of insurance brokers, week ending 30th June, 19..:

Class division (£)	Number of brokers (f)	Class mark (m)	Product (fm)
50– 99.99	3	75	225
100–149.99	7	125	875
150–199.99	14	175	2 450
200–249.99	18	225	4 050
250–299.99	3	275	825
300–349.99	1	325	325
	$\Sigma f = 46$		$\Sigma fm = £8\,750$

$$\bar{x} = \frac{\Sigma fm}{\Sigma f}$$

$$= \frac{£8\,750}{46}$$

$$= £190.22$$

6.7 Exercises: the arithmetic mean from grouped data

1 The following sales distribution was extracted from the record books of milkmen in an industrial area in the North of England. Calculate the mean weekly sales per customer, to the nearest litre.

Number of litres sold per week	Number of customers
1– 5	20
6–10	32
11–15	48
16–20	74
21–25	93
26–30	80
31–35	37
36–40	26
41–45	12

2 The following data were obtained from the personnel records of a manufacturing company. Calculate the mean number of working days lost by employees in the industry. Answer correct to the nearest day.

Number of working days absent in a year	Number of employees
1– 4	16
5– 8	21
9–12	29
13–16	15
17–20	10
21–24	4
25–28	2
29–32	1

3 The sales achieved by a team of representatives were as shown below. Calculate the mean sales from the data. Answer to the nearest £100.

Sales (£ '000)	Number of representatives
Under 10	4
10 and under 20	12
20 and under 30	15
30 and under 40	18
40 and under 50	14
50 and under 60	3

4 The sales achieved by a team of representatives were as shown below. Calculate the mean sales from the data. Answer to nearest £100.

Sales (£ '000)	Number of representatives
Under 10	8
10 and under 20	12
20 and under 30	10
30 and under 40	8
40 and under 50	6
50 and under 60	4

5 The hourly earnings of full-time employees in a certain industry are given in the table below. Calculate the mean earnings (to nearest penny).

Hourly earnings (pence)	Number of employees
100 but under 150	12
150 but under 200	56
200 but under 250	84
250 but under 300	90
300 but under 350	112
350 but under 400	46
400 but under 450	40

6   The hourly earnings of full-time employees in a certain industry are given in the table below. Calculate the mean earnings (to nearest penny).

Hourly earnings (pence)	Number of employees
100 but under 150	42
150 but under 200	65
200 but under 250	71
250 but under 300	37
300 but under 350	27
350 but under 400	15

6.8   The arithmetic mean calculated from an assumed mean

The methods of finding the arithmetic mean described above are quite satisfactory, but when the values and numbers are very large the calculations become tedious, and it is helpful if the figures actually being processed can be made simpler. This is the advantage of calculating from an 'assumed mean'. Usually it is possible to see, from even quite complex sets of figures, roughly where the arithmetic mean will be. If we then take this figure as the 'assumed mean', we have only to find how far away from the 'assumed mean' the 'true mean' is. A simple example will demonstrate the method.

Example 6.4   Find the arithmetic mean of 17, 25 and 36. From a quick inspection of these figures we can see that the average is somewhere above 25. Let us guess 27. This is now the 'assumed mean'.

If we now compare the original numbers with the assumed mean, we find in relation to it, as follows:

$$17 = -10$$
$$25 = -2$$
$$36 = +9$$

These differences add up to -3 ($-12 + 9$).

Dividing by the number of numbers (which is 3), we find that our true mean is -1 from the assumed mean.

$$\therefore \text{ True mean is } 26$$

$$\left(\text{Check:} \frac{17 + 25 + 36}{3} = \frac{78}{3} = 26 \right)$$

We will now repeat the method with a more difficult example.

Example 6.5   Earnings of insurance brokers, week ending 30 June, 19..:

Class (£)	Numbers of brokers (f)	Midpoints	Deviation from assumed mean (in class intervals) (d)	Product (f × d)
50– 99.99	3	75	−3	−9
100–149.99	7	125	−2	−14
150–199.99	14	175	−1	−14
200–249.99	18	225	0	0
250–299.99	3	275	+1	+3
300–349.99	1	325	+2	+2
	$\Sigma f = 46$			$\Sigma fd = -32$

Notes

1   The 'sssumed mean' has been taken as 225. Any point may be taken, but the midpoint of a fairly central group is the most sensible, especially if f is large in that group. (In this example $f = 18$.)

2   The sum of the deviations from the 'assumed mean' is -32 class intervals. As the class interval is £50 this means the total deviation is $-32 \times £50 = -£1\,600$.

3   Dividing by the number of brokers ($\Sigma f = 46$) we find that the true mean

$$= -\frac{£1\,600}{46} \text{ from the 'assumed mean'.}$$

$$= £34.78 \text{ from } £225$$

$$= \underline{\underline{£190.22}}$$

4   Clearly the figures generated using this method are much smaller than those using the other methods, and therefore are more easily handled.

The formula using this short-cut method is

$$\bar{x} = A + \frac{\Sigma fd \times i}{\Sigma f}$$

where A is the assumed mean (which is the midpoint of the group where the assumed mean is given the value of 0 class intervals), f the number of cases within a group, d the deviation from the assumed mean in class intervals, i the size of the class interval which is normal for the table (see below for abnormal class intervals), Σf the total number of cases (i.e. the sum of the frequencies), and Σ 'the sum of'.

Some students find it difficult to decide what the class interval is. The answer is very simple. Look at the lowest point of any class (50 in the lowest class of Example 6.5). Now look at the lowest point in the next class above (100 in Example 6.5). Take the lower figure from the higher figure $(100 - 50)$ and it is clear the class interval is 50. This is true of all the class intervals of Example 6.5 – but if we look at example 6.6, the last interval $(250 - 349.99)$ is 100. The problems this causes are explained in the next paragraph.

Difficulties where the class intervals are not uniform

The table used in Example 6.5 had class intervals which were consistent throughout. However, it is possible for the class intervals in a table to vary. Where this occurs, the procedure is to select a 'standard class interval' for the table. In Example 6.6 this 'standard class interval' is 50: a reflection of the majority of intervals. The method is to express any deviation from this in terms of multiples by such a 'standard'. Thus the last interval is 100 – which is two class intervals.

This approach is shown in Example 6.6. Before we look at this example a further problem must be briefly referred to.

Open-ended distributions

Sometimes the last interval of a group distribution is open-ended, e.g. '100 and over'. This suggests that some items occurred which were well beyond 100. Clearly it is impossible to deal with such an interval unless we make an assumption as to its size. One popular assumption is that this final interval is the same size as the other intervals. A more cautious assumption (and therefore probably better) is to regard this last class interval as twice as big as the other intervals that precede it. Whichever is chosen, the final result can only be approximate, for we can never know the true mean without knowing every item.

The problem with open-ended distributions and class intervals that are of abnormal size is to find the class mark for such an interval, i.e, the midpoint, and hence decide how many class intervals it is from the assumed mean. It is really easy enough: The procedure is

1   Obtain the class mark (the midpoint) of the unequal group. In Example 6.6 this is 300.
2   Subtract the assumed mean from this midpoint (i.e. 300–225). The answer is 75.

3 Now divide this result by the 'standard class interval' – in this case 50. $75 \div 50 = 1\frac{1}{2}$

4 Therefore the deviation from the assumed mean is $1\frac{1}{2}$ standard class intervals.

5 With an open-ended class it is usual to assume it is two class intervals, since it clearly must be more than one class interval or there would have been no need to designate it 'open-ended'.

Example 6.6 Earnings of insurance brokers, week ending 30 June, 19..:

Class (£)	Numbers of brokers (f)	Midpoints	Deviation from assumed mean (in class intervals) (d)	Product (f × d)
50– 99.99	3	75	-3	-9
100–149.99	7	125	-2	-14
150–199.99	14	175	-1	-14
200–249.99	18	225	0	0
250–349.99	4	300	$+1\frac{1}{2}$	$+6$
	$\Sigma f = 46$			$\Sigma fd = -31$

Once the deviations from the assumed mean have been calculated, the working is exactly the same as in Example 6.5. Hence

$$\bar{x} = A + \frac{\Sigma fd \times i}{\Sigma f}$$

$$= £225 + \left(\frac{-31 \times £50}{46} \right)$$

$$= £225 + (-£33.70)$$

$$= \underline{\underline{£191.30}}$$

Because of the slight rearrangement of the data to include one non-standard class, the result of the calculations is marginally different from that in Example 6.5. This serves to illustrate the slight inaccuracy of the method. For most practical purposes this inaccuracy is insignificant.

6.9 Exercises: the arithmetic mean from an assumed mean

1 From the data given below calculate, using the 'assumed mean' method, the mean mortgage granted to members by the XYZ Building Society in 19.. Answer to nearest £100.

Mortgages granted (£)	Number of members
10000 and under 20000	381
20000 and under 30000	275
30000 and under 40000	162
40000 and under 50000	35

2   The following table gives the length in centimetres of a number of steel rods. Calculate the mean length of rod, using the 'assumed mean' method.

Length in centimetres	Number of rods
20–29.99	4
30–39.99	16
40–49.99	31
50–59.99	64
60–69.99	40
70–79.99	25
80–89.99	15
90–99.99	5

3   Find the arithmetic mean of the information in the table below, which relates to the distances travelled daily by trains in an imaginary region. Use the 'assumed mean' method and give the answer correct to one decimal place.

Km	Frequency
400 and under 420	13
420 and under 440	27
440 and under 460	34
460 and under 480	24
480 and under 500	15
500 and under 520	8

4   The following table shows the earnings of a group of machinists. Compute the mean earnings, using the 'assumed mean' method, correct to the nearest penny.

Weekly earnings (£)	Number of employees
50 and under 75	20
75 and under 100	30
100 and under 125	50
125 and under 150	20
150 and under 200	10

5   The following table shows the length in centimetres of a number of copper pipes used in the construction of a housing estate. Using the 'assumed mean' method, calculate the mean length in centimetres correct to one decimal place.

Length (cm)	Number of pipes
Under 30	10
30 and under 60	26
60 and under 90	26
90 and under 120	16
120 and under 150	9
150 and under 180	6
180 and under 240	10

6.10   The weighted arithmetic mean

In some enquiries certain statistics may be relatively more important than others, and are said to carry more 'weight'. Thus if the average householder always buys bread, and only very rarely buys caviare, an enquiry into household expenditure would give more 'weight' to purchases of bread.

It is sometimes necessary to calculate a 'weighted' arithmetic mean where the frequencies, considered in Section 6.4 above, are replaced by weights. These weights are intended to reflect the relative importance of the various items in the data – the larger the weight (in a given series of weights) the greater the significance of the item bearing it. In the Index of Retail Prices, published in the *Monthly Digest of Statistics*, the total weighting given to all items is 1 000. The subgroup meat and bacon is given a weighting of 37, while fish has a weighting of 7.

When finding 'weighted arithmetic means' the formula used is very similar to that used to find the mean of a frequency distribution, except that the letter w (weight) is substituted for f (frequency)

$$\text{Weighted mean} = \frac{\Sigma wx}{\Sigma w}$$

The total of wx is divided by the sum of the weights – it is important to remember this.

Example 6.7 shows how the formula is used.

Example 6.7   A student's work for a certain course is graded as follows: final examination 62 per cent, homework 72 per cent, classwork 66 per cent. If the weights given each grade are 7, 2 and 1 respectively, calculate the student's weighted grade.

Score %(x)	Weight (w)	wx
62	7	434
70	2	140
66	1	66
	$\Sigma w = 10$	Σwx 640

$$\text{Weighted mean} = \frac{640}{10} = 64 \text{ per cent}$$

Weighted arithmetic means are perhaps met most often in the form of index numbers. Chapter 13 deals with these and shows how the weighted mean is put to use.

6.11   Exercises: weighted arithmetic means

1   In an educational course a weighting of 3 is given to the final examination, a weighting of 2 is given to course work and a weighting of 1 to homework. Calculate the mean score of the following individuals (correct to one decimal place):

   (a) A. Brown, whose final examination total is 54 per cent, whose course work was awarded 84 per cent and whose homework award is 92 per cent.

   (b) C. Dark, whose final examination total is 44 per cent, whose course work was awarded 81 per cent and whose homework award is 68 per cent.

2 In an educational course a weighting of 5 is given to the final examination, a weighting of 3 is given to course work and a weighting of 2 to homework. Work out the mean score of the following individuals:

(a) M. Lark, whose final examination total is 46 per cent, whose course work was awarded 67 per cent and whose homework award is 58 per cent.
(b) T. Sparrow, whose final examination total is 64 per cent, whose course work was awarded 94 per cent, and whose homework award is 86 per cent.

3 In a motorcycle three-day event the weighting is as follows:

Care and presentation of machine	4
Reliability in cross-country performance	3
Speed tests	5
Knowledge of road safety	3

Two competitors scored as follows:

	Mr Y (%)	Mr Z (%)
Care and presentation of machine	76	85
Cross-country performance	54	65
Speed tests	84	71
Knowledge of road safety	42	90

Calculate their weighted mean scores (correct to one decimal place) and hence show which was the better competitor.

4 At a county agricultural show weighting in the animal judging was as follows:

Condition of the animal	3
Special breed characteristics	2
Weight	2

Each aspect was judged out of 100. The three best in show scored as follows:

	A	B	C
Condition	84	82	79
Breed characteristics	70	85	90
Weight	78	84	81

Calculate their weighted mean scores (correct to one decimal place) and hence determine which animal was 'Best in Show'.

6.12   The median

Although the arithmetic mean is the commonest average used, the median is a useful measure of centrality. It is defined as the value of the middle item of a distribution, when the items are arranged in ascending order of size.

For ungrouped data the method of calculation of the median is very simple. The process is as follows:

1   Arrange the data in order of size, i.e. so that they run from the smallest to the largest. Such an arrangement is called an **array**.
2   Find the middle item. The formula for finding the middle item is

$$\frac{n+1}{2}$$

where n is the number of items. Hence where there are seven items

$$\frac{n+1}{2} = \frac{7+1}{2} = 4$$

The fourth item would give us the median value. We know this to be the case, since in an array of seven there are three items on either side of the fourth one – it is therefore in the middle.

Where the number of items is even, it is not possible to isolate an actual item which is the middle one. Thus where there are eight items in an array

$$\frac{n+1}{2} = \frac{8+1}{2} = 4\frac{1}{2}$$

The middle item is now the $4\frac{1}{2}$th item, and it is necessary to find the average of the fourth and fifth items to find the median value.
3   Find the value of the middle item.

Important note   Statisticians sometimes refer to the 'median' item. Strictly speaking this is not correct. The median is, by definition, the value of the middle item in an array. In an array with an odd number of items the median value will coincide with the middle item in the array. In an array with an even number of items it will be the average of the two middle items. The danger is that a student may say that in an array of 27 numbers, 14 is the median. It is of course the **value** of the fourteenth number in that array that is the median.

Example 6.8 The salaries per month of seven bank employees are £380, £960, £520, £790, £648, £660 and £925. Find the median salary.

(*a*) Arrange data in order of value:

1	2	3	4	5	6	7
£380	£520	£648	£660	£790	£925	£960

(*b*) Find the middle item. With seven items this is the fourth, $\frac{n+1}{2}$.

(*c*) Find the median value. Value of fourth item is £660.

$$\therefore \quad \text{median value} = \underline{\underline{£660}}$$

If an extra salary of £856 were added, there would be no single median item. It would then be necessary to find the average value of items 4 and 5.

Example 6.9 The monthly salaries of eight bank employees are given as £420, £810, £746, £548, £912, £926, £462 and £685. Find the median salary.

(*a*) Arrange the data in order of size:

1	2	3	4	5	6	7	8
£420	£462	£548	£685	£746	£810	£912	£926

(*b*) Find the middle item

$$\frac{n+1}{2} = \frac{9}{2} = 4\tfrac{1}{2}$$

There is no single item: 4 and 5 are 'in the middle'.
(*c*) The median value will be the average of these items

$$= \frac{£685 + £746}{2}$$

$$= \frac{£1\,431}{2}$$

$$= \underline{\underline{£715.50}}$$

6.13   Exercises: the median

1   Calculate the median life of an electric light bulb based on the following nine examples: (*a*) 236 hours, (*b*) 11 hours, (*c*) 248 hours, (*d*) 25 hours, (*e*) 1 294 hours, (*f*) 728 hours, (*g*) 5 hours, (*h*) 1 hour, (*i*) 483 hours.

2   Farmer Brown's hens laid as follows in one year: Lucy 236 eggs, Speckly 426 eggs, Mary 156 eggs, Crooked Leg 184 eggs, Dainty 156 eggs, Brownie 84 eggs, Polynesia 203 eggs and Margaret 225 eggs. Calculate the median output.

3   The orders received from the representatives of Cosmetics Ltd are as follows for the month of July:

	£		£
Mr A	8 540	Mr F	15 230
Mr B	12 720	Miss G	27 460
Mr C	16 230	Mr H	14 250
Mrs D	18 710	Mrs Y	1 850
Miss E	5 950		

Calculate the median value.

4   The orders received from the representatives of Icepak Ltd are as follows for the month of June:

	£		£
Mr A	18 540	Mr F	8 417
Mr B	12 760	Miss G	19 325
Mr C	29 250	Mr H	28 612
Mrs D	13 286	Mrs Y	14 713
Miss E	48 716	Mrs J	8 450

Calculate the median value.

6.14   Calculating the median from grouped data

When dealing with a grouped frequency distribution, finding the median value is slightly more complicated, since the value of the median item may not be known. We do not know the individual values of each occurrence within a group.

It is therefore necessary to make an assumption and then calculate the median value. The assumption is that the items in a group are evenly spread throughout the group, though in fact we cannot be sure of this. They might all be bunched at the lower end or bunched at the upper end of the group. Having made this assumption, we can then tell, if we build up a cumulative frequency table as shown in Example 6.10, which group the median item is in, and how far up the group it is.

Example 6.10

Find the median salary of bank employees per month from the information given in the following table:

Earnings (£)	Number of employees	Cumulative frequency
300 and under 400	13	13
400 and under 500	45	58
500 and under 600	209	267
600 and under 700	101	368
700 and under 800	78	446
800 and under 900	42	488
900 and under 1 000	12	500

With grouped data, for fairly complex reasons, we must use the formula $\frac{n}{2}$ for the median, instead of $\frac{n+1}{2}$. The explanation is that in assuming that the items are evenly spread within the group, with one item in each subdivision, the formula $\frac{n+1}{2}$ finds the upper end of the subdivisions, not the middle of them. We must therefore go back half an interval and use $\frac{n}{2}$, not $\frac{n+1}{2}$. This explanation need not concern students unduly, but you should use the formula $\frac{n}{2}$ for the median of grouped data. This makes the median item the 250th item.

The median item is clearly located in the £500–£600 class interval. In order to find the median item it is necessary to take 192 cases from within the £500–£600 class (which when added to the preceding 58, makes 250). Using this information we have:

$$\text{Median} = £500 + \left(\frac{192}{209} \times £100\right)$$

where (a) £500 is the bottom of the class interval in which the median is located, (b) £100 is the size of the class interval, and (c) $\frac{192}{209}$ represents the median item – the 192nd item in the £500–£600 class. Therefore

$$\text{Median item} = £500 + (0.91866 \times 100)$$
$$= £500 + £91.87$$
$$= £591.87$$

The same data idea can be expressed by the following formula:

$$\text{Median } (M) = Lm + \frac{C}{fm}\left(\frac{n}{2} - fm^{-1}\right)$$

where Lm is the lower limit of the group in which the median is to be found, C is the class interval, fm is the frequency in this group, n is the sum of all the frequencies $\left(\text{so } \frac{n}{2} \text{ is the median item in the group}\right)$ and fm^{-1} is the cumulative frequency of all the item in the table up to the upper limit of the class below the one with the median item in it.

Substituting in the values given in Example 6.10, we have

$$\text{Median} = £500 + \frac{£100}{209}\left(\frac{500}{2} - 58\right)$$
$$= £500 + \frac{£100}{209} \times 192$$
$$= £500 + £91.87$$
$$= £591.87$$

This is the same answer as was arrived at formerly. The basic method is so easy to work out from common-sense principles that the formula is hardly worth committing to memory.

The reader should recognize that the result is only an approximation of the true median – an approximation which reflects the assumption we have made about the distribution of the items within the class interval where the median is known to lie. Again, any error will be minimized if the number of frequencies is large.

6.15   Exercises: medians from grouped data

1   From the grouped frequency data given below calculate the median price of calves for the day.

Prices of calves at a country market July 14

Prices (£)	Number of bargains struck	Cumulative frequency
25–49.99	13	13
50–74.99	38	51
75–99.99	79	130
100–124.99	44	174

2   From the grouped frequency data given below calculate the cumulative frequency and hence the median price of cattle for the day.

Prices of cattle at a country market July 21

Prices (£)	Number of bargains struck	Cumulative frequency
125–149.99	9	?
150–174.99	59	?
175–199.99	168	?
220–224.99	34	?

3   From the grouped frequency data given below calculate the median passenger load carried on aircraft leaving Cosmo Airport in August. Answer correct to the nearest whole number.

Passengers carried in August

Groups of passengers	Number of aircraft	Cumulative frequency
150–199	27	27
200–249	41	68
250–299	56	124
300–349	184	308
350–399	194	502
400–449	127	629
450–499	13	642

4   From the grouped frequency data given below calculate the cumulative frequency and the median cost of operations:

Cost of operations – County Health Service

Cost per operation (£)	Number of operations	Cumulative frequency
0– 99.99	2 728	?
100–199.99	3 856	?
200–299.99	4 250	?
300–399.99	1 247	?
400–499.99	349	?
500–599.99	217	?
More than £600	584	?

6.16 Obtaining the median from a cumulative frequency curve (ogive)

A relative simple method of finding a median from a grouped frequency distribution is by the construction of a cumulative frequency curve or **ogive**. The word 'ogive' is the architectural term for a Gothic arch, and cumulative frequency curves tend to be shaped rather like Gothic arches. A cumulative frequency curve is plotted from a frequency distribution table on which a cumulative frequency column has been added (see Example 6.11 below). The cumulative frequency for each group is plotted

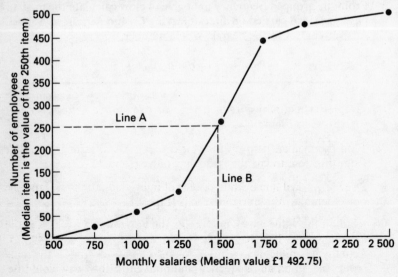

Figure 6.1 A cumulative frequency curve (ogive)

on the graph, and becomes the upper limit of the group. The points are joined by straight lines, as shown in Figure 6.1.

Where a table has one group which is larger than the general groups in the table (as with the last group in Table 6.11), it is treated exactly like the other groups, but care must be taken to plot the extra size of the group on the horizontal scale. If a distribution has an open-ended class, it is usually taken to be twice as large as the normal groups in the table. In any case it has no effect on the median item.

Example 6.11
From the table of salaries given below find the median salary.

Monthly Earnings of Computer Programmers

Earnings (£)	Number of employees	Cumulative frequency
500 and under 750	24	24
750 and under 1 000	32	56
1 000 and under 1 250	46	102
1 250 and under 1 500	156	258
1 500 and under 1 750	184	442
1 750 and under 2 000	33	475
2 000 and under 2 500	25	500

(a) Graph the cumulative frequencies on a cumulative frequency curve (ogive), as in Figure 6.1.

(b) Find the median item on the vertical axis. Draw a horizontal line from this item to cut the frequency ogive (Line A).

(c) Draw a vertical line from the point of intersection of line A and the ogive curve, to the horizontal axis (Line B).

(d) Read off the value where line B cuts the horizontal axis. This is the median value. This has been shown on the graph as £1492.75. Actually it is difficult to read off the median exactly unless the scale is very large and an answer within about £10 either way would be acceptable to examiners.

Quartiles, Deciles and Percentiles

Besides reading off the median from a cumulative frequency curve it is possible to read off other measures of position. For example, the **quartiles** divide the series into four parts, and may be read off in Fig. 6.1 from the 125th item (lower quartile or Q_1) and the 375th item (upper quartile or Q_3). The formula for the lower quartile is $\dfrac{n}{4}$ and for the upper quartile is $\dfrac{3n}{4}$.

Similarly, the **deciles** (Latin *decem* = 10) divide the series into 10 equal parts and the **percentiles** into 100 equal parts. The formula for any particular decile or percentile is similar to the formula for quartiles. For example, the fourth decile is found by $\dfrac{4n}{10}$ and the 63rd percentile by $\dfrac{63n}{100}$.

In Figure 6.2 below an ogive curve shows the profitability of 500 small firms in Ruralarea. Study the diagram and then answer the questions below the diagram.

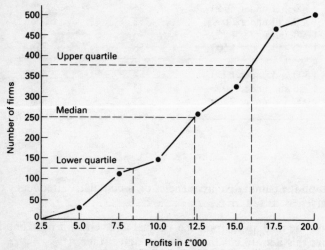

Figure 6.2   Small firm profitability in Ruralarea

Questions (for answers see top of page 155)

1 Read off the median profit.
2 Read off the lower quartile profit.
3 Read off the upper quartile profit.
4 How many firms made less than £10 000 profit?
5 How many firms made less than £15 000 profit?

Answer section   Answers can only be approximate.

1   £12 375,   2   £8 475,   3   £15 938,   4   147 firms,   5   323 firms

6.17   Exercises: obtaining the median from ogive curves

1   From the grouped frequency data given below calculate the cumulative frequency; draw an ogive curve and then read off the value of the median item in the group.

Prices at auction of bankrupt's stock, July 19..

Prices £	Number of bargains struck	Cumulative frequency
25– 49.99	264	?
50– 74.99	127	?
75– 99.99	318	?
100–124.99	59	?
125–149.99	44	?
150–174.99	136	?
175–199.99	89	?
200 and over	65	?

2   From the grouped frequency data given below calculate the cumulative frequency. Draw an ogive curve and then read off the value of the median item in the group.

Ages of marathon runners at Capital City, May 19..

Ages runners	Number of frequency	Cumulative frequency
10–19	2 959	?
20–29	5 386	?
30–39	4 122	?
40–49	2 366	?
50–59	748	?
60–69	390	?
70 and over	29	?

3   (*a*) From the grouped frequency data given below calculate the
cumulative frequency; draw an ogive curve and then read off
the value of the median item in the group.

Prices of houses on offer in Laburnum Village, April 19..

Price range (£'000)	Number of properties	Cumulative frequency
20 and under 30	3	?
30 and under 40	5	?
40 and under 50	18	?
50 and under 60	23	?
60 and under 70	25	?
70 and under 80	9	?
80 and under 90	12	?
90 and under 100	15	?
100 and under 110	35	?
110 and under 120	60	?
120 and under 130	18	?
130 and over	27	?

(*b*) Now read off the values of the lower quartile property and the
upper quartile property.
(*c*) Finally, read off the values of the tenth percentile property and
the sixtieth percentile property.

6.18   The mode

The mode is defined as that value in a set of figures which occurs most
often. To arrive at the mode, then, one needs only to find the item
having the greatest frequency. When working with ungrouped data,
this merely necessitates counting the frequencies to discover which one
predominates.

What is the mode of the data given in Example 6.12?

Example 6.12(a)   Staff employed in a travel agency are aged as follows:

23   29   27   24   29   63   30   26

The modal age is 29 years, because this value occurs more often (twice)
than any other value.

(*b*) In the football season Wildebeeste Wanderers score goals as follows:

$$2, 5, 0, 3, 0, 1, 2, 4, 11, 6, 5, 2, 4, 3, 2, 5, 2$$

The modal score is 2 goals, since this value occurs five times in the season. With a frequency distribution, as shown in Example 6.13, the modal item is the most frequent item.

Example 6.13   Weekly contributions to pension fund of employees

Contribution (£)	Number of employees
4	11
6	18
8	29
10	16
15	10
20	3

The most common payment, made by 29 employees, is £8; therefore this is the modal contribution.

Sometimes it is possible to have bi-modal statistics. Had there been 29 people paying £15 per week, it would have been a bi-modal series. A series can also be multi-modal.

Where data are presented in the form of a grouped frequency distribution, the mode can be taken as the midpoint of the class interval with maximum frequency. However, because it is likely that the occurrences within a class interval will not be evenly distributed, finding the midpoint alone will tend towards inaccuracy. In many sets of grouped statistics, for example, the group which occurs most frequently (the modal group) may have below it a group which also has a large number of items, whereas the group above it may have only a few. In such circumstances the midpoint of the modal group would probably be an unsatisfactory mode to pick, for the chances are that there are more items below it than above it, judging from the groups on either side.

To overcome this difficulty two methods can be adopted to find the mode: (*a*) calculation, and (*b*) use of a histogram. Since both these methods can give the same result, and since the second is much easier to undertake, this is the one demonstrated first in Example 6.14 below.

Example 6.14

The earnings of 180 bank employees are as follows. Find the modal salary.

Earnings (£)	Number of employees
Under 4 000	10
4 000 and under 8 000	25
8 000 and under 12 000	40
12 000 and under 16 000	55
16 000 and under 20 000	30
20 000 and under 24 000	20

(*a*) Construct a histogram – as in Figure 6.3.
(*b*) Find the modal class – this is represented by the tallest rectangle.
(*c*) Join the top left-hand corner of the modal rectangle to the top left-hand corner of the adjacent rectangle, as shown, and similarly with the top right-hand corner to the top right-hand corner of the adjacent rectangle, as shown. These lines will intersect.
(*d*) The mode occurs at the intersection.

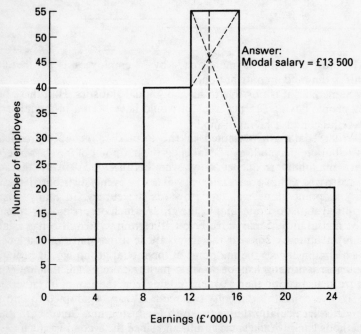

Answer:
Modal salary = £13 500

Figure 6.3   Using a histogram to find the modal earnings of 180 bank employees

This method clearly demonstrates that the distribution of items within the modal class will probably not be centrally located within that class. Rather there will be a tendency for the maximum distribution of items within the modal class to be biased towards the boundary of the adjacent class with more frequencies.

A second method is to calculate the modal salary by means of the following formula:

$$\text{Mode} = L + \frac{(B - A)}{(B - A) + (B - C)} \times \text{class interval}$$

where L = lower limit of the modal group,
         B = frequency in the modal group,
         A = frequency of the group preceding the modal group,
         C = frequency of the group following the modal group.

In Example 6.14 the modal group is clearly the '£12 000 and under £16 000' group. Therefore $L = £12 000$, $B = 55$, $A = 40$, $C = 30$. The class interval is £4 000. Substituting in our formula we have

$$\text{Mode} = £12 000 + \frac{(55 - 40)}{(55 - 40) + (55 - 30)} \times £4 000$$

$$= £12 000 + \frac{15}{40} \times £4 000$$

$$= £12 000 + £1500$$

$$= £13 500$$

6.19   Exercises: the mode

1 In the following cricket scores which is the modal score for each batsman?

   Batsman A: 27, 0, 14, 162, 27, 5, 27, 16, 27
   Batsman B: 5, 15, 38, 5, 72, 91, 106, 4, 3, 0, 5
   Batsman C: 27, 14, 36, 7, 21, 9, 19, 36

2 In the following lists of bowling performance which is the modal performance for each bowler?

   Bowler A: Wickets taken 4, 3, 1, 4, 4, 5, 3, 1, 2, 4, 5
   Bowler B: Wickets taken 2, 2, 2, 0, 1, 7, 3, 2, 2, 1, 5
   Bowler C: Wickets taken 5, 1, 4, 7, 1, 1, 3, 2, 3, 3, 4

3   Houses in Newtown have the following number of bedrooms. Which is the modal-sized house?

Number of rooms	1	2	3	4	5	6
Frequencies	27	272	1 954	825	430	36

4   (*a*) Draw a histogram to represent the following data and hence find the modal payment:

Commission paid to travellers, January (£)	Number of salesmen
200 and under 300	8
300 and under 400	13
400 and under 500	14
500 and under 600	16
600 and under 700	5
700 and under 800	4

(*b*) Now check your answer by using the formula in Section 6.18 above.

5   (*a*) Draw a histogram to represent the following data and hence find the modal income in the town investigated:

Range of incomes (£)	Number of families
Under £3 000	5
3 000 and under 6 000	127
6 000 and under 9 000	856
9 000 and under 12 000	1 327
12 000 and under 15 000	459
15 000 and under 18 000	449
18 000 and under 21 000	389
21 000 and over	484

(*b*) Now check your answer by means of the formula in Section 6.18 above.

6.20 Comparison of the averages

The **arithmetic mean** is the main average used, because it is readily understood, fairly easy to calculate, takes into account all the data, and is capable of algebraic manipulation. However, there are certain sets of data for which the arithmetic mean does not fulfil its function of adequate representation. Consider the following illustrations:

1 Imagine there is an enquiry into the average age of students at a college, classified according to whether they are day-release or evening. The following results might occur: arithmetic average age of day-release students, 20 years, and arithmetic average age of evening-class students, 20 years. Obviously the mean age is identical, but the day-release average may have been computed from a class of 150 students, each one aged 20 years, and the evening-class average from a class of 100 students, of which 90 were each aged 17 years and 10 each aged 47 years. Clearly, the mean age of 20 is not representative of the evening class but is representative of the day-release group. Therefore if data contain extreme items, the arithmetic mean will tend to distort and incorrectly describe the situation.
2 The arithmetic average number of children per household might easily be calculated at 2.2 for Great Britain. This is a meaningful average for statisticians but many ordinary people find such a figure unrealistic, since obviously no family actually *has* 2.2 children. The mean number of legs per dog in the United Kingdom may be approximately 3.9, but this conjures up a strange picture of a dog. Clearly the mode conveys the best impression of a dog, and in that enquiry would be the best average to choose.

In the two cases above, to a greater or less extent, the arithmetic mean would appear to be unsatisfactory as a means of description and the **median** would probably be a better choice, since:

1 In the case of data with extreme items the median will not be affected by them and will possibly be more representative. Returning to our two classes of students, the median ages would be 20 for the day-release group and 17 for the evening group – a more accurate picture of the situation.
2 The median number of children per household in Great Britain is 2, which is a more realistic indication of the average family than 2.2.

Unfortunately, one of the characteristics of the median which is particularly useful in some circumstances, that of concentrating on the middle item, is a disadvantage in the majority of cases, because, in the main, all data relevant to the problem should be taken into account. Also the median is unsuitable for further mathematical calculation.

The **mode** is of limited use, because, although it has some of the advantages and all of the disadvantages associated with the median, there is, in addition, the difficulty of distributions which have no mode or two modes (bi-modal). For example, the data 2, 3, 8, 9, 12 and 13 have no mode; the data 2, 3, 3, 3, 5, 7, 8, 8, 8, 9 and 10 have two modes, 3 and 8.

In summary, it is a good rule-of-thumb guide to use the arithmetic mean in all those cases where it adequately represents the data. Where this is not the case, the median is usually the best alternative.

6.21   Exercises: comparison of averages

1   One hundred farmers, taken at random, were asked to submit figures relating to yields of wheat from one hectare on their farms. The results were as follows:

Yield (tonnes)	Number of farms
2 and under 4	8
4 and under 6	6
6 and under 8	12
8 and under 10	23
10 and under 12	20
12 and over	31

Calculate the arithmetic mean of the yields (correct to one decimal place). Is the arithmetic mean the best average to use for this distribution of figures? Give reasons for your conclusion.

2   Give a definition of (*a*) the arithmetic mean, (*b*) the median, (*c*) the mode.

Using the following as the basis of a frequency distribution, illustrate the answers given to (*a*), (*b*) and (*c*) above: 11, 16, 4, 7, 6, 13, 2, 5, 8, 10, 6.

3   The following table gives the numbers of those who die as a result of physical attacks in a large city, in a 12-month period, classified by age:

Age	Number
Under 1	28
1 but under 5	18
5 but under 10	13
10 but under 20	22
20 but under 35	59
35 but under 50	46
50 but under 70	35
70 but under 85	10

(*a*) Show these figures in the form of a histogram. (*b*) Calculate the mean age at death (correct to the nearest year). (*c*) Are there any other appropriate measures of central tendency? Give reasons for your conclusions.

4   The following data relate to the weekly earnings of 300 insurance brokers:

Earnings (£)	Number of brokers
250 and under 300	15
300 and under 350	25
350 and under 400	40
400 and under 450	108
450 and under 500	92
Over 500	20

(*a*) Compute the median earnings of the brokers (correct to one decimal place). (*b*) Which average do you consider to be the most appropriate to represent the data? Give your reasons.

6.22   Summary of Chapter 6

1   A measure of central tendency is an average, which shows the central point around which the data is spread. There are five possible measures: the arithmetic mean, the median, the mode, the geometric mean and the harmonic mean.

2   The most widely used mean is the arithmetic mean. In the simplest case we add up the variables and divide by the number of variables.

The symbol for the arithmetic mean is $\bar{x}$ (x bar) and the simplest formula is:

$$\bar{x} = \frac{\Sigma x}{n}$$

3   With a frequency distribution we multiply the value of each group by the number in that group, add the total values and divide by the total frequencies. The formula is therefore:

$$\bar{x} = \frac{\Sigma fx}{\Sigma f}$$

4   If data are grouped, it is usual to assume that they are evenly spread within the group, and therefore the midpoint of the group may be taken as the value of the group. This is called the class mark (m), but it is often referred to as m = midpoint. To find the mean we multiply the frequency by the class mark and divide the total result by the number of frequencies. The formula is therefore:

$$\bar{x} = \frac{\Sigma fm}{\Sigma f}$$

5   Where grouped data have very large numbers, the calculations become laborious and it is better to work from an assumed mean (usually designated A). We judge where A is from an inspection of the data, how many in the various groups etc.? We then call the midpoint of that group 0 and designate the groups below and above it -1 and $+1$ respectively. This continues up and down the group. These figures are called the 'deviations' because they show deviations of the groups from the assumed mean. Multiplying the frequencies by the deviations, we get products fd. Some are minus and some are plus. When we add these up, we get the total deviation from the mean in class intervals. Divide this by the sum of the frequencies and we find the deviation from the assumed mean, and hence the mean. The formula is

$$\bar{x} = A + \frac{\Sigma fd \times i}{\Sigma f}$$

where i is the class interval.

6   Open-ended classes need care here, because we have to make an assumption about their size. It is usual to assume that an open-ended class is *two* class intervals (because it clearly must be more than one class interval or there would be no need to have it open-ended).

7   The median is the value of the central item of an array when it has been arranged in ascending order of size. To calculate the median item of ungrouped data we use the formula $\frac{n+1}{2}$. If the result has a $\frac{1}{2}$ in it – say the $14\frac{1}{2}$ item in the array – we take the values of the items on either side (the 14th and 15th items) and find the midpoint between them.

8   With grouped data we use $\frac{n}{2}$ $\left(\text{not } \frac{n+1}{2}\right)$. We build up a cumulative frequency table, find the $\frac{n}{2}$ item and we can then see where the median item is located. The formula is

$$\text{Median } (Me) = Lm + \frac{C}{fm}\left(\frac{n}{2} - fm^{-1}\right)$$

where Lm is the lower limit of the group where the median is located, C is the class interval, fm is the frequency in the group where the median is located, n is the total frequency $\left(\text{so } \frac{n}{2} \text{ is the median item}\right)$ and fm^{-1} is the cumulative frequency in all the groups up to the upper limit of the class below the one with the median in it.

9   An ogive curve is a cumulative frequency curve. It can be used to read off the median, the quartiles and any percentile group.

10 The mode is that value in a set of data that occurs most often. In an ungrouped set of data it may be found by inspection. In a grouped set of data it may be found by drawing a histogram, when the modal item will be found to exist in the modal group, by joining the top left-hand corner of that group to the highest left-hand point of the group above, and by joining the top right-hand corner of the model group to the top right-hand corner of the group below. Where these lines intersect is the modal item, whose value we are seeking to find (see Figure 6.2 to revise this idea).

Alternatively the modal group may be found by the formula:

$$\text{Mode} = L + \frac{(B - A)}{(B - A) + (B - C)} \times ci$$

where L is the lower limit of the modal group,
        B is the frequency in the modal group,
        A is the frequency of the group preceding the modal group,
        C is the frequency of the group following the modal group,
        ci is the class interval.

7
Measures of dispersion

7.1 Averages and dispersion

While the various averages described in Chapter 6 tell us where the centre of a distribution lies, we are also interested in the dispersion of the individual items around the central point. For example, if we were told that the average income in a certain area was £15 000 per annum, we have an informative measure of central tendency, but how the individual incomes are spread around that central point could be even more informative. Suppose that 1 000 people have been questioned about their incomes to arrive at this average. What shall we find when we investigate the dispersion of those 1 000 incomes around the average? Suppose we find that nobody has an income of less than £12 500 per annum and that the highest income of all is only £17 500 per annum. It means that all the people are very close to the average income, and we have a very egalitarian society. There are no very poor people and no very rich people. Such a situation might have very important implications for business. It would appear that diamond tiaras would have very little chance of selling in such an area, since one has to very rich to afford them, whereas items of average price have a ready market. them, whereas items of average price have a ready market.

Suppose by contrast that we find the dispersion of incomes around the central position is much more widespread. Hundreds of families have incomes below £5 000 per annum, and most people have incomes of less than £10 000. One or two millionaires have brought the average up to £15 000. The market for diamond tiaras might be quite good in such an unfair society, whereas the mass market required for electronic gadgets might not be present. Perhaps television sets might sell well, but video machines would be less acceptable and compact disc players might be in quite poor demand.

Consider the following situation. You are the traffic manager of a bus company and have received complaints about the reliability of a certain service. You suspect that it may have something to do with the particular driver in charge and therefore carry out an investigation into the time taken by the two drivers concerned over a period of 100 journeys each. See Table 7.1.

Table 7.1   Journey times for Drivers A and B

Driver A: Times to nearest minute

32	30	28	26	31	29	33	29	31	30
28	29	30	28	31	29	30	29	31	31
29	33	28	29	31	30	28	29	28	27
30	31	32	30	30	33	31	27	31	32
31	32	30	27	31	30	31	31	28	26
30	33	29	30	27	30	29	31	29	30
29	28	31	34	29	30	28	29	30	31
31	30	28	30	30	34	32	30	33	29
31	31	31	29	32	29	32	30	27	30
30	29	30	29	32	32	30	32	29	30

Driver B: Times to nearest minute

30	30	31	29	30	30	30	31	31	31
29	30	30	30	29	28	30	31	30	30
30	29	30	29	30	29	31	30	29	31
29	30	30	30	29	30	30	30	30	30
31	29	31	30	30	29	30	31	30	30
30	30	30	30	30	30	29	30	30	30
30	30	32	31	30	30	30	30	30	31
30	30	30	30	30	30	30	32	30	30
30	30	29	30	30	31	31	28	29	30
30	30	31	29	31	30	30	30	30	29

The mean time for each driver is 30 minutes (you should check this figure) but, as with all statistical investigations, we could further analyse the data using a table, graph and/or diagram. The frequency distribution will be as shown in Table 7.2

Table 7.2   The data arranged as two frequency distributions

	Journey time (to nearest minute)			
Time in minutes	Driver A		Driver B	
	Frequency	Cumulative frequency	Frequency	Cumulative frequency
26	2	2	–	0
27	5	7	–	0
28	10	17	2	2
29	20	37	16	18
30	26	63	64	82

31	20	83	16	98
32	10	93	2	100
33	5	98	–	100
34	2	100	–	100
	———			
	100		100	
	═══		═══	

It is obvious from the table that the times of Driver A vary more than those of Driver B, although both have the same mean time (and also the same median and mode). Therefore we will need to consider how the data is spread or dispersed around the average, and we can measure this variation by means of one (or more) of the following measures:

1   The range.
2   The interquartile range.
3   The quartile deviation.
4   The mean deviation.
5   The standard deviation.

As with the averages, each measure has both advantages and disadvantages, and so we must look at each measure of dispersion in turn.

7.2   The range

This measures the difference between the highest and lowest values of the data. Therefore we have:

(*a*)   The range of Driver A's times was $34 - 26 = 8$ minutes.
(*b*)   The range of Driver B's times was $32 - 28 = 4$ minutes.

Therefore the times of Driver B were more concentrated around the average of 30 minutes than were those of Driver A, and indeed it follows that the average was more representative of Driver B's actual times than it was of Driver A's times.

The usefulness of the range is limited and therefore has few practical applications. These will be discussed later in this chapter.

7.3   The interquartile range and the quartile deviation

In Section 6.16 reference was made to the finding of the upper and lower quartiles by reading them off from the cumulative frequency curve (the ogive). The lower quartile item is found by the formula $\dfrac{n+1}{4}$ and the upper quartile item is found by the formula $\dfrac{3(n + 1)}{4}$. Since in each case in the example above we took the records of 100 trips, the lower quartile item is $\dfrac{101}{4} = 25\frac{1}{4}$, the $25\frac{1}{4}$th journey made when the times are arranged as a frequency distribution. Similarly the upper quartile is the $\dfrac{3 \times 101}{4} = 75\frac{3}{4}$ the $75\frac{3}{4}$th journey made when the times are arranged as a frequency distribution. Calling the lower quartile $Q1$ and the upper quartile $Q3$, we have for Drivers A and B the following:

Driver A: $Q1 = 29$ minutes $Q3 = 31$ minutes
Driver B: $Q1 = 30$ minutes $Q3 = 30$ minutes

As far as Driver B is concerned, both the $25\frac{1}{4}$th journey and all journeys up to the $75\frac{3}{4}$th journey were made in 30 minutes exactly.

The interquartile range

This is the range between Q1 and Q3 and is found by working out $Q3 - Q1$. For our two drivers the interquartile range is:

Driver A: $Q3 - Q1 = 31 - 29 = 2$ minutes
Driver B: $Q3 - Q1 = 30 - 30 = 0$ minutes

This is in many ways a more significant figure than the range, for it tells us the length of the interval that contains the central half of the data. The central half of any spread of data is usually the most meaningful. It is not affected by extreme items, very small or very large items, which do not appear in it at all.

The quartile deviation

This is a measure of the way the central half of the data is spread out on either side of the median. (But we cannot say it is central around the median because the median could be anywhere between Q1 and Q3 – it is not necessarily half way.) The quartile deviation is sometimes called the **semi-interquartile range**, which gives a clue to the manner of its calculation. This is:

$$QD = \frac{Q3 - Q1}{2}$$

In the very simple example given above above we have

$$\text{Driver A:} \quad QD = \frac{31-29}{2} = \frac{2}{2} = 1$$

$$\text{Driver B:} \quad QD = \frac{30-30}{2} = \frac{0}{2} = 0$$

In other words the central half of all the times taken for the journey made by Driver A lay within 1 minute of the mean time of 30 minutes. With Driver B the central half of all the journeys made was made in exactly the mean time of 30 minutes – no dispersion at all around the average. Driver B can only be described as a very steady driver indeed. All fifty journeys in the inter-quartile range were made in the exact time permitted.

We could define the quartile deviation as a measure of variation that tells us the average amount by which the two quartiles differ from the median, or the mean.

We must now take some further examples, because we must be prepared to calculate both the interquartile range and the quartile deviation for ungrouped data, frequency distributions and grouped data.

(a) Ungrouped data
Example 7.1

An investigation shows the number of days which each of ten drivers spent in a depot in a particular month. Time spent in the depot is wasted time as far as driving is concerned. You are asked to calculate the quartile deviation from the following information

Driver:	A	B	C	D	E	F	G	H	I	J
Days in:	9	1	4	5	6	7	11	7	3	12

The $Q1$ position will be $\frac{n+1}{4}$, where n is the number of items of data.

We have ten items of data and therefore $\frac{n+1}{4} = \frac{11}{4} = 2\frac{3}{4}$. You will recall that the data must be rearranged in order of magnitude

| 1 | 3 | 4 | 5 | 6 | 7 | 7 | 9 | 11 | 12 |

The second item is 3 and the third item is 4, so the $2\frac{3}{4}$th item will be $\frac{3}{4}$ of the interval between 3 and 4 = $3\frac{3}{4}$. Therefore the $Q1$ value will be 3.75 days.

Similarly, the $Q3$ position will be $\frac{3(n+1)}{4} = \frac{33}{4} = 8\frac{1}{4}$.

The eighth item in order of magnitude is 9 and the ninth item is 11. The $8\frac{1}{4}$th item is therefore one quarter of the way from 9 to 11. One quarter of $2 = \frac{1}{2}$. Therefore the Q_3 position is $9\frac{1}{2}$, i.e. 9.5 days.

$$\text{Therefore} \quad QD = \frac{9.5 - 3.75}{2} = \frac{5.75}{2} = 2.875 \text{ days}$$

The interquartile range is 5.75 days and the QD is 2.875 days.

(b) Frequency distribution

Example 7.2
The numbers of accidents occurring at a road junction in one year were as follows:

Accidents at Pye Crossroads in 19..

Accidents in a week	Number of weeks when this number occurred	Cumulative frequency
0	10	10
1	17	27
2	11	38
3	7	45
4	3	48
5	2	50
6	2	52
7	0	52
	52	

Calculate the quartile deviation.

The first stage is to arrange the data into a cumulative table, and this has already been done in the table above.

$$Q1 \text{ position} = \frac{n+1}{4} = \frac{52+1}{4} = \frac{53}{4} = 13\frac{1}{4}$$

The $13\frac{1}{4}$th item in the cumulative frequency table is in the 1 accident a week class. Hence the $Q1$ value will be 1 accident per week

$$Q3 \text{ position} = \frac{3(n+1)}{4} = \frac{159}{4} = 39\frac{3}{4}$$

This lies in the 3 accidents per week class. Hence the $Q3$ value will be 3 accidents, and the $QD =$

$$\frac{3-1}{2} = 1 \text{ accident per week}$$

The central half of the accidents which occurred were in the range of 1–3 accidents per week, and the $Q1$ and $Q3$ positions were only on average 1 accident per week away from the median position.

(c) Grouped frequency distributions

Example 7.3
The weights of package transported by an express van service were as follows:

Weight of packages (kg)	Number of packages
Less than 2	2
2 and under 4	7
4 and under 6	8
6 and under 8	13
8 and under 10	16
10 and under 12	32
12 and under 14	36
14 and under 16	20
16 and over	10

Calculate the quartile deviation.

As with the previous example, the first procedure is to obtain the cumulative frequency table:

Weight (kg)	Frequency (f)	Cumulative frequency
Less than 2	2	2
2 and under 4	7	9
4 and under 6	8	17
6 and under 8	13	30
8 and under 10	16	46

10 and under 12	32	78
12 and under 14	36	114
14 and under 16	20	134
16 and over	10	144
	Σf 144	

The $Q1$ position $= \dfrac{\Sigma f}{4} = \dfrac{144}{4} = 36$.

The 36th item in the cumulative frequency table will be the 6th item in the '8 and 10' group. Since there are 16 items in the group, the value of the 36th item will be $8 + \left(\dfrac{6}{16} \text{ of } 2 \right) = 8 + \frac{3}{4} = 8.75\text{kg}$. The $Q3$ position $= \Sigma f \times \frac{3}{4} = \dfrac{144 \times 3}{4} = 108$.

The $Q3$ value will be in the '12 and under 14' group. It will be the 30th item in that group $(108 - 78)$ and it will be $\dfrac{30}{36}$ of the way up the group. Therefore:

$$Q3 \text{ value} = 12 + \left(\frac{30}{36} \times 2 \right)\text{kg}$$

$$= 12 + \frac{(5 \times 2)}{6}$$

$$= 12 + 1\tfrac{2}{3}$$

$$= \underline{\underline{13.67\text{kg}}}$$

Therefore the quartile deviation is:

$$QD = \frac{13.67 - 8.75}{2} = \frac{4.92}{2} = 2.46\text{kg}$$

Remember, the quartile deviation tells us the average amount by which the two quartiles vary from the median. The centre half of all the packages were in the range of weights between 8.75kg and 13.67kg. You will recall that we can obtain the quartiles either by calculation (as above) or from the ogive, the cumulative frequency group. You would be well advised to repeat this example using the graph in order to obtain your $Q3$ and $Q1$ values (see Figure 6.1, p. 152).

7.4   Questions on the range, the interquartile range and the quartile deviation

1   What is meant by the concept of dispersion? List the measures of dispersion.

2   In a particular week ten small factories making similar components for an assembly plant turned out the following outputs.

(a) 4 850 units	(b)	480 units
(c) 5 325 units	(d)	9 596 units
(e) 7 562 units	(f)	10 000 units
(g) 8 426 units	(h)	1 240 units
(i) 5 525 units	(j)	385 units

Find (i) the average output (arithmetic mean) (answer correct to the nearest whole number), and (ii) the range of the data.

3   Attendances at soccer matches in Ruralville are as follows at the thirteen fixtures in the pre-Christmas season: 1 569, 2 342, 8 564, 7 325, 9 116, 4 297, 3 583, 2 416, 11 594, 12 726, 6 345, 5 924, and 3 816.

Find (a) the arithmetic mean attendance (answer to the nearest whole number), and (b) the range of attendances.

4   Two employees paid on a piecework basis are being compared for efficiency. Mr A is often late and frequently absent; Mr B is punctual and regular in attendance. They work on identical products. Output is as follows in the month of March:

Mr A's output per day					*Mr B's output per day*				
5	56	48	46	0	27	26	29	31	30
0	72	0	56	0	31	29	24	32	29
0	68	60	78	0	33	32	36	31	25
42	70	84	68	0	24	27	35	29	30

Find (a) The total outputs of each worker.

(b) The range of outputs of each.
(c) The median output of each.
(d) The interquartile range of each.
(e) The quartile deviation.
(f) How helpful is this data in deciding which of the workers should be made redundant if the question arises?

5   Do-it-yourself shops are investigated for profitabiity, and the following information is obtained:

Profits made (£)	Number of outlets	Cumulative frequency
Less than £10 000	426	?
10 000–14 999.99	733	?
15 000–19 999.99	1 238	?
20 000–24 999.99	664	?
25 000–29 999.99	372	?
30 000–34 999.99	365	?
35 000–39 999.99	422	?
40 000 and over	588	?

Find (a) The cumulative frequency total.
   (b) The median profit (answer correct to nearest £1).
   (c) The lower quartile and the upper quartile values (correct to nearest £1).
   (d) The interquartile range of profits.
   (e) The quartile deviation.

6 Fifty television sets sold with a 3-year free service guarantee have to be repaired at the costs (in £) shown below:

18	14	12	3	6	7	9	29	5	84
4	25	27	6	18	8	25	10	16	17
19	5	15	39	48	46	9	18	56	29
17	24	25	16	7	11	19	13	14	36
36	12	17	9	18	26	12	43	19	40

Find (a) The range of the data.
   (b) The mean cost of a repair.
   (c) The median value, the first quartile value and the third quartile value.
   (d) The interquartile range.
   (e) The quartile deviation (answer correct to the nearest penny).

7 A major grocery firm investigates twenty-five retail grocery businesses to identify target firms for takeovers. The number of branches of the firms investigated were as follows:

Number of outlets	36,	18,	7,	5,	16
	49,	19,	38,	72,	60
	41,	43,	16,	9,	46
	127,	86,	73,	11,	84
	29,	16,	17,	14,	38

Find (*a*) The range of outlets.
     (*b*) The average of outlets (arithmetic mean).
     (*c*) The upper and lower quartiles.
     (*d*) The interquartile range.
     (*e*) The quartile deviation.

8   Students in a class examination achieve the following results out of 100:

Score	Number of students
Over 90	3
80 to 89.9	4
70 to 79.9	6
60 to 69.9	10
50 to 59.9	13
40 to 49.9	8
30 to 39.9	3
20 to 29.9	1
10 to 19.9	1
0 to 9.9	1

Draw an ogive curve and use it to find:

(*a*) The median score.
(*b*) The $Q1$ and $Q3$ scores.
(*c*) The interquartile range.
(*d*) The quartile deviation.

9   The following table gives the distribution by seating capacity of new bus and coach registrations during Spring 19..;

Seating capacity	No. of Vehicles
15–19	123
20–24	142
25–29	269
30–39	890
40–49	1 823
50–59	125

Calculate the quartile deviation.

7.5 The mean deviation

In both measures that we have calculated (the range and the quartile deviation) only two values have been taken into account in each case – the maximum and minimum values for the range, and Q_1 and Q_3 for the quartile deviation. It would obviously be better if each item of data could be taken into account and both the mean and standard deviations do this, but with different results. Let us consider the mean deviation first. It is the arithmetic mean of the deviations of each item of data from the data average (which is usually the arithmetic mean but sometimes the median), with all deviations being counted as positive.

The last sentence is not easy to understand, and an illustration may help.

Suppose the average score in an examination is 56.5, and no student actually has that score. Then all students will have a score which is either above or below that 'mean' score, e.g.

Candidate A has 81 marks. His deviation from the mean is + 24.5 marks.
Candidate B has 93 marks. Her score deviates from the mean by + 36.5 marks.
Candidate C has 40.5 marks and deviates from the mean by − 16 marks.
Candidate D only scored 27.5 marks and deviates by − 29 marks.

If we want to understand the dispersion of the marks around the average score of 56.5 marks, we shall get the clearest idea if we find the 'mean deviation', i.e. the average amount by which marks vary from the average score. To do this we add up all the deviations and divide by the number of students, but then we run up against a difficulty. Since some are above average and some below average the + and − scores cancel one another out. We find ourselves trying to find an average of nothing. Therefore we have to regard all the deviations as positive if we are to get a clear picture. Using the very limited example given above, the mean deviation is (ignoring the minus signs):

$$\frac{24.5 + 36.5 + 16 + 29}{4} = \frac{106}{4} = 26.5 \text{ marks}$$

The average deviation from the mean score is 26.5 marks.

As before, we must be able to calculate the mean deviation for ungrouped data, frequency distributions and grouped data.

Ungrouped data

Example 7.4
Using the data from example 7.1, calculate the mean deviation for driver time in the depot.

The arithmetic mean ($\bar{x}$) is $\dfrac{65}{10}$ days $= 6.5$ days.

Driver	Number of days (x)	Deviation from mean (x − x̄)	|x − x̄|
A	9	+2.5	2.5
B	1	−5.5	5.5
C	4	−2.5	2.5
D	5	−1.5	1.5
E	6	−0.5	0.5
F	7	+0.5	0.5
G	11	+4.5	4.5
H	7	+0.5	0.5
I	3	−3.5	3.5
J	12	+5.5	5.5
	65		27.0

The sign $|x - \bar{x}|$ is an instruction to take the modulus of the value, i.e. make it positive irrespective of the original sign.

The method for calculating the mean deviation is:

1   Calculate the mean, if not already given

$$\bar{x} = \frac{65}{10} = 6.5$$

2   Find the deviations from the mean $(x - \bar{x})$, i.e.

$9 - 6.5 = 2.5$

$1 - 6.5 = -5.5$ etc.

3   Make all these deviations absolute deviations from the mean by having them all positive.

4   Calculate the mean deviation:

$$\text{MD} = \frac{\Sigma |x - \bar{x}|}{n} = \frac{27}{10} = 2.7 \text{ days}$$

We cannot calculate the mean deviation by simply averaging the deviations $(x - \bar{x})$, because the sum of the deviations will always be zero. As explained earlier, when you calculate an average, the items above and below average always equal one another when they are totalled, and sum to zero. As a result, the mean of these deviations will also always be zero, i.e. $\dfrac{\Sigma(x - \bar{x})}{n} = 0 \left(\text{you should check that } \dfrac{\Sigma(x - \bar{x})}{n} = 0\right.$ in our example$\left.\right)$. This is the reason why we have to use the modulus of the deviation value.

Frequency distribution

The general procedure, as outlined in the previous example, applies both to the frequency distribution and the grouped frequency distribution, except that the deviations are weighted by their respective frequencies before averaging.

Example 7.5

Using the data in Example 7.2, calculate the mean deviation. The mean is 1.81 (see below):

Accidents at Pye Crossroads in 19 . .

Accidents in a week	Number of weeks (f)	fx	Deviation from mean $x - \bar{x}$	Modulus $\|x - \bar{x}\|$	$f\|x - \bar{x}\|$
0	10	0	−1.81	1.81	18.1
1	17	17	−0.81	0.81	13.77
2	11	22	+0.19	0.19	2.09
3	7	21	+1.19	1.19	8.33
4	3	12	+2.19	2.19	6.57
5	2	10	+3.19	3.19	6.38
6	2	12	+4.19	4.19	8.38
7	0	0	+5.19	5.19	0
	52	94			63.62

The method for calculating the mean deviation from a frequency distribution is:

(*a*) Calculate the mean ($\bar{x}$):

$$\bar{x} = \frac{\Sigma fx}{\Sigma f} = \frac{94}{52} = 1.81 \text{ accidents}$$

(b) Obtain the deviations of each class from the mean ie $x - \bar{x}$.
    For example $0 - 1.81 = -1.81$; $1 - 1.81 = -0.81$, etc.
(c) Make all the deviations positive i.e. $|x - \bar{x}|$. So -1.81 becomes 1.81, etc.
(d) Multiply each deviation by its respective frequency, to give the total deviations of the group in each case.
(e) Add up the total deviations and find the mean deviation

$$MD = \frac{\Sigma f(|x - \bar{x}|)}{\Sigma f} = \frac{63.62}{52} = 1.22 \text{ accidents}$$

We can therefore say that on average the number of accidents in any week varied from the mean number of 1.81 accidents a week by 1.22 accidents.

Grouped frequency distributions

The procedure is as in Example 7.4, except that the deviations are taken from the class mark (the midpoint of the class)

Example 7.6
Using the data in Example 7.3, calculate the mean deviation.

Weight of packages (kg)	Number of packages (f)	d	fd
0 to under 2	2	-5	-10
2 to under 4	7	-4	-28
4 to under 6	8	-3	-24
6 to under 8	13	-2	-26
8 to under 10	16	-1	-16
10 to under 12	32	0	0
12 to under 14	36	1	36
14 to under 16	20	2	40
16 and over	10	$3\frac{1}{2}$	35
	144		+7

(a) Calculate the mean. We have used the assumed mean method and assumed that all the items in a group are equally distributed around the midpoints. We have also assumed that the open-ended class is twice as big as the other classes. (Students who are unsure of the figure of $3\frac{1}{2}$ class intervals difference in the d column should reason it out as follows. The midpoint of the group chosen as the assumed mean is 11, and is designated A. The midpoint of the open-ended group 16–20 is 18. Therefore, since the class interval is 2 and the difference between 11 and 18 is 7, the midpoint of the open-ended group is $3\frac{1}{2}$ class intervals above the assumed mean).

Using the formula $\bar{x} = A + \left(\dfrac{\Sigma fd}{\Sigma f} \times \text{Class interval}\right)$, we have

$$\bar{x} = 11 + \left(\frac{7}{144} \times 2\right)$$

$$= 11 + 0.10$$

$$= \underline{\underline{11.10}}$$

You will see that the mean of 11.10 is given correct to two decimal places.

(b) In order to obtain the deviations from the mean $(x - \bar{x})$ we assume (as usual) that the class marks (the midpoints) represent the group. Subtract the mean from each in turn, making them all positive.

(c) Multiply the deviations by their respective frequencies to give $f(|m - \bar{x}|)$. The table now looks like this:

Class mark (m)	Modulus $\lvert m - \bar{x} \rvert$	Number of packages (f)	Total deviations $f(\lvert m - \bar{x} \rvert)$
1	10.10	2	20.20
3	8.10	7	56.70
5	6.10	8	48.80
7	4.10	13	53.30
9	2.10	16	33.60
11	0.10	32	3.20
13	1.90	36	68.40
15	3.90	20	78.00
18	6.90	10	69.00
		$\Sigma f = 144$	431.20

(d)   Calculate the mean of the deviations:

$$MD = \frac{\Sigma f(|m - \bar{x}|)}{\Sigma f}$$

$$= \frac{431.20}{144}$$

$$= \underline{\underline{2.99 \text{kg}}}$$

Remember that we can do the calculation without using the 'assumed mean' method.

7.6   Exercises about the mean deviation

1   The total incomes of persons residing in Coronation Close are as follows:

House number	Incomes per annum in total (£)
1	15 600
2	4 840
3	17 550
4	23 820
5	8 560
6	12 620
7	5 940
8	13 200
9	7 760
10	5 900
11	8 400

Find (a) the mean income, and (b) the mean deviation around the mean income (answer correct to the nearest £1)

2   Analysis of export trade to North America in 19.. by originating areas in the UK, differentiating between deep-sea container movements and air freight, reveals the following:

Location area	Deep-sea container ('000 tonnes)	Air freight ('000 tonnes)
London	160	24
East Anglia	64	20
South West	82	6
West	36	8
Wales	120	4
Midlands	230	26
North West	65	5
North East	50	12

Calculate from the *total* tonnage by originating area, irrespective of the mode of transport used:

(a) The average tonnage of exports from the eight areas.
(b) The mean deviation from that average figure.

3 Calculate the mean age of council tenants and the mean deviation, given the following:

Age distribution of council tenants in Port Town in 19..

Age group	Number
Over 15 but under 25	1 825
Over 25 but under 35	2 342
Over 35 but under 45	875
Over 45 but under 55	260
Over 55 but under 65	180
Over 65 but under 75	1 958
Over 75	946

You may assume that the last class interval is twice as big as the other groups.

4 Sales by representatives of a UK firm in the USA in 19.. were as follows:

Classes ($'000)	Number of salesmen
Under 10	3
Over 10 but under 20	5
Over 20 but under 30	6
Over 30 but under 40	8
Over 40 but under 50	9
Over 50 but under 60	10
Over 60 but under 70	6
Over 70 but under 80	6
Over 80 but under 90	4
90 and over	3

(a) Calculate the mean sales and the mean deviation of sales volumes. You may assume the last class interval to be *three* times the size of the other classes.

(b) State what you understand about the set of data from your answers.

7.7 The standard deviation

All the measures of dispersion discussed up to now have serious defects as methods of describing any distribution, for the following reasons.

First, the range is of little use since it only mentions the first and last items in the distribution, and neither of these is particularly representative of the distribution as a whole. For example a class of 17-year-old students with one septuagenarian in attendance is not well described if we say 'the age range is from 17–74.' An extreme item at either end of a distribution makes the 'range' unrepresentative.

Second, the interquartile range is better, because it does at least tell us where the centre half of the distribution is located, and the quartile deviation tells us the average amount by which $Q1$ and $Q3$ vary from the median. Unfortunately that is not a very clear way of describing the centre half of a distribution, because we do not know where the centre is, except that it is somewhere between $Q1$ and $Q3$. The median, being the central item in the array, may not be at the centre, equidistant from $Q1$ and $Q3$, because the various items may be bunched close to $Q1$, or close to $Q3$. So all we can say is that on average they are spread around by the amount of the quartile deviation.

Third, the mean deviation is better. If we use the arithmetic mean as the central point, the mean deviation tells us the average amount by which the individual statistics vary from the arithmetic mean of the whole set of data. Unfortunately, to arrive at the mean deviation we have to ignore the signs of the deviations, because some will be above the average and some below the average, and when we add them all together, the result will be zero. So we cannot find an 'average' deviation unless we ignore signs and use the modulus (the deviations with all signs positive), as explained in Section 7.5 above. The trouble then, as far as the use of the mean deviation in higher level statistics is concerned, is that the mean deviation is not suitable for mathematical manipulation. This is a great disadvantage, which the **standard deviation** avoids, and you will find that the standard deviation is the main measure used in advanced statistical work. The standard deviation avoids the problem by squaring the deviations in order to make them all positive. It then takes the square root of the answer. Note that in many textbooks the standard deviation is designed by the Greek letter σ (lower case sigma). We have simply used SD. Once again we must be able to calculate the standard deviation for ungrouped data, frequency distributions and grouped data.

The standard deviation of ungrouped data

We must be prepared to calculate the standard deviation when the mean is either (*a*) an exact figure or (*b*) an approximated figure.

Example 7.7

We will calculate the standard deviation, using the data from Example 7.1, which was about the number of days spent in the depot by certain drivers. In the table below, x is the number of days the drivers spent in the depot, d stands for the deviation from the arithmetic mean and d^2 means the square of the deviation so found. When we square a negative number, the answer is positive, so that all the d^2 figures are positive. The method is explained below the table.

x	d	d^2
9	2.5	6.25
1	−5.5	30.25
4	−2.5	6.25
5	−1.5	2.25
6	−0.5	0.25
7	0.5	0.25
11	4.5	20.25
7	0.5	0.25
3	−3.5	12.25
12	5.5	30.25
65		108.50

(a)   Calculate the mean ($\bar{x}$)

$$\bar{x} = \frac{65}{10} = 6.5 \text{ days}$$

(b)   Obtain the deviations from the mean ($x - \bar{x}$) and call the results d.
(c)   Square the deviations to give d^2.
(d)   Calculate the average of the deviations. This is known as the **variance**. In this case it is $\frac{108.5}{10} = 10.85$.
(e)   Take the square root of the variance to give the standard deviation:

$$\sqrt{10.85} = 3.29 \text{ days}$$

(f)   Put as a general formula, we have:

$$\text{Variance} = \frac{\Sigma d^2}{n} = \frac{108.5}{10} = 10.85 \text{ days}$$

$$\text{SD} = \sqrt{\frac{\Sigma d^2}{n}}$$

$$= \sqrt{\frac{108.5}{10}}$$

$$= \sqrt{10.85}$$

$$= \underline{\underline{3.29 \text{ days.}}}$$

In Example 7.7 the mean came out exactly to 6.5 days, but it may not do so, and we will be forced to abbreviate it to a given number of places of decimals. We then have the difficulty that when we calculate the deviations, they will all be slightly wrong. It is therefore better to use the assumed mean method, taking the assumed mean as the whole number closest to the abbreviated mean we have found. Consider Example 7.8:

Example 7.8
Seven drivers spent days in the depot as shown below. The total number of days lost is shown to be 43, and the $\bar{x}$ is therefore $43 \div 7 = 6.14$ days. As this is going to give very awkward (and slightly wrong) figures for the deviations from the mean d, we use the assumed mean method and take 6 as the assumed mean. The method is explained below the table.

x	d	d^2
9	3	9
1	-5	25
4	-2	4
5	-1	1
6	0	0
7	1	1
11	5	25
43	$+1$	65

(a) Calculate the mean ($\bar{x}$)

$$\bar{x} = \frac{43}{7} = 6.14 \text{ days}$$

You will see that we have had to approximate the mean to two decimal places and therefore the mean is not exact.

(b) Choose an assumed mean (A) – the nearest whole number to the approximated mean; in this case 6.

(c) Obtain the deviations from the assumed mean, ($x - A$). Call these d and add them together, Σd. You will recall that deviations from an exact mean will always sum to zero, but in this case $\Sigma d = 1$.

(d) Square the deviations to give d^2.

(e) Calculate the variance, using the formula:

$$\text{Variance} = \frac{\Sigma d^2}{n} - \left(\frac{\Sigma d}{\Sigma n}\right)^2$$

The second part of the formula applies a correction to take account of the fact that the deviations do not sum to zero.

Substituting in on this formula we have:

$$\text{Variance} = \frac{65}{7} - \left(\frac{1}{7}\right)^2$$

$$= 9.29 - 0.02$$

$$= \underline{9.27 \text{ days}}$$

(e) Take the square root of the variance to give the standard deviation:

$$\text{SD} = \sqrt{\text{variance}} = \sqrt{9.27} = \underline{3.04 \text{ days}}$$

We can therefore describe the distribution of the data in the following way. The average number of days drivers spent in the depot was 3.14 days, and the standard deviation around this central point was 3.04 days.

Set out as a general formula, the formula for finding the standard deviation by the assumed mean method is:

$$SD = \sqrt{\frac{\Sigma d^2}{\Sigma n} - \left(\frac{\Sigma d}{\Sigma n}\right)^2}$$

The $-\left(\dfrac{\Sigma d}{\Sigma n}\right)^2$ in the formula is sometimes referred to as the **correction factor**, because it is correcting for the fact that we have obtained our deviations from an assumed mean, not the true mean. The correction factor is always minus.

Actually you could use the SD formula given above for any calculation, whether it was from an exact mean or an assumed mean, because where the mean is exact, the correction factor would simply come to 0. Try it with the data of Example 7.7 and prove to yourself that the term does come to 0.

The standard deviation from a frequency distribution

Again we have the two situations, when (a) the mean is exact and (b) the mean is approximate.

Example 7.9 – with an exact mean

A stretch of motorway on which accidents occur regularly is found to have accidents per week as follows:

Number of accidents in a week (x)	Number of weeks (f)	fx
0	13	0
1	11	11
2	12	24
3	7	21
4	3	12
5	2	10
6	2	12
7	2	14
	52	104

If we calculate the mean from the formula, we get

$$\bar{x} = \frac{\Sigma fx}{\Sigma x} = \frac{104}{52} = 2.0$$

We find the mean to be 2.0 exactly. Our table can then be extended as follows: the last term fd^2 is the product of the squares of the deviations and the group frequency. The method is explained after the following table:

x	f	fx	d $(x-\bar{x})$	d^2	fd^2
0	13	0	-2	4	52
1	11	11	-1	1	11
2	12	24	0	0	0
3	7	21	1	1	7
4	3	12	2	4	12
5	2	10	3	9	18
6	2	12	4	16	32
7	2	14	5	25	50
	52	104			182

(a) Calculate the mean ($\bar{x}$)

$$\bar{x} = \frac{\Sigma fx}{\Sigma f} = \frac{104}{52} = 2.0 \text{ accidents}$$

(b) Obtain the deviations of the mean from each class $(x - \bar{x})$, i.e. d.
(c) Square these deviations to give d^2.
(d) Multiply the squared deviations by their respective frequencies.
(e) Calculate the mean of these weighted squared deviations to give the variance:

$$\text{Variance} = \frac{\Sigma fd^2}{\Sigma f} = \frac{182}{52} = 3.5 \text{ accidents}$$

(b) Take the square root of the variance to obtain the standard deviation:

$$\text{SD} = \sqrt{\text{variance}} = \sqrt{3.5} = 1.87 \text{ accidents}$$

We may therefore describe the data about accidents on this stretch of motorway as revealing that in an average week there were 2 accidents and the standard deviation of the number of accidents around that figure was 1.87 accidents.

Example 7.10 – with an approximate mean

If the mean is not exact, it is best to use the assumed mean method to obtain both the mean and the standard deviations. Consider this situation in a small factory.

The number of rejected parts per shift were recorded over a period of several weeks. Calculate the mean number of rejected parts per shift and the standard deviation. The method is shown after the table.

Number of rejected parts per shift x	Number of shifts f	d	fd	fd^2
0	5	−1	−5	5
1	31	0	0	0
2	28	1	+28	28
3	2	2	+4	8
4	1	3	+3	9
	67		+30	50

(a) Choose an assumed mean (A). We have chosen 1 but any of the classes will do.
(b) Obtain the deviations of each class from the assumed mean, $(x - A)$, i.e. d.
(c) Multiply these deviations by their respective frequencies (fd) and total them.
(d) Square the deviations (d^2), and multiply by their respective frequencies (fd^2) and total them. The easy way to do this is to multiply fd by d to get fd^2
(e) Calculate the mean:

$$\bar{x} = A + \left(\frac{\Sigma fd}{\Sigma f}\right) = 1 + \left(\frac{30}{67}\right) = 1.45 \text{ parts rejected per shift}$$

Calculate the standard deviation:

$$SD = \sqrt{\frac{\Sigma fd^2}{\Sigma f} - \left(\frac{\Sigma fd}{\Sigma f}\right)^2}$$

$$= \sqrt{\frac{50}{67} - \left(\frac{30}{67}\right)^2}$$

$$= \sqrt{0.7463 - 0.2005}$$

$$= \sqrt{0.5458}$$

$$= 0.74 \text{ parts}$$

We can therefore describe the distribution by saying that the average number of rejected parts per shift is 1.45 parts, with the distribution of results around that central point averaging out at 0.74 parts.

In examinations, it would clearly be a waste of valuable time to calculate the mean first to see if it is exact or not. It is better to use the second method always, and if the mean does turn out to be exact, then the correction factor $\left(\dfrac{\Sigma fd}{\Sigma f}\right)^2$ will be zero. Use the assumed mean method for Example 7.9 to satisfy yourself that the answers are the same.

Grouped frequency distributions

With frequency distributions, there were two possible methods which could be employed, but it was suggested that method 2 be used. With grouped data, the assumed mean approach is best and the formulae are very similar to those in Example 7.10.

Example 7.11

The following data show the speeds of lorries checked as they moved along a stretch of dual carriageway:

Speed (mph)	Number of lorries
20 to under 25	4
25 to under 30	6
30 to under 35	8
35 to under 40	9
40 to under 45	10
45 to under 50	12
50 to under 55	14
55 to under 60	16
60 to under 65	12
65 and over	9
	100

192 Statistics for Business

Find the arithmetic average speed and the standard deviation. You may assume that the last group is twice as large as the other groups. The method is given after the table below, which shows the various calculations. The mean speed has been assumed to be 42.5mph, the midpoint of the '40 to under 45' group.

Speed mph	Number of lorries f	d	fd	fd²
20 to under 25	4	−4	−16	64
25 to under 30	6	−3	−18	54
30 to under 35	8	−2	−16	32
35 to under 40	9	−1	−9	9
40 to under 45	10	0	0	0
45 to under 50	12	1	12	12
50 to under 55	14	2	28	56
55 to under 60	16	3	48	144
60 to under 65	12	4	48	192
65 and over	9	$5\frac{1}{2}$	$49\frac{1}{2}$	272.25
	100		$+126\frac{1}{2}$	835.25

(a) Calculate the mean using the formula:

$$\bar{x} = A + \left(\frac{\Sigma fd}{\Sigma f} \times \text{class interval} \right)$$

$$= 42.5 + \left(\frac{126.5}{100} \times 5 \right)$$

$$= 42.5 + (1.265 \times 5)$$

$$= 42.5 + 6.325$$

$$= \underline{\underline{48.825\text{mph}}}$$

(b) Multiply the fd column by the d column to give fd^2, by so doing we make the weighted deviations all positive (a minus multiplied by a minus become a plus).

(c) Total the fd^2 column and use in the formula:

$$SD = \sqrt{\frac{\Sigma fd^2}{\Sigma f} - \left(\frac{\Sigma fd}{\Sigma f} \right)^2} \times CI \text{ (class interval)}$$

$$= \sqrt{\frac{835.25}{100} - \left(\frac{126.5}{100}\right)^2} \times \text{CI}$$

$$= \sqrt{8.3525 - (1.265)^2} \times \text{CI}$$

$$= \sqrt{8.3525 - 1.6023} \times \text{CI}$$

$$= \sqrt{6.7502} \times \text{CI}$$

$$= 2.598 \times 5$$

$$= \underline{\underline{12.990\text{mph}}}$$

The most common error made by students in examinations is to multiply $\frac{\Sigma fd^2}{\Sigma f} - \left(\frac{\Sigma fd}{\Sigma f}\right)^2$ by the class interval and then take the square root. This is wrong and will give an incorrect answer, as you can prove for yourself.

7.8 The coefficient of variation

Suppose a transport company has two depots whose weekly usage of diesel is as follows:

	Mean	Standard deviation
Depot A	5 000 gallons	500 gallons
Depot B	500 gallons	100 gallons

Clearly the standard deviation of A is larger in absolute terms than B, but equally it is clear that in relative terms the variability of diesel usage is greater in B than in A. This would be important in terms of policies of stocking and reordering supplies, and therefore it is sometimes helpful to employ a measure of the *relative* dispersion of the data around the mean known as the **coefficient of variation**. The coefficient of variation may be defined as a measure which shows the magnitude of the variation relative to the size of the quantity that is being measured.

$$\text{Coefficient of variation (CV)} = \frac{\text{Standard deviation}}{\text{Arithmetic mean}}$$

$$\text{CV} = \frac{\text{SD}}{\text{AM}}$$

Example 7.12

Using the data above, calculate the coefficients of variation:

Depot A $\quad$ CV $= \dfrac{500}{5\,000} = 0.1$

Depot B $\quad$ CV $= \dfrac{100}{500} = 0.2$

It is usual to express the coefficients in percentage terms and therefore:

Depot A $\quad$ CV $= 10\%$

Depot B $\quad$ CV $= 20\%$

You can see that the CV is independent of the units of measurement, and this enables us to compare the variability of data which has been measured in different units.

Example 7.13

A garage reports its average weekly use of two particular spare parts as follows:

	Mean	Standard deviation
Part A	121 units	23 units
Part B	638 kilos	104 kilos

Calculate the coefficients of variation:

Part A $\quad$ CV $= \dfrac{23}{121} \times 100 = 19.01\%$

Part B $\quad$ CV $= \dfrac{104}{638} \times 100 = 16.30\%$

Clearly there is more variability in the use of Part A than Part B.

7.9 A comparison of the four measures of dispersion

The range

It is the easiest measure to calculate, but as it is derived by looking at the extreme items, and pays no attention to any other items, it can give a misleading view. There is no indication of the distribution throughout the range – items could be bunched anywhere. It can be misleading in other ways too. Suppose you were told that the range of earnings per week at garage A was £50 and at garage B £10, then reasonably you would consider that the variability of earning at garage A was very much greater than at garage B. However, the actual earnings may have been:

Garage A (£) 180, 180, 180, 180, 180, 180, 180, 230
Garage B (£) 189, 188, 185, 184, 182, 181, 180, 185

These figures suggest that the range values are not very indicative of the comparative variability of the data.

Furthermore, the range is to some extent dependent on the number of items of data taken, because there tend to be more extreme values as the amount of data is increased. This may be important in sampling.

The quartile deviation

This measure suffers from the same disadvantage as the range, in that it only takes into account two values $Q1$ and $Q3$ and ignores the rest. It also is not so easy to understand, although it does have some advantages over the range because it can be calculated for grouped data and for open-ended distributions. It also ignores extreme items, dealing only with the central half of the range. The major disadvantage is that it is not suitable for mathematical manipulation.

The mean deviation

It must be an advantage to base the calculation of the spread of the data on every item of data. This occurs with the mean deviation, but unfortunately, in its calculation, we had to make all the deviations positive, which inhibits its use in further statistical calculations. If our aim is merely to obtain a representative measure which is easily understood, then the mean deviation is particularly suitable. Otherwise we must use our fourth measure.

The standard deviation

This is widely used because it not only takes into account each item of data but is also mathematically acceptable for further statistical calculations. Other calculations may be based upon it.

7.10   Questions on the standard deviation and the coefficient of variation

1   The rateable values of business premises in the United Kingdom are given in the table below. Calculate the arithmetic mean valuation and the standard deviation.

Rateable value (£)	Percentage of premises
Under 1 000	23
1 000 and under 2 000	15
2 000 and under 3 000	14
3 000 and under 4 000	10
4 000 and under 5 000	8
5 000 and under 6 000	6
6 000 and under 7 000	5
7 000 and under 8 000	4
8 000 and under 9 000	4
9 000 and under 10 000	3
Over 10 000	8

You may assume that the open-ended group is as large as *five* other groups.

2   A hundred 'long-life' candles are tested for longevity and the results are as follows:

Lifetime in hours	Frequency
Under 20	18
20–29.99	23
30–39.99	37
40–49.99	19
50 and over	3

Find the average life and the standard deviation. You may assume that the open-ended group is twice as large as the other groups.

3   Candidates at an intermediate accountancy examination are awarded marks as follows:

Marks	Frequency
Under 30	326
30– 39	1 539
40– 49	1 726
50– 59	2 381
60– 69	865
70– 79	773
80– 89	124
90–100	49

You may assume that no candidate scored less than 20 marks.

Calculate the arithmetic mean score, and the standard deviation.

4 Recruits to the armed forces at age 18 are found to have heights as shown below:

Height (*in metres*)	Frequency
Below 1.60	58
1.60 and under 1.65	143
1.65 and under 1.70	209
1.70 and under 1.75	224
1.75 and under 1.80	336
1.80 and under 1.85	295
1.85 and under 1.90	276
1.90 and under 1.95	191
1.95 and under 2.00	86
2.00 and over	64
	1882

Calculate the arithmetic mean and the standard deviation, assuming that in each case the open-ended groups are twice as large as the other groups.

5 Daily sales of pizzas in a pizza parlour are found to be as follows:

Type	Mean sales	Standard deviation
Thin and crispy	464	56
Deep pan	1 124	285

Calculate the coefficients of variation. What do these coefficients tell you about the variability of demand for the two types of pizza.

6   An insurance company is comparing two garages for the repair of motor vehicles which are the subject of claims by insured drivers. They discover the following:

Garage A   Mean charge £385   Standard deviation £23
Garage B   Mean charge £325   Standard deviation £105

Calculate the coefficients of variation and comment on the results.

7   Discuss the case of 'mean deviation versus standard deviation' as a means of measuring group dispersion.

7.11   Summary of Chapter 7

1   Dispersion is the way that a group of data is spread around on either side of the central point. They may be closely packed near to the central item, or widely dispersed on either side of the centre. There are five measures of dispersion: the range, the interquartile range, the quartile deviation, the mean deviation and the standard deviation.

2   The range measures the difference between the highest and lowest values in a set of data. It is therefore greatly affected by the extreme items, and tells us nothing about the way the items in a group are distributed within the range.

3   The interquartile range measures the distance between the upper and lower quartiles of a set of data. It is found by the formula $Q3 - Q1$. It is a more satisfactory measure than the range, since it deals with the central half of a distribution only, and is not affected by extreme items. On the other hand, it does not tell us where the centre of the data is, except that it is somewhere between $Q1$ and $Q3$.

4   The quartile deviation is half the interquartile range and is sometimes called the semi-interquartile range. It is a measure of the way the central half of the data is spread out around the centre, but we do not know where the centre is, which is rather unsatisfactory. It could be nearer to $Q1$ than $Q3$, or vice versa. The quartile deviation tells us the average amount by which the two quartiles vary from the median, or the mean.

The formula for the quartile deviation is $\dfrac{Q3 - Q1}{2}$.

5   The mean deviation is the arithmetic mean of the deviation of each item from the centre point of a distribution. The centre point is usually the arithmetic mean of the data, but the median can be used in some cases as well. We find the central point of the data

(say the arithmetic mean) and then measure the distance of each item of data from that point. We then find the average distance from the centre, ignoring the signs. We have to ignore the signs because, since some items are above the midpoint and some below it, the data actually sum to zero. If we ignore the signs, we do get a meaningful average deviation from the central position. The sign $|x - \bar{x}|$ (the deviations from the mean ignoring the signs) is called the **modulus**. The disadvantage of the mean deviation is that it cannot be used in higher mathematical statistics, because we have ignored signs when arriving at the mean deviation.

6 The formula for the mean deviation for ungrouped data is:

$$MD = \frac{\Sigma|x - \bar{x}|}{n}$$

For a frequency distribution it is:

$$MD = \frac{\Sigma f(|x - \bar{x}|)}{\Sigma f}$$

For a grouped frequency distribution it is:

$$MD = \frac{\Sigma f(|m - \bar{x}|)}{\Sigma f}$$

where m is the class mark (the midpoint of each class).

7 The standard deviation measures the dispersion of data around the arithmetic mean without the difficulty of ignoring the signs. The differences from the mean are squared – thus giving positive figures for all the data – and the square root is then taken. In this way we arrive at a deviation which is susceptible to mathematical manipulation in more advanced work.

8 For ungrouped data with an exact mean the formula for the standard deviation is:

$$SD = \sqrt{\frac{\Sigma d^2}{n}}$$

where d is the difference from the mean.

For ungrouped data where the mean is not an exact number we need to take into account a correction factor to correct for the fact that the mean does not sum to zero. The formula is

$$SD = \sqrt{\frac{\Sigma d^2}{\Sigma n} - \left(\frac{\Sigma d}{\Sigma n}\right)^2}$$

For a frequency distribution with an exact mean it is:

$$SD = \sqrt{\frac{\Sigma fd^2}{\Sigma f}}$$

For a frequency distribution with an approximate mean we use:

$$SD = \sqrt{\frac{\Sigma fd^2}{\Sigma f} - \left(\frac{\Sigma fd}{\Sigma f}\right)^2}$$

For grouped data we use:

$$SD = \sqrt{\frac{\Sigma fd^2}{\Sigma f} - \left(\frac{\Sigma fd}{\Sigma f}\right)^2} \times CI \text{ (class interval)}$$

Be careful to find the final square root value before multiplying by the class interval.

9   A **coefficient of variation** is a measure which shows the relative dispersion of data around the mean. It is a number, usually expressed as a percentage, showing the magnitude of the variation relative to the size of the quantity that is being measured.

10   The formula for the coefficient of variation is:

$$CV = \frac{SD}{AM}$$

In books where the standard deviation is designated σ (little sigma) this formula would be given as:

$$CV = \frac{\sigma}{\bar{x}}.$$

8
Skewed and normal distributions

8.1 Skewed and symmetrical distributions

So far, we have calculated averages and measures of dispersion in order
to describe any data collected, but it could be that we have three sets
of data, each having the same mean and standard deviation, but yet
they are different. Suppose we have three garages in our company and
their average weekly pay statistics are as follows:

Garage	Mean	Standard deviation
A	£80	£10
B	£80	£10
C	£80	£10

The wages structure appears to be the same but if we plotted the data
as three frequency curves, the graphs might be as shown in Figure 8.1.

8.2 Normal distribution curves

The concept of a 'normal' distribution curve is a very important one
in statistics. Whether we find the average by the mean, the median or
the mode, we need to know how the data that make up the distribution
under discussion are spread around the average chosen. Are they
symmetrically arranged around the average or are they asymmetrically
arranged (in other words skewed)? Even if they are symmetrically
arranged, are they widely spread or narrowly spread? For example, if
we take five pieces of data:

$$98 \quad 99 \quad 100 \quad 101 \quad 102$$

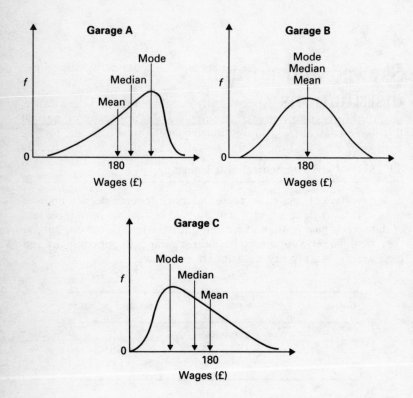

Figure 8.1   Normal and skewed distributions

Notes:
1   Garage B shows a normal distribution curve which is symmetrical about the central line. The mean, median and mode coincide at the central point in a normal distribution, and the data are symmetrically arranged on either side.
2   Garage A shows a negatively skewed distribution. With a negatively skewed distribution the mean is moved to the left, where a long tail of smaller values exerts an influence to drag the mean to the left of the modal position. The median lies between the mean and the mode, which is of course situated at the high point of the diagram (since the mode reflects the most numerous item).
3   The data for Garage C are skewed positively, with a long tail of high value items pulling the mean to the right of the mode, and the median again somewhere between the two.
4   The differences between the mean and the mode increase with the degree of skewness. This can be measured with a **coefficient of skewness**.

The average is clearly 100 (total $500 \div 5$) and the data are closely clustered around the average. By contrast, consider the following five pieces of data:

25   50   100   150   175

The average is still 100 ($500 \div 5$) but now the data are widely spread around the average.

Both sets of data are symmetrically distributed around the average, but the distributions are far from alike. In any case of normal distribution the three averages must by definition coincide, for the arithmetic mean and the central item (the median) of a symmetrically arranged distribution must coincide; while the fact that the mode is the most frequent item and is always to be found at the high point of the curve will also mean that it is centrally placed.

Consider an experiment in which ten truly balanced coins are tossed into the air. We would expect to have five heads and five tails, but in any actual experiment we might have other results, such as 6:4, or 7:3, or, rather more rarely, 10:0. If we can repeat this experiment 100 times, we might find the results shown in Table 8.1. We could draw this set of data as a histogram as shown in Figure 8.2 and described in the notes below it. Study this illustration now.

Table 8.1   One hundred experiments tossing ten coins

| | Number of heads | | | | | | | | | | |
	0	1	2	3	4	5	6	7	8	9	10
Frequency	1	3	5	12	16	24	17	11	7	3	1

When we consider the sort of curve which might result from a very large number of experiments with a large number of coins, we could expect a normal distribution curve something like Figure 8.3.

Characteristics of the normal curve

The characteristics of a normal curve are the following:

1   It is bell-shaped.
2   It is symmetrical about the mean.
3   It extends indefinitely in both directions, but in practice it is indistinguishable from the horizontal axis once we get more than three standard deviations either side of the mean.

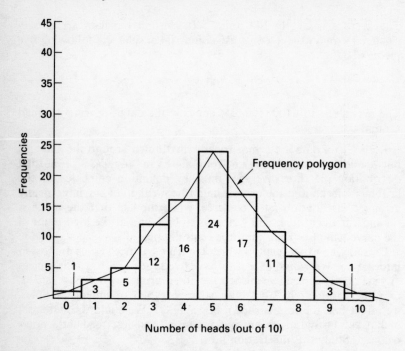

Figure 8.2 Histogram of results (100 experiments tossing ten coins each time)

Notes:

1 The steps of the histogram are fairly erratic, and do not exactly make a 'normal' distribution, though they do show a tendency that way, with the high point at the centre and falling away to a single item at either side.
2 If we had tossed 100 coins each time there would have been 100 steps in the histogram and this would have smoothed out the curve.
3 It would have smoothed it out even more if we had tossed the 100 coins 10 000 times – the more experiments you do the more likely it is that all the various combinations of results will be arrived at.
4 By joining up the midpoints of the tops of the blocks, we get a **frequency polygon** which shows the rather erratic curve of distribution of this set of data.

4 The parts of the curve which approach the horizontal axis are called the tails.
5 If we know the mean and the standard deviation of the curve, the curve is completely determined mathematically. However, this is beyond the scope of the present book.

To conclude this introductory look at the normal curve we may just compare the two normal curves drawn in Figure 8.4.

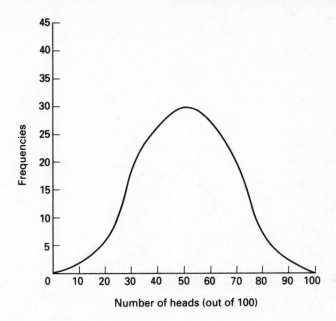

Figure 8.3 A normal distribution curve (resulting from a large number of experiments)

Note:
Students might like to refer to the characteristics of the normal curve given on pages 203–4 and notice how this bell-shaped symmetrical curve conforms to the characteristics listed. Then turn to page 206 and consider the two curves illustrated there, and the notes below them.

Skewed data

Although the normal distribution is an important theoretical distribution, it is unlikely to be met in real life. However, a number of sets of data do tend towards normality e.g. educational data, sample quality control measurements, or some market research information, particularly where the numbers concerned are very large. Most sets of data will display some skewness, and if the reader refers to Figure 8.1 he/she will see that this causes some separation between the mean, the median and the mode. Since we find it helpful when trying to describe any set of data to know where the 'average' is, it follows that our three averages (if they do not coincide to give a normal distribution) may give us some clues as to the extent of the skewness they display. It is this observed difference between the averages which is used to measure skewness.

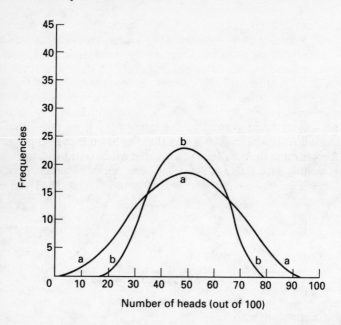

Figure 8.4   Normal curves with different distributions but the same mean

Notes:
1   Both sets of data have a mean of 50.
2   In the *aaa* distribution the data are spread widely around the mean (i.e. the standard deviation is larger than with the *bbb* curve and the dispersion of the data is wider). Consequently the height of the bell shaped curve is not as great as with the *bbb* curve.
3   With the *bbb* curve the dispersion around the mean is less, and consequently the height of the bell is greater but the tails on either side are less.

8.3   Pearson's Coefficients of Skewness

A measure of skewness is a measure which can tell us the degree of asymmetry in a distribution. Since in a symmetrical distribution the mean and the mode and the median are all in the same place, and any asymmetry results in the mean and the median moving away from the mode, it should be possible to devise a measure of asymmetry using the relative positions of these averages.

Professor Pearson devised a coefficient of skewness which can be used in two forms. **Pearson's No. 1 Coefficient of Skewness** is:

$$\text{Coefficient of Skewness} = \frac{\text{mean} - \text{mode}}{\text{SD}}$$

What we are doing is calculating the difference between the mean and the mode as a fraction of the standard deviation (in other words as a fraction of the average spread of the data around the mean). Since all three measurements will be in the units of the data (whatever they happen to be in the particular distribution we are studying), the units will cancel one another out and leave us with the skewness expressed as a number only – in other words as a coefficient. Thus if we measure a dispersion as being skewed to the extent of $+\frac{1}{3}$, we mean that the distribution is skewed in such a way that the mean is moved positively (to the right) one-third as much as a standard deviation.

The trouble with Pearson's No. 1 Coefficient of Skewness is that it uses the mode, which is not a particularly useful average. There may not be a mode, or we could have two modes, etc. For this reason it is usual to revise the formula to restate the expression without the mode. This is possible because in the vast majority of cases the median is positioned about two-thirds of the way from the mode to the mean. In other words

$$\text{mode} - \text{median} = 2\,(\text{median} - \text{mean})$$

Transposing, we have:

$$\text{mode} = 2\,(\text{median} - \text{mean}) + \text{median}$$
$$= 2\,\text{median} - 2\,\text{mean} + \text{median}$$
$$= 3\,\text{median} - 2\,\text{mean}$$

Substituting in this value for the mode, we have:

$$SK = \frac{\text{mean} - (3\,\text{median} - 2\,\text{mean})}{SD}$$
$$= \frac{\text{mean} - 3\,\text{median} + 2\,\text{mean}}{SD}$$
$$= \frac{3\,\text{mean} - 3\,\text{median}}{SD}$$
$$= \frac{3\,(\text{mean} - \text{median})}{SD}$$

This formula is known as **Pearson's No. 2 Coefficient of Skewness**. The sign of the calculated coefficient indicates the direction of skewness and its value the strength of the skewness, e.g. a symmetrical distribution would have a coefficient of 0.

Example 8.1

Calculate the coefficients of skewness for the data given below. The first set of data refers to an investigation of vehicles carrying bulk sugar from a refinery in East Anglia. The second refers to the data collected about the daily consumption of sugar in a classroom of 12-year-old pupils in the London area

	Lorry speeds (mph)	*Consumption (grams)*
Mean	33.61	224.87
Median	37.45	218.70
Mode	41.50	214.57
SD	7.23	17.92

In the first case

$$SK = \frac{3(\text{mean} - \text{median})}{SD} = \frac{3(33.61 - 37.45)}{7.23}$$

$$= \frac{3(-3.84)}{7.23}$$

$$= \frac{-11.52\text{mph}}{7.23\text{mph}}$$

$$SK = \underline{\underline{-1.59}}$$

In the second case

$$SK = \frac{3(\text{mean} - \text{median})}{SD} = \frac{3(224.87 - 218.70)}{17.92}$$

$$= \frac{3(+6.17)}{17.92}$$

$$= \frac{18.51 \text{ grams}}{17.92 \text{ grams}}$$

$$SK = \underline{\underline{1.03}}$$

The first distribution is negatively skewed, with a 'tail' of the distribution to the left and mean less than the median. The second distribution is positively skewed, though not as much as the first example, with the mean to the right of the median and greater than it.

8.4 Bowley's Coefficient of Skewness

A further coefficient of skewness, devised by Professor Bowley, uses calculations based upon the relative positions of the quartiles and the median. Since in a symmetrical distribution the median would lie at the central point of the distribution and the quartiles would be equally on either side, we could say:

$$(Q3 - M) - (M - Q1) = 0$$

If the distribution was skewed either positively or negatively, the equation shown above would obviously not be true. If $(Q3 - M)$ was greater than $(M - Q1)$, we would have a positively skewed distribution; while if $(M - Q1)$ was the greater, we would have a negatively skewed distribution.

Rearranging the formula we have $Q3 - M - M + Q1 = 0$. Therefore $Q3 + Q1 - 2M = 0$.

If the distribution is normal, $Q3 + Q1 - 2M$ will be equal to zero, and any skewness (found by expressing this formula as a fraction of the distribution of the data around the median) will be zero too. Thus with a normal distribution

$$\frac{Q3 + Q1 - 2M}{\dfrac{Q3 - Q1}{2}} = 0 = \text{SK}$$

If the distribution is not normal it will be skewed and the equations can be simplifed to read:

$$\text{SK} = \frac{2(Q3 + Q1 - 2M)}{Q3 - Q1}$$

This will also be a coefficient (i.e. a number only) because the original units (whatever the data were) will have been cancelled out as the fraction was solved. **This is Bowley's Coefficient of Skewness**.

Using the figures given earlier in Example 7.3 (see p. 172) for the weights of packages transported by an express van service, we had:

M = value of the 72nd item = 26th item in the 10–12 group

$$= 10 + \left(\frac{26}{32} \times 2\right)$$

$$= \underline{\underline{11.625 \text{ kg}}}$$

$Q1 = \underline{8.75 \text{ kg}}$

$$Q3 = 13.67 \text{ kg}$$

$$SK = \frac{2(13.67 + 8.75 - 2(11.625) \text{ kg}}{13.67 \text{ kg} - 8.75 \text{ kg}}$$

$$= \frac{2(22.42 - 23.25)}{4.92}$$

$$= \frac{-1.66}{4.92}$$

$$= \underline{\underline{-0.34}}$$

In other words, the data is slightly negatively skewed, to the extent of 0.34 of a quartile distribution from the normal.

The reader will appreciate that as Bowley's Coefficient of Skewness relates to the quartile deviation and not the standard deviation, it is not, strictly speaking, comparable with the two Pearson's Coefficients of Skewness, but is an alternative to them for describing the skewness of a distribution.

8.5 Questions on coefficients of skewness

1   What is meant by the statistical term 'skewness? How does a skewed distribution vary from a normal distribution?
2   (a) Give the formula for Pearson's No. 1 Coefficient of Skewness
    (b) Speeds of motorway lorries are measured on a particular stretch of motorway and the figures collected give the following results.

Mode	60.3mph
Median	48.7mph
Mean	46.5mph
Standard deviation	10.5mph.

Calculate the coefficient of skewness correct to one decimal place, using Pearson's No. 1 Coefficient of Skewness. Explain what this tells us about the distribution of the data we have collected.
3   The wage bill in a certain business with 100 employees is such that the mean wage is £650 per month, but the modal wage is £450 per month. The standard deviation is £300. Find Pearson's No. 1 Coefficient of Skewness for this set of data and explain what it tells us about this set of data.
4   (a) What is Pearson's No. 2 Coefficient of Skewness?
    (b) Why is it more useful than Pearson's No. 1 Coefficient?
    (c) The following data are available for cars travelling on (i)

minor roads and (ii) motorways. Calculate the coefficient of
skewness in each case, using Pearson's No. 2 Coefficient, and
describe each set of data using this coefficient.

	Minor roads (i) (speeds in mph)	Motorways (ii) (speeds in mph)
Mean	38.6	54.6
Median	29.1	62.6
SD	10.6	8.5

5   Scores for the 200 candidates in an examination were spread as
    follows:

No of marks	No of candidates
24	6
32	6
37	7
39	6
44	15
47	16
49	10
54	35
56	22
59	11
64	26
67	13
68	12
73	9
77	2
84	4
	200

Find the mean score, the median score and the standard deviation.
From these figures find the coefficient of skewness according to
Pearson's No. 2 formula.

6   Using the data given in Question 5 above, calculate Bowley's Coefficient of Skewness for the distribution.

7   Students in a professional examination achieve the following scores out of 100:

Score	Number of Students
Over 90	5
80–89.99	11
70–79.99	14
60–69.99	26
50–59.99	86
40–49.99	93
30–39.99	35
20–29.99	12
10–19.99	3
0– 9.99	0

Complete the table with a cumulative frequency column, and then find (*a*) The median score; (*b*) the $Q3$ and $Q1$ scores; and (*c*) the coefficient of skewness of the data. (Answers correct to 2 decimal places.)

8.6   Summary of Chapter 8

1   The way in which a particular set of data is dispersed about the average is called the 'distribution' of the data.

2   It is possible to have sets of data which have the same average, say the same arithmetic mean, and the same average distribution around that mean (i.e. the same standard deviation) and yet have very dissimilar distributions. This is because distributions can be normal or skewed.

3   A normal distribution is one where the data are distributed symmetrically around the central position. All the averages – the mean, the median and the mode – coincide at the central position and the distribution is bell-shaped. The high point of the bell will then depend upon the standard deviation of the data around the central point.

4   If a distribution is not 'normal', then it will be skewed – in other words, the distribution of the data will have more above the central point than below it (negatively skewed) or more below the central point than above it (positively skewed).

5   The words 'negative' and 'positive' in this connection refer to the position of the mean relative to the mode. With negatively skewed distributions the mean is to the left of the mode (closer to the origin of the graph), while with positively skewed distributions the mean is to the right of the mode (further from the origin).

6   We can measure the differences between the mean and the mode with a coefficient of skewness. There are two such measures: Pearson's Coefficient of Skewness and Bowley's Coefficient of Skewness.

7   Pearson's Coefficient of Skewness is in two forms:

$$\text{First formula: Coefficient of Skewness} = \frac{\text{mean} - \text{mode}}{\text{SD}}$$

What this does is measure the distance of the mean from the mode in terms of the standard deviation. How far is the mean from the mode measured in standard deviations? This tells you the extent of the skewness.

8   The trouble with Pearson's No. 1 formula is that it uses the mode, a rather awkward average, and there may be no mode, or we could have a multi-modal set of data.

9   Pearson's No. 2 formula is based on the fact that in most cases the median lies about two-thirds of the way from the mode to the mean. By substituting this fact in the No. 1 formula, we get:

$$\text{Pearson's No. 2 formula: SK} = \frac{3(\text{mean} - \text{median})}{\text{SD}}$$

10   A symmetrical distribution has a coefficient of skewness of 0 (the mean, the median and the mode all coincide)

11   A coefficient of skewness such as -1.59 is negatively skewed, with the mean to the left of the mode by 1.59 standard deviations.

12   A coefficient of skewness of .37 is positively skewed, with the mean to the right of the mode to the extent of .37 of a standard deviation.

13   Bowley's Coefficient of Skewness uses the relative positions of the quartiles and the median. The formula is:

$$\text{SK} = \frac{2(Q3 + Q1 - 2M)}{Q3 - Q1}$$

where M stands for the median and $Q1$ and $Q3$ for the quartiles.

9

Elements of probability

9.1 What is probability?

Probability in statistics is a measure of the likelihood of some event happening. It is an attempt to quantify uncertainty. Since we need a measure which can be easily understood, it is usual to present probabilities as percentages, either in the form of a percentage figure (there is a 50 per cent chance that a coin tossed into the air will land showing the side with the head on it) or as a figure with two decimal places (the probability that the coin will land showing the head is 0.50).

It is important to mention that any statement about probability refers to 'the very long run', because in fact no sequence of events may follow the probability we have predicted exactly. Thus if we say that 90 per cent of Post Office deliveries will arrive next day, any business person seeking to check the statistics might have to wait a very long time before 90 out of 100 of the letters delivered on any day actually were 'next day' deliveries. He/she might find that in the batches of 100 letters investigated the numbers meeting the promised deadline for delivery were 78, 88, 95, 99, 32, 46, 89, 91, etc.

In real life, and particularly in business life, the nearest we can get to certainty is often only a statement of probability. People who won't do anything unless they are certain it will be successful will never do anything at all. If I ask a bank manager, a business consultant or an enterprise agency whether the tourist attraction I propose to establish will be successful, it is no good expecting a 'Yes' or 'No' reply, unless the circumstances are so obviously favourable, or so manifestly unfavourable that the expert's opinion is not needed anyway. There are so many factors entering into the 'success' of any enterprise that a more guarded reply must be expected. For example, the success of tourist attractions depends upon such factors as the degree of prosperity in the economy, the tax system at the moment, the political stability of the country concerned, the competition from other attractions, etc. To give a particular proposal a 95 per cent success probability means that, in the long run, out of every 100 similar enterprises established it is likely that 95 will succeed and 5 will fail. It is this envisaged 'relative frequency of the event happening' which is the probability of success.

In dealing with probabilities we cannot just pick figures out of the air somewhere between 0 and 100 and assign the figure chosen to the probability of an event occurring. Our estimate of probability has to be based on observation and perhaps experiment over a considerable period of time. In some cases, e.g. insurance, the collection of a long series of records is the basis on which the probability of any event occurring is estimated. Such knowledge is called 'empirical knowledge' – knowledge based on experience alone. Even a very long series of evidence may be upset, however, by new factors entering the situation. Empirical evidence may show that in the long run the population of the United Kingdom is law-abiding, and a visit to Trafalgar Square to feed the pigeons may be a safe and memorable event for one's grandchildren; but it cannot entirely override the chance that some political event may make Trafalgar Square the last place to take one's grandchildren, with policeman on horseback seeking to control a violent and turbulent mob.

Where empirical evidence is not much help in predicting the probability of some event occurring, or where new circumstances have arisen, new policies are being proposed, or a change of course in business is envisaged, we may need to base our estimates of probability on *a priori* reasoning. The words *a priori* mean 'based on what has gone before'. *A priori* reasoning may be described as reasoning from cause to effect. Thus if we say that wages will rise by 10 per cent in real terms, we may, based on that statement, be able to argue that leisure spending will increase and tourist attractions will prove more popular and therefore the probability that a proposed development will succeed is increased. This type of reasoning is widely used in predicting probabilities, and a succession of predictions might offer a range of probabilities depending upon whether wages in real terms rose by 5, or 10, or 15 per cent, etc. Probability is a substitute for certainty, and a range of estimates of probability may be more helpful than a single prediction, where unknown factors enter into the situation.

To conclude, we may define probability as *the relative frequency with which a particular event will occur in the long run.* It is found by comparing the frequency of the event occurring with the total number of events, and is usually expressed for convenience in percentage terms.

9.2   Some terms used in probability

Probability statements

It is usual to make statements about probability in the form

$$P(A) = \ldots\ldots$$

This is read as 'The probability of an event A happening is …'. Thus the probability of drawing a diamond when we take one card from a pack of cards is expressed as

$$P(D) = \frac{13}{52} = .25 \ (25\%)$$

This is because there are 13 diamonds in a pack of 52 cards and the probability of drawing a diamond is therefore a 1 in 4 chance. The probability of drawing a queen would be expressed as

$$P(Q) = \frac{4}{52} = .077 \ (\text{or a } 7.7\% \text{ chance})$$

There are only 4 queens in a pack of 52 cards.

The smallest value a probability statement can have is 0 (there is no chance of the event occurring) and the largest value it can have is 1, meaning the event is bound to occur. Presenting the information above in generalized form, we may say that the probability of an event A happening is a (the number of times the event will occur) over b the total number of experiments, observations or possible events):

$$P(A) = \frac{a}{b}$$

If we toss a coin into the air fifty times we would expect, if the coin is balanced, to get 'heads' quite as often as we get 'tails'. Therefore

$$P(A) = \frac{25}{50} = .50 \ (\text{or } 50\%)$$

Sample space

When discussing probabilities, we often use the term 'sample space' to refer to the set of all possible outcomes. Thus when taking cards from a pack, the sample space is 52, because there are only 52 cards in a pack (once the two jokers have been removed). Similarly there are only 12 signs of the zodiac, so the sample space for astrologers is 12.

Joint and disjoint outcomes

In many situations events are **disjoint**, or **mutually exclusive**. For example, if we consider picking aces and kings from a pack of cards, the two events are mutually exclusive. If we do pick a king, it can never be an ace, and if we do pick an ace, it can never be a king. However, if the two events we are concerned with are a king and a spade, it would be possible to pick one card which fulfilled both events, the king of spades. Such events are said to be **joint** or **non-exclusive**.

Independent and dependent outcomes

In calculating probabilities the question whether events are dependent on one another or independent sometimes arises. With independent events the results of one trial or outcome have no effect on other trials or outcomes – every further trial starts from the same situation. Thus if we toss a coin into the air, the result (a head or a tail) does not influence the next time we toss the coin; there is still the same long run probability of .50 for every experiment. With the removal of an ace from the pack of cards, the chances of getting a second ace are reduced (there are only three aces left). The chances of getting an ace change each time we draw one, unless we restore the selected ace to the pack and re-shuffle.

The successive chances of picking an ace would be:

$$\text{Full pack} \quad P(A) = \frac{4}{52} = .077$$

$$\text{One ace gone} \quad P(A) = \frac{3}{51} = .059$$

$$\text{Two aces gone} \quad P(A) = \frac{2}{50} = .040$$

$$\text{Three aces gone} \quad P(A) = \frac{1}{49} = .020$$

9.3   The rules of probability

We have already stated the first rule of probability, that the smallest value a probability can have is 0 and the highest probability is 1. For example, it is not possible for rain to fall on more than 100 per cent of the days in the sample space we are considering, nor to fall on less than 0 per cent of the days.

This leads us to the second rule, that if the probability of an event occurring is P(E) the probability that it will *not* occur is $1 - P(E)$. Thus if the probability of drawing a queen from a pack of cards is:

$$P(Q) = \frac{4}{52} = .077$$

then the probability of not drawing a queen is $1 - .077 = .923$. We can check that this is true because the probability of not drawing a queen is 48 chances out of 52:

$$P(NoQ) = \frac{48}{52} = .923$$

Thus if the probability that an airliner will fail to meet its ETA (estimated time of arrival) is .65, then the chance that it will arrive on time or early is $1 - .65 = .35$.

Addition rules

There are two rules of addition in probability theory, the **special rule of addition** and the **general rule for addition** of probabilities. The special rule applies to the addition of probabilities where the events are mutually exclusive or disjoint. Thus in choosing cards from a pack of cards the chances of getting a king or a queen are mutually exclusive events. Therefore the chances of getting either a king or a queen are found by adding the probabilities.

$$P(K \text{ or } Q) = \frac{4}{52} + \frac{4}{52}$$

$$= .077 + .077$$

$$= .154$$

The general rule of addition is used where events are not mutually exclusive, as with the selection of a queen or a spade. Since the chance of getting a queen is $\frac{4}{52} = .077$ and the chance of getting a spade is $\frac{13}{52} = .25$, it might be thought that the chances of getting either a queen or a spade are $.077 + .25 = .327$. However, this would be too great a probability, because the occurrence of a joint event (drawing the Queen of Spades) is being counted twice. We must therefore reduce the probability by the probability of getting both events at once. The general formula is therefore for this sequence of events:

$$P(Q \text{ and } S) = \frac{4}{52} + \frac{13}{52} - \frac{1}{52} = \frac{16}{52} = 0.308$$

The probability of getting a queen is $\frac{4}{52}$; the probability of getting a spade is $\frac{13}{52}$; but there is one chance out of 52 that we will get both at once.

Multiplication rules

Where events are independent – the occurrence of one event having no possible connection with, or influence upon, the occurrence of the other – the probability that both will happen is the product of their probabilities, in other words one probability multiplied by the other. Thus if A's chance of promotion this year is reckoned to be .2 and the chance that the company will earn a Queen's Award to Industry this year is put at .05, the chance that both events will happen this year is:

$$P(P \text{ and } A) = P(P) \times P(A)$$
$$= .2 \times .05$$
$$= .01$$

This is called the special rule of multiplication.

Similarly, if a member of staff's chances of achieving full professional qualification this year are given as .6, and if his son's chances of passing the driving test at the first attempt are rated as .35, then the probability that both events will occur is $.6 \times .35 = .21$. Notice that the chance that both events will occur is always smaller than the chance that either one will occur on its own.

Where events are not independent, but one influences the other, the probability that the dependent event will take place if the influential event has already taken place is greater than the probability that it will take place on its own.

Thus if A stands for investment in advertising and S stands for an increase in sales, the chance that S will follow A is called the conditional probability of S relative to A. This is written symbolically as $P(S/A)$ – the probability that S will increase if A has already taken place. Thus if $P(A)$ is .6 and $P(S)$ is .3, then (S/A) will be more than .3, say .45. The probability of both events happending is not the product of $P(A)$ and $P(S)$ but the more favourable $P(A) \times P(S/A)$.

We therefore have

$$P(A \text{ and } B) = P(A) . P(S/A)$$
$$= .6 \times .45$$
$$= .27$$

Similarly, if we consider the chance of drawing a king from a pack of cards to have a probability of $\frac{4}{52} = .077$, what are the chances of drawing a second king from the pack. This must be $\frac{3}{51}$, because there are only three kings left out of a possible 51. The joint probability of drawing two kings from the pack in this way is:

$$P(K \text{ and } K) = P(K).P(K2/K1)$$

$$= \frac{4}{52} \times \frac{3}{51}$$

$$= .077 \times .059$$

$$= \underline{\underline{.0045}}$$

9.4   Tree diagrams

A tree diagram is a technique for investigating probabilities which starts from a beginning point and branches as we consider each of the possible outcomes. Thus if we investigate the possibility of drawing an ace from a pack of cards, the tree will look as shown in Figure 9.1.

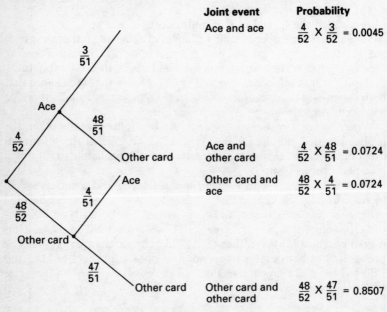

Figure 9.1   A tree diagram – probability of selecting an ace from a pack of cards

Notes:
1   At the first choice there are 4 chances out of 52 of selecting an ace and 48 chances out of 52 of selecting some other card. These are shown as right angle branches on the probability tree.
2   If we continue with a second choice of a card we have two possible selections, with four possible results. Thus if we select an ace the first time the chances of getting a joint event (ace, ace) are 3 out of 51, but the chances of getting a joint event (ace, other card) are 48 out of 51. These probabilities are .0045 and .0724 respectively.
3   Notice that all the probabilities sum to 1.00, since there is always a 100 per cent chance of getting one of the four outcomes.

If we now extend the diagram to a third selection of a card, this is going to give eight possible results with the probabilities shown in Figure 9.2.

1st choice	2nd choice	3rd choice	Joint event	Probabilities			Probability
	Ace	Ace	Ace, Ace, Ace	$\frac{4}{52}$	$\frac{3}{51}$	$\frac{2}{50}$	.0001809
		Other card	Ace, Ace, Other card	$\frac{4}{52}$	$\frac{3}{51}$	$\frac{48}{50}$	.0043438
	Other card	Ace	Ace, Other card, Ace	$\frac{4}{52}$	$\frac{48}{51}$	$\frac{3}{50}$	.0043438
		Other card	Ace, Other card, Other card	$\frac{4}{52}$	$\frac{48}{51}$	$\frac{47}{50}$	.0680542
Ace							
Other card	Ace	Ace	Other card, Ace, Ace	$\frac{48}{52}$	$\frac{4}{51}$	$\frac{3}{50}$	.0043438
		Other card	Other card, Ace, Other card	$\frac{48}{52}$	$\frac{4}{51}$	$\frac{47}{50}$	.0680542
	Other card	Ace	Other card, Other card, Ace	$\frac{48}{52}$	$\frac{47}{51}$	$\frac{4}{50}$	.0680542
		Other card	Other card, Other card, Other card	$\frac{48}{52}$	$\frac{47}{51}$	$\frac{46}{50}$	.7826243
							.9999992

Figure 9.2 Further probabilities of drawing an ace

9.5   Exercises on simple probabilities

Where necessary give the answer correct to three decimal places.

1   What are the chances of selecting from a full pack of cards:

  (*a*) The jack of spades?
  (*b*) Any jack?
  (*c*) Any spade?

2   A new pack of cards is taken and all the cards discarded except the aces, kings, queens, jacks and tens. What are the chances of selecting from this reduced pack:

  (*a*) Any queen?
  (*b*) Any diamond?
  (*c*) The queen of hearts?

3   The probability that a train will arrive on time or early is put at 0.78. What is the probability that it will arrive late?

4   What is the probability of not drawing an ace from a full pack of cards?

5   I have just drawn a diamond from a pack of cards, plus another diamond. My third selection also proves to be a diamond. What are the chances that if I draw another card, it too will be a diamond?

6   (*a*) State the special rule of addition in probabilities.
  (*b*) State the chance of getting a head when tossing a coin.
  (*c*) State the chance of getting a tail.
  (*d*) State the chance of getting either a head or a tail.

7   (*a*) State the general rule for addition of probabilities.
  (*b*) What is the chance of getting either a queen or a king when selecting a card from a pack of cards?
  (*c*) What is the chance of getting a queen or a spade?

8   If the probability of throwing a 7 with a pair of dice is $\frac{1}{6}$, what is the probability of throwing:

  (*a*) Two sevens in a row?
  (*b*) Three sevens in a row?

9   The general rule for multiplication of probabilities is

$$P(A \text{ and } B) = P(A) . P(B/A)$$

  If P(S) (the probability of a family man saving) is given as .25 and P(I) (the probability of an increased income for employees of his age and trade) is given as .4, but the probability of this man saving if the increased income is forthcoming P(S/I) is deemed to be .35, what is the probability of both I and S being achieved?

10 Bearing in mind the multiplication rule given in Exercise 9 above, we are told that (*a*) the probability of an East European state relaxing its import controls is given as P(I) = .60, (*b*) the probability of an exporter securing an order is P(0) = .35, and the probability of securing an order if the East European state does relax import controls is P(O/I) = .5. What is the prospect that both the relaxation of import controls and the order to the exporter will materialize?

11 Twenty discs exactly similar in all but colour are put into a hat and drawn out by a blindfolded person. Four of the discs are blue, 4 red, 4 white, 4 yellow and 4 green. Draw a tree diagram to illustrate the probability of drawing: (*a*) a green disc, (*b*) 2 green discs, one after the other, and (*c*) 3 green discs in succession.

9.6 Summary of Chapter 9

1 Probability is a way of measuring the likelihood of some event happening. It seeks to give some measure of certainty in situations which are largely uncertain.

2 Probabilities are always stated in percentage terms, either as an actual percentage figure or as a decimal to two places (e.g. the chance that A will precede B is .95.

3 Statements of probability are always understood to refer to 'the very long run'.

4 Statements about probability must be based on observations or evidence of some sort. We cannot just pick figures out of the air. Where hard evidence is not forthcoming, we may still be able to make a statement based on *a priori* reasoning, i.e. based on 'what has gone before'. Thus if past experience shows that wage increases lead to inflation, we may argue that an expected bout of pay rises will prove inflationary.

5 P(A) means 'The probability that A will occur ...'

6 The smallest value a probability can have is 0 – the event can never happen. The largest value it can have is 1 – the event is bound to happen.

7 The 'sample space' in any consideration of probabilities is the set of all possible outcomes. If events are mutually exclusive, they are said to be disjoint. If they can occur at the same time, they are said to be non-exclusive; a joint outcome is possible.

8 The rules of probability are:

   (*a*) If the probability of an event occurring is P(E), the probability that it will not occur is 1 − P(E).
   (*b*) With mutually exclusive events the probability of two events

occurring is the sum of their individual probabilities. This is the special rule of addition.

(c) With non-exclusive events the general rule of addition applies. This rule says that the probability of two events occurring is the sum of their individual probabilities, less the probability that they will occur together.

(d) Where events are independent, i.e., the occurrence of one event has no influence on the probability that the other will occur, the probability that both will occur is the product of their individual probabilities. This is the special rule of multiplication. The probability that both events will occur is always smaller than the probability that either of them will occur.

(e) Where events are not independent, and the occurrence of one influences the probability that the other will occur, we have a more favourable situation that both will occur. The probability that both will occur is then found by the formula:

$$P(A \text{ and } B) = P(A) \cdot P(B/A)$$

(where B/A is called the conditional probability that B will occur, given that A has already occurred.)

9 A tree diagram is a technique for investigating probabilities. It starts from one point, and branches as we consider each of the possible probabilities.

10
Correlation and regression 1

10.1 The association of two variables

A very important tool which the statistician can provide for management
is the establishment of an objective measurement of the degree to which
pairs of data are associated and dependent one on another. If it can be
shown that there is, for example, a close association (correlation)
between the cost of a tyre and its life, then management will be better
able to make correct decisions about the purchasing of tyres. If an
agricultural institute shows that there is a correlation between the use
of a new type of fertilizer and the yield of a particular market garden
crop, it will encourage smallholders to use it. The relations between
the two variables is said to be **causal** – changes in one variable cause
changes in the other. For example, increased use of fertilizer causes
increased crop yield. We would also describe such a correlation as
positive, because both sets of data move in the same direction – increased
fertilizer causes increased output. It is also possible to have **negative
correlations**, e.g. the relation between speed of working and product
quality might be a negative correlation. If increased speed leads to a
reduction of quality and less perfect assemblies being made, then we
have a negative correlation.

It is possible to be mistaken about the relation between two variables,
and draw incorrect conclusions, called **spurious correlations**. An often
quoted example is the relation between live births in Germany just
before the Second World War and the increase in the stork population
observed at that time. Both sets of data did increase but there was no
connection between them.

One final piece of correlation vocabulary is the designation of
variables with a close association as **dependent variables** and **independent
variables.** If high rainfall causes high sugar-beet yields, the dependent
variable is the yield of sugar beet and the independent variable is the
rainfall. If a rise in community policing reduces crime, the number of
police employed in this way is the independent variable on which the
reduction in crime statistics depends.

In Chapter 5 we saw how scatter diagrams can be used in establishing whether there is evidence of any association and whether this relation is linear. Clearly, we would only be confident about making decisions based on these relations if such a relation were close, and to that end we can calculate a **measure of association** known as the **correlation coefficient**. This measure is called **Pearson's Product Moment Correlation Coefficient**.

Before looking at this measure of association in Chapter 11, we must first revise our ideas on scatter diagrams.

10.2   Scatter diagrams

A scatter diagram is a graph in which pairs of observations have been plotted against one another. If one of the variables is dependent and the other independent, it is usual to use the horizontal axis for the independent variable and the vertical axis for the dependent variable. Suppose we have data for profitability from various jobs of different sizes, as in Table 10.1. When Table 10.1 is produced as a scatter diagram, we have a scatter as shown in Figure 10.1. Study this diagram and the notes below it now.

Table 10.1   Order size and profitability

Job no.	Size of order in units	Profitability (£)
1	20,000	14 800
2	2,000	1 200
3	5,000	2 600
4	10,000	7 700
5	4,000	2 600
6	3,000	1 500
7	9,000	5 400
8	20,000	11 400
9	18,000	11 800
10	500	400

10.3   Drawing in the 'line of best fit'

The 'line of best fit' or regression line, is important because such a straight line can be expressed as a mathematical equation, and when this is done, we refer to it as the **regression equation**. All statistical techniques have as their objective the provision of accurate and relevant data, clearly presented and fully analysed, so that management is aided in the decision-making process. Scatter graphs and the calculation of the correlation coefficients referred to earlier seek to establish whether data are associated, because, if they are, we may be able to make valid predictions of a dependent variable, given an independent variable. For instance, we may be able to make an accurate prediction of the profits likely to accrue from an order of any given size. The problem is how to obtain this line and there are five possible methods.

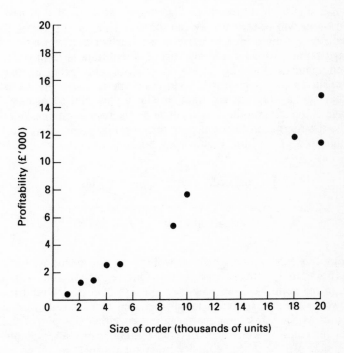

Figure 10.1   A scatter diagram showing reasonably close correlation

Notes:
1   We can see that there is reasonably close correlation between the size of an order and its profitability, because all the small orders are barely profitable (profits are low on them all) while the large orders give much larger profits.
2   If profits bore an exact relation to the size of orders all the scatter points would lie on a straight line which would run from the origin (no order, no profit) up to some fairly high position on the right of the graph. Such a relation is called a **linear relation**.
3   If profits do not bear this exact relation to size of order we should still be able to find a line which runs reasonably close to the scattered points, in an average position, with some points on one side and some on the other. Such a line is called the **line of best fit**, or regression line. See text.

By eye

This is the easiest way, though probably the least accurate. It simply requires that you look at the scatter diagram, guess where the line will be and draw it in accordingly. If two or three people tried to draw in such a line, it is highly likely that their lines would be slightly different from one another.

By the stretched cotton method

This is a slightly better method of getting an accurate line of best fit, because – as will be shown – we can see both sides of our 'ruler'. First though, it is a good idea to draw in one further scatter point – the average point where the average of one set of data (size of order) is plotted against the average of the other set of data (profit earned). It can be shown (although it is beyond the scope of your syllabus to do so) that this average of the data on the y axis plotted against the average of the data on the x axis will lie on the regression line. In other words, the regression line will pass through this point. If we do this calculation we find: from Figure 10.2

$$\text{Average order size} = \frac{91\,500}{10} = 9\,150$$

$$\text{Average profit} = \frac{£59\,400}{10} = £5\,940$$

Plotting this extra point, which we will call M (for mean), we have an extra point in Figure 10.2 as shown. Our regression line will pass through the point M. If we now take a length of cotton wound round our two hands and stretched taught between them, and hold it over the point M, we can see the scatter points on either side of it. The line of best fit is a line which has an 'equal' number of scatter points on either side of it, but this equality must take into account not only the number of points but their distance from the line of best fit, measured as a vertical distance. Thus three points 2 mm from the line each would balance up one point 6 mm from the line. Having observed closely where our piece of cotton indicates the best line to be, we set it aside and draw in the line. This is a slightly better method than using eyesight alone.

If we repeat this activity with a second set of data, we shall see that it is not always so easy to draw a line of best fit, and consequently different people might have different ideas of where the line would lie. The data given are the result of a series of observations made at a factory during the loading of metal castings on to lorries. If we plot this information on to a scatter diagram and draw the regression line by eye, we find it is much more difficult.

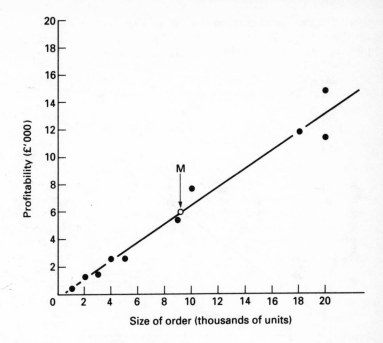

Figure 10.2   Drawing in a 'line of best fit'

Number of castings in load	Time taken to load in minutes
4	8
19	11
14	12
11	12
20	18
32	19
15	20
29	24
34	29
39	30

There is more scatter of the data in this example and therefore the position of the line drawn in will be very subjective, and vary accordingly. Therefore, at best, this method is only likely to provide an approximate line of best fit and may not be accurate enough for making predictions. The scatter is illustrated in Figure 10.3. Even if we calculate the average vlue for each set of data and plot this mean point M (as shown) at 21.7 castings loaded in 18.3 minutes, it is not all easy to plot the line of best fit with the wide scatter shown on the graph.

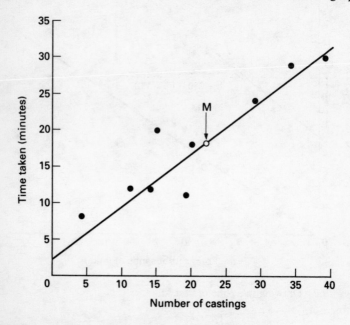

Figure 10.3   A line of best fit where the scatter is wide

Before turning to consider more accurate methods of fitting a regression line to a scatter diagram, we must first consider the **regression equation**, which is an expression of the regression line in mathematical form. Since we are only concerned with linear relations, we can use the mathematical equation for any straight line:

$$y = a + bx$$

where a and b are constants for any particular line. The intercept of the regression line on the y axis is a and the slope of the regression lines is b. By slope, or gradient, we mean the increase in y per unit of x. The procedure for obtaining a and b from a graph is shown in the Figure 10.4.

The point at which the line crosses the y axis is called the y intercept and therefore $a = 1\,250$. The slope or gradient is calculated using the fraction $\dfrac{P}{b}$ and therefore $b = \dfrac{800}{110} = 7.3$. The equation of the regression line will be $y = 125 + 7.3x$.

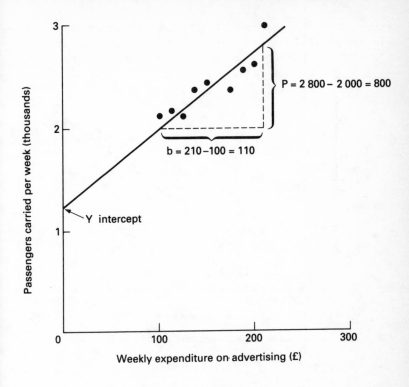

Figure 10.4   Deriving a regression equation from a regression line

Using the same procedure on Figure 10.3, we find the equation of the line to be $y = 2.5 + 0.71x$.

In both examples, the slope is positive, but in Figure 10.5 the slope is negative. The regression line is easy to draw because all the plots lie on a straight line and the equation of this line will be:

$$y = 43 - 0.6x$$

The calculation for b is as before, i.e. $\dfrac{9}{15} = 0.6$, but in this instance a minus sign is inserted into the equation to show that the slope is negative. Similarly the a value can be negative, as in Figure 10.6, where the intercept on the y axis is -1.

The equation of the line in this case is:

$$y = -1 + 2x$$

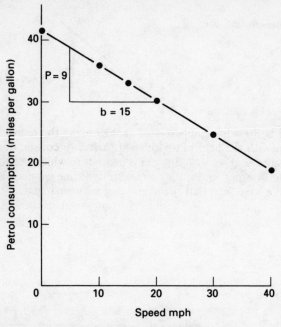

Figure 10.5   A regression line with negative slope

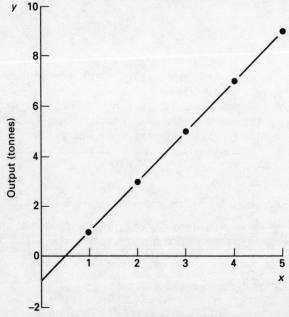

Figure 10.6   A regression line with a negative intercept on the *y* axis

The points plotted are

$$x = 1, 2, 3, 4, 5$$
$$y = 1, 3, 5, 7, 9$$

The two-point method

You will by now have appreciated that drawing the regression line by eye, even with the help of a stretched thread of cotton, does not give exact results, and we would prefer a procedure which provides greater precision. In order to draw a precise straight line we need at least two points. We have seen that the average of x plotted against the average of y gives one point. In examination questions, the examiners must include details of a second point if you are to be able to use this two-point method. Consider Example 10.1.

Example 10.1

A vehicle repair shop has ten machines of similar type and management wishes to find out whether there is any relation between the number of hours of maintenance per month of these machines and their age. Draw a scatter diagram and on it the regression line when one point on the line has a machine aged 25 months requiring 4.5 hours of maintenance. The figures are:

Machine	Age in months	Maintenance in hours
A	42	6.3
B	45	6.5
C	56	8.5
D	48	7.8
E	42	6.9
F	35	5.9
G	58	9.4
H	40	6.2
I	39	6.8
J	50	8.7

The first requirement is to calculate the average age and average maintenance time:

$$\text{Average age} = \frac{455}{10} = 45.5 \text{ months}$$

$$\text{Average maintenance} = \frac{73.0}{10} = 7.3 \text{ hours}$$

We can now plot the scatter diagram (Figure 10.7), including the average positions plotted against one another, and the figure given in the example of 25 months and 4.5 hours of maintenance. The regression line can then be drawn by joining these two points and extending the line. You might like to work out the equation of the regression line.

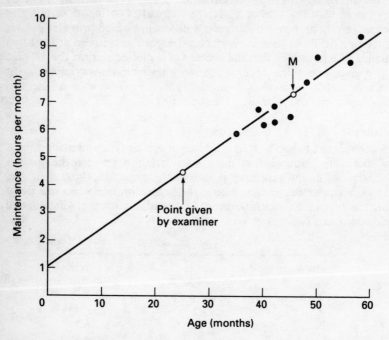

Figure 10.7   Finding regression lines by the two-point method

The three-point (or arithmetic mean) method

The procedure required for this method is as follows:

(a) Rearrange the pairs of data so that the x values are in ascending order of magnitude.
(b) Calculate the mean of the x values and the mean of the y values.
(c) Calculate the mean of all the x values which exceed the mean of x, and the mean of their corresponding y values.
(d) Do likewise for all the x values (and their corresponding y values) which are less than the mean of x.
(e) Plot the three pairs of means on the scatter graph. They should be close to a straight line, which can then be drawn by eye.

Example 10.2

Consider the following data for fifteen firms in the retail trade. Their turnover per annum is shown against the net profit resulting from the trading activities concerned:

Retail outlet	Turnover (£ '000)	Net profit (£ '000)
1	42	17
2	37	13
3	39	16
4	56	23
5	175	49
6	73	25
7	281	95
8	79	28
9	49	31
10	12	9
11	29	19
12	41	24
13	47	29
14	67	32
15	172	58

Rearranged in order of turnover size and corresponding net profits, we have:

12– 9	42–17	73–25
29–19	47–29	79–28
37–13	49–31	172–58
39–16	56–23	175–49
41–24	67–32	281–95

$$\text{Average turnover} = £\,\frac{1\,199('000)}{15} = £79.9('000)$$

$$\text{Average net profit} = \frac{468('000)}{15} = £31.2('000)$$

The items with a turnover greater than £79.9('000) are the three items:

$$172–58$$
$$175–49$$
$$281–95$$

The average turnover of these is $\dfrac{£628}{3} = £209.3$ ('000), and the corresponding average net profit $= \dfrac{£202}{3} = £67.3$ ('000).

The items with a turnover less than £79.9('000) are the first twelve items. Taking these items and finding the average turnover and the average net profit, we have:

$$\text{Average turnover} = \frac{£571}{12} = £47.6 \text{ ('000)}$$

$$\text{Average net profit} = \frac{£266}{12} = £22.2 \text{ ('000)}$$

If we now plot the scattergraph and then plot these three sets of means on it as well, we should find the means are close to a straight line and can be joined (or nearly joined) by a straight line. This gives us a scatter diagram as in Figure 10.8.

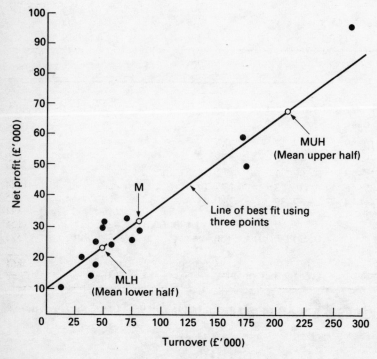

Figure 10.8   A regression line by the three-point method

Regression lines by the 'least squares' method

The first four methods are not very satisfactory from the practical point
of view, and are largely for use in examination questions. They are
either imprecise or use information which in reality is not available,
and therefore we need a method which *will* give the regression line
accurately. The least squares procedure enables us to calculate the y
intercept a and the slope b, using the two following equations:

$$b = \frac{n\Sigma xy - \Sigma x\Sigma y}{n\Sigma x^2 - (\Sigma x)^2}$$

$$a = \bar{y} - b\bar{x}$$

where $\bar{y}$ is the average of y, $\bar{x}$ is the average of x, and n is the number
of pairs of data.

These formulae are derived from mathematical calculations which
are beyond the scope of this book. However, we can see that they give
a correct answer if we use them in a typical example, such as the one
used earlier in Figure 10.3.

Using this data, we can calculate the regression equation and plot
the regression line on the scatter diagram, as follows:

No. of castings in load (x)	Time taken to load (y)	xy	x^2
4	8	32	16
19	11	209	361
14	12	168	196
11	12	132	121
20	18	360	400
32	19	608	1024
15	20	300	225
29	24	696	841
34	29	986	1156
39	30	1170	1521
217	183	4661	5861

Substituting in on the formula, we have:

$$b = \frac{n\Sigma xy - \Sigma x\Sigma y}{n\Sigma x^2 - (\Sigma x)^2}$$

$$= \frac{10 \times 4\,661 - 217 \times 183}{(10 \times 5\,861) - (217)^2}$$

$$= \frac{46\,610 - 39\,711}{58\,610 - 47\,089}$$

$$= \frac{6\,899}{11\,521}$$

$$= \underline{0.599}$$

$$a = \frac{183}{10} - \left(0.599 \times \frac{217}{10}\right)$$

$$= 18.3 - 12.998$$

$$= \underline{\underline{5.302}}$$

Therefore the regression equation will be:

$$y = 5.302 + 0.599x$$

In order to plot the line of regression on to the scatter diagram, we require two points. We could in fact use $a = 5.302$ as one of the points, because that is the point where the intercept on the y axis is going to occur. However, in some diagrams we might use a broken scale and the intercept on the y axis might not then be usable. Ignoring this possibility then we will substitute two values for x in the regression equation. Any two values will do but in order to help us draw the line accurately, we will take one low value of x and one high value.

Point 1   Let $x = 5$

$$y = 5.302 + (0.599 \times 5)$$

$$= 5.302 + 2.995$$

$$= \underline{\underline{8.297}}$$

Point 2   Let $x = 40$

$$y = 5.302 + (0.599 \times 40)$$

$$= 5.302 + 23.96$$

$$= \underline{\underline{29.262}}$$

This is illustrated in Figure 10.9. Note that the intercept on the y axis does occur at 5.3.

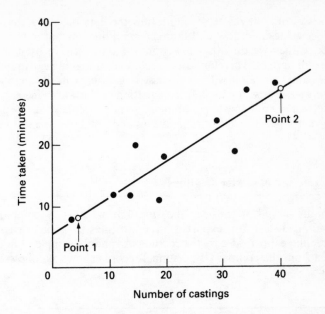

Figure 10.9 Plotting a regression line by the 'least squares' method

Some further points on the 'least squares' method

You will recall that the purpose of obtaining the regression equation was to enable us to make predictions of the value of a dependent variable, given the value of an independent variable. For example, we would be able to make an estimation of the time which would be taken to load 25 castings, using our calculated equation as follows:

$$\text{Let} \quad x = 25$$
$$y = 5.30 + (0.599 \times 25)$$
$$= \underline{\underline{20.275}}$$

Therefore it would take just over 20 minutes to load the 25 castings. Of course, we would also have to calculate the correlation coefficient in order to find out if there was a sufficiently close association between the number of castings in the load and the time taken to load to enable us to have confidence in our estimation.

The value of 25 castings is within the range of observed values and this process is known as **interpolation**. If we had taken a value outside the range, say 60, then we would have used **extrapolation**.

There is always the possibility of error in our predictions, but it is more likely with extrapolated estimates than with interpolated estimates.

We can see from our scatter diagram how the data behave within our range of x values and how well the regression line fits, but outside the observed values we do not know how the data behave or if linear relation still applies. Therefore care is required in making extrapolated estimates and this point will be discussed again later in the chapter.

Please note that you may find the equation of a straight line is given in the form $y = mx + c$, where m replaces b and c replaces a. We have used $y = a + b$ because most examinations and syllabuses use this form.

10.4   Exercises on scatter diagrams

1   You are asked to answer the question whether a company's recruitment test for export staff constitutes a good basis for predicting export sales by the recruits. A random sample of figures taken from the company's personnel records shows as follows:

Code name of staff	Score in test on recruitment (max. = 100)	Sales in year 3 after recruitment (£ '000)
A	64	227
B	72	294
C	95	386
D	63	280
E	56	214
F	51	295
G	88	321
H	76	384
I	48	368
J	86	400
K	76	328
L	58	462

Plot these points on a scatter diagram and draw in a line of best fit, using the 'stretched cotton' method. What is your opinion of the usefulness of the initial recruitment test as a guide to salesmanship?

2   Franchisees operating franchised pizza parlours have rates of stock turnover and profit figures as follows:

Code name of outlet	Number of times stock turns over in a year	Profit of outlet (£ '000)
A	21	18
B	24	22
C	46	50
D	32	38
E	18	12
F	19	15
G	27	33
H	38	35
I	42	41
J	50	47

Plot these points on a scatter diagram and draw in a line of best fit, using the 'two-point' method. Comment on the closeness of the relation between rate of stock turnover and profitability.

3   The following data relate to the age of 'Wide Frontier' motor vehicles and their 'write-off' value as offered by insurance companies in a recent year:

Age (years)	Write-off value (£)
1	7 250
2	5 800
4	3 250
6	1 750
10	500
3	4 500
5	2 250
1	6 500
6	1 500
7	1 000

Use the formulae given in the 'least squares' method (p. 237) to calculate the regression line and the scatter points on a scatter diagram.

4   A trade association is analysing the sales of communication equipment
    by its members relative to the incomes of firms in their catchment
    areas. To this end it calculates the median profit of firms in twelve
    areas chosen at random and the sales achieved by its members in
    these areas. The results are as follows:

Area	Median profits (£ '000)	Sales (£ '000)
1	38	96
2	34	82
3	26	72
4	39	84
5	42	98
6	50	120
7	19	38
8	12	28
9	17	38
10	46	100
11	26	60
12	28	72

Using the formula given in the 'least squares' method (p. 237), calculate
the regression equation of the regression line and hence draw in a line
of best fit to the set of data on a scatter diagram, showing the pairs of
related data given above.

10.5 Summary of Chapter 10

1   An association between two sets of data is called a correlation.
2   Correlations may be positive (both sets of data change in the
    same way) or negative (an increase in one set is associated with a
    decrease in the other).
3   Correlations may be causal (changes in one set of data cause the
    changes in the other set).
4   A spurious correlation is an incorrect conclusion about the association
    between two variables.
5   A scatter diagram is a graph in which pairs of observations are
    plotted against one another to reveal whether there is any pattern
    in the relation between them. A perfect correlation would be
    indicated by the plotted points all appearing to lie in a straight line.

6   If a scatter diagram reveals a less than perfect correlation between the data, we may be able to draw a straight line on the graph which fits the data fairly well. This is called a **regression line**. It may be drawn in five ways:

(a) *By eye* (a subjective impression by the one drawing the line as to where the line should be).

(b) *By the stretched cotton method*. A slightly improved subjective estimate of where the line should be, because we can see the plotted points of the scatter on either side of the piece of cotton. To fix one point on the line we can plot the mean of one set of data against the mean of the other and hold the stretched cotton over that point.

(c) *By the two-point method*. Here the mean position is one point, and the other point must be given to us (in an examination).

(d) *By the three-point method*. Here we not only find the mean position, but we also find the mean of the points above the mean and the mean of the points below the mean. This gives us three points through which we can draw a straight line, or at least a line of best fit.

(e) *By the 'least squares' method*. The equation for any straight line is $y = a + bx$, where a is the intercept on the y axis and b is the slope of the line (the increase in y per unit of x). The y intercept (a) and the slope (b) can be calculated from the formulae:

$$b = \frac{n\Sigma xy - \Sigma x \Sigma y}{n\Sigma x^2 - (\Sigma x)^2}$$

and

$$a = \bar{y} - b\bar{x}$$

where $\bar{y}$ is the average of y, $\bar{x}$ is the average of x, and n is the number of sets of data.

   The regression line can then be drawn in by plotting any two points (of which one can be the intercept on the y axis).

7   Once we have a regression line, we can predict the value of a dependent variable for any values of the independent variable. However, while these will be reasonably accurate within the set of data plotted, i.e. if we interpolate, they become less reliable if we extrapolate, i.e. estimate values outside our present observed sets of data.

11
Correlation and regression 2

11.1 Pearson's product moment correlation coefficient

If there is a relation between two variables, it can be used to make predictions about them which are useful in business, management, science, etc. These predictions will only by accurate if the relation between the variables is close, and it is helpful if we have some measure of this closeness. Such a measure is Pearson's Product Moment Correlation Coefficient, which is usually denoted by the letter r (you can remember this by regarding the letter r as standing for 'relation'). When we talk about a 'coefficient', we mean a number, and the relation between the two variables must lie between -1 and $+1$, so r is always a number between -1 and $+1$. For example, if there is no relation between the two variables, r will be 0. If there is a perfect positive relation between them r will be $+1$, or if there is a perfect negative relationship r will be -1. The degree of relation is shown by the value of r.

What the correlation coefficient tells us is the extent to which the points on a scatter diagram of observed relations cluster around a sloping straight line drawn through the points, and which best fits the data. The formula we shall use is particularly appropriate for use with electronic calculators. It reads:

$$r = \frac{n\Sigma xy - \Sigma x \Sigma y}{\sqrt{[n\Sigma x^2 - (\Sigma x)^2][n\Sigma y^2 - (\Sigma y)^2]}}$$

In this rather difficult equation $n =$ number of pairs of data, $x =$ the various values of the independent variable and $y =$ the various values of the dependent variable.

Consider the pairs of data in the Example 11.1.

Example 11.1
The following figures are available for the weekly expenditure on advertising for a local bus service in Liverpool and the number of passengers carried:

Expenditure on advertising (£)	Number of passengers	Expenditure on advertising (£)	Number of passengers
100	1 200	160	2 180
120	1 418	170	2 240
136	1 682	195	2 690
140	1 840	205	2 760

You are asked to establish whether there is any association between advertising and passenger numbers. The scattergraph drawn using the data (see Figure 11.1) indicates a fairly close correlation between the two sets of information but this is only a visual impression and to obtain a more objective assessment we will calculate the coefficient of correlation.

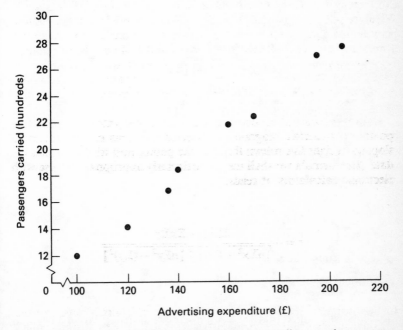

Figure 11.1 A scatter diagram of advertising expenditure and passengers carried

The figures for the calculation can be found from the following table:

Weekly expenditure on advertising (£) x	Number of weekly passengers y	xy	x^2	y^2
100	1 200	120 000	10 000	1 440 000
120	1 418	170 160	14 400	2 010 724
136	1 682	228 752	18 496	2 829 124
140	1 840	257 600	19 600	3 385 600
160	2 180	348 800	25 600	4 752 400
170	2 240	380 800	28 900	5 017 600
195	2 690	524 550	38 025	7 236 100
205	2 760	565 800	42 025	7 617 600
$\Sigma x = 1\ 226$	$\Sigma y = 16\ 010$	$\Sigma xy = 2\ 596\ 462$	$\Sigma x^2 = 197\ 046$	$\Sigma y^2 = 34\ 289\ 148$

$$r = \frac{n\Sigma xy - \Sigma x \Sigma y}{\sqrt{[n\Sigma x^2 - (\Sigma x)^2][n\Sigma y^2 - (\Sigma y)^2]}}$$

$$= \frac{(8 \times 2\ 596\ 462) - (1\ 226 \times 16\ 010)}{\sqrt{[(8 \times 197\ 046) - (1\ 226)^2][8 \times 34\ 289\ 148 - 16\ 010^2]}}$$

$$= \frac{20\ 771\ 696 - 19\ 628\ 260}{\sqrt{[1\ 576\ 368 - 1\ 503\ 076][274\ 313\ 184 - 256\ 320\ 100]}}$$

$$= \frac{1\ 143\ 436}{\sqrt{(73\ 292)(17\ 993\ 084)}}$$

$$= \frac{1\ 143\ 436}{270.725 \times 4\ 241.8255}$$

$$= \frac{1\ 143\ 436}{1\ 148\ 368.2}$$

$$= 0.996$$

$$\therefore \quad r = \underline{\underline{0.996}}$$

Students will notice that these numbers are horribly large. They can be made smaller by transforming the figures. This is a mathematical trick by which we move the axes of a graph without altering the pattern of points relative to each other. In our example we will deduct 100 from all the *x* values (bringing the first *x* value as low as possible, i.e. 0) and deduct 1 200 from all the *y* values (bringing the first *y* value to 0. The result is the rather easier set of data given below:

x	y	xy	x^2	y^2
0	0	0	0	0
20	218	4 360	400	47 524
36	482	17 352	1 296	232 324
40	640	25 600	1 600	409 600
60	980	58 800	3 600	960 400
70	1 040	72 800	4 900	1 081 600
95	1 490	141 550	9 025	2 220 100
105	1 560	163 800	11 025	2 433 600
$\Sigma x = 426$	$\Sigma y = 6\,410$	$\Sigma xy = 484\,262$	$\Sigma x^2 = 31\,846$	$\Sigma y^2 = 7\,385\,148$

$$r = \frac{n\Sigma xy - \Sigma x \Sigma y}{\sqrt{[n\Sigma x^2 - (\Sigma x)^2]\,[n\Sigma y^2 - (\Sigma y)^2]}}$$

$$r = \frac{(8 \times 484\,262) - (426 \times 6\,410)}{\sqrt{[(8 \times 31\,846) - 426^2]\,[8 \times 7\,385\,148 - 6\,410^2]}}$$

$$= \frac{3\,874\,096 - 2\,730\,660}{\sqrt{[254\,768 - 181\,476] \times [59\,081\,184 - 41\,088\,100]}}$$

$$= \frac{1\,143\,436}{\sqrt{(73\,292) \times (17\,993\,084)}}$$

$$= \frac{1\,143\,436}{270.725 \times 4\,241.826}$$

$$= \frac{1\,143\,436}{1\,148\,368}$$

$$r = \underline{\underline{0.996}}$$

The calculated coefficients are the same because the transformation process has merely moved the axes without altering the pattern of the points relative to each other. Therefore, if either or both of the pairs of data are very large, this procedure can be of benefit.

The correlation coefficient can range from -1 to $+1$, with both these values of 1 indicating **perfect correlation**. This would be shown on a scatter diagram with all the points on a straight line, and in practice is unlikely to occur. The closer the coefficient is to 1, the better the correlation between the two sets of data, and the closer to 0, the worse the correlation. In our example, 0.996 means very good correlation, and confirms our visual impression that there is a very close relation between the amount spent on advertising and the number of passengers carried. Furthermore, the coefficient is $+0.996$, with the plus sign indicating that there is **positive correlation**. This means that as the independent variable (x) increases, so does the dependent variable (y), and therefore not only is there a close relation between advertising and passengers carried, but also as the amount spent on advertising increases, so does the number of passengers carried.

If our coefficient had been -0.996, the association between the pairs of data would have still been very strong, but the minus sign indicates that there would have been **negative** or **inverse correlation**. This would mean that as the amount spent on advertizing increased, the number of passengers carried decreased.

At this stage it is appropriate to issue a word of warning about the interpretation and conclusions which may be drawn from a correlation coefficient. A high value for r does not necessarily imply a cause and effect relation, and certainly does not prove that there is one. What it does is to add weight to any theory about relations between data and sometimes to suggest causal relations in areas in which some association was not suspected, e.g. in medical research. Similarly, a low coefficient value does not always mean a low level of association, because we are measuring the strength of a linear relation, and it could be that we have a close association but curvilinear. This is why it is important always to draw a scatter diagram at the beginning in order to see if the relation is linear or curvilinear.

Therefore we must be on our guard against **spurious correlation**, which shows a high coefficient value but no causal connection. For example, if we calculated the correlation coefficient between the amount spent on agriculture by the EEC and the number of car accidents in the UK in the decade 1973–83, the value would be high and positive. Clearly there can be no direct connection between the two sets of data, except that both are increasing. In this example spurious correlation is obvious, but sometimes the situation can be confused by a third linking factor. You may suspect that a certain brand of tyre gives better value than another, and the calculation of a correlation coefficient may confirm your ideas. However, it may be that the link between the life of a tyre and brand lies in the driver, the make of lorry, or the price, and further investigations may be necessary in order to establish what is the causal relation.

Our studies of correlation and regression started with a consideration of scatter diagrams and the visual impressions they can create of a relation between the two sets of data. We then moved to seeking a more formal measure of association, the correlation coefficient. We must now consider a measure of correlation which is useful in those situations where precise measurements of data are not possible, since it is difficult to measure objectively the attributes under consideration, and the best we can do is rank the variables in order, one against the other. This measure is called the **Rank Correlation Coefficient**, and since the most commonly used formula was devised by Professor Spearman, it is usually called **Spearman's Rank Correlation Coefficient**. Before we consider it, try the exercises in Section 11.2.

11.2 Exercises on Pearson's Product Moment Correlation Coefficient

1 What is meant by the term 'correlation'? How can correlation analysis help management?
2 What are (*a*) positive correlation, (*b*) negative correlation, (*c*) spurious correlation?
3 What is Pearson's Correlation Coefficient? How big can the coefficient be? Explain the relation between two variables whose correlation coefficient $r = 0.34$.
4 The following figures refer to the importation of malting barley and the export of whisky in the Country of Caledonia. Find the correlation coefficient between these two events and discuss whether the correlation is causal or spurious.

Year	Barley imports (£m)	Whisky exports (£m)	Year	Barley imports (£m)	Whisky exports (£m)
1	2	5	6	6	14
2	2	6	7	7	16
3	3	7	8	7	22
4	4	8	9	8	28
5	5	9	10	9	33

5 The following figures refer to the import of leather and skins into Technologia and its export of shoes and other leather products over the 8-year period. Find the correlation coefficient of the two sets of figures and discuss whether it is likely to be a causal or a spurious correlation.

Year	Imports (£m)	Exports (£m)	Year	Imports	Exports
1	2.5	8	5	6.5	15
2	3.2	9	6	7.8	19
3	3.7	11.5	7	9.5	23
4	4.8	12	8	10.0	25

6   The following data give the rent per square metre of business premises in fifteen towns, and the percentage of unemployed in the population. Calculate the correlation coefficient and discuss whether the relation is causal or spurious.

Name of town	Rent per sq. metre (£)	Unemployment level (%)
A	24	12
B	17	5
C	16	6
D	8	4
E	3	16
F	15	19
G	5	10
H	4	12
I	2	3
J	6	13
K	15	11
L	19	8
M	22	3
N	16	10
O	12	7

11.3   Spearman's Rank Correlation Coefficient

In order to calculate Pearson's Product Moment Coefficient we required measurements for our independent (x) and dependent (y) variables, but there are occasions when such measurement is impossible.

Suppose your company wishes to appoint a transport manager and has set up a panel of four people to interview a short list of six applicants. Certain measurements may be relevant in the interviews, such as age, length of experience, educational qualifications, etc., but many of the attributes required of a manager are not capable of precise measurement. As a member of the panel, you may well be able to place the applicants in some sort of order of suitability, i.e. rank them, without being able to give an objective measure to each. You may be lucky enough to be asked to take part in a wine-tasting panel in which you have to rank a certain number of wines in order of preference. This is clearly a matter of personal taste and is not capable of precise measurement. In such examples our data is placed in order, or ranked, and we use the Rank Correlation Coefficient (denoted by the capital letter R) in order to measure the strength of the association between the variables. The most commonly used formula is Spearman's and is as follows:

$$R = 1 - \frac{6\Sigma d^2}{n(n^2 - 1)}$$

where d is the difference in ranks, and n is the number of pairs of data.

Example 11.2
Two motorists were asked to place ten colours in order of preference as a car colour. Given that the rankings are shown in the table below, and that the difference is calculated by regarding Motorist No. 1's views as the starting point, work out the Rank Correlation Coefficient.

Colour Code	Motorist No. 1	Motorist No. 2	d	d^2
A	2	3	-1	1
B	1	2	-1	1
C	3	1	$+2$	4
D	4	4	0	0
E	6	6	0	0
F	5	7	-2	4
G	8	5	$+3$	9
H	7	9	-2	4
I	10	10	0	0
J	9	8	$+1$	1
				$\overline{\underline{24}}$

Using the formula,

$$R = 1 - \frac{6\Sigma d^2}{n(n^2-1)}$$

$$= 1 - \frac{6 \times 24}{10(100-1)}$$

$$= 1 - \frac{144}{990}$$

$$= 1 - 0.15$$

$$= \underline{\underline{0.85}}$$

It would appear that the two motorists have similar colour preferences.

Sometimes you may be asked to calulate the Rank Correlation Coefficient from measured variables, and in this case you have to rank the data before applying the formula. Consider Example 11.3.

Example 11.3

The following data relate to the average scores of all students taking mathematics and economics in each of ten colleges in the United Kingdom:

College	Average maths score (%)	Average economics score (%)
A	67.2	72.5
B	58.5	61.5
C	86.3	79.8
D	91.1	84.6
E	79.2	63.2
F	59.8	68.6
G	71.4	52.5
H	63.4	71.4
I	54.6	84.7
J	84.2	79.6

Ranking these in order we have:

College	Maths ranking	Economics ranking	d	d^2
A	6	5	+1	1
B	9	9	0	0
C	2	3	−1	1
D	1	2	−1	1
E	4	8	−4	16
F	8	7	+1	1
G	5	10	−5	25
H	7	6	+1	1
I	10	1	+9	81
J	3	4	−1	1
				128

$$R = 1 - \frac{6\Sigma d^2}{n(n^2 - 1)}$$

$$= 1 - \frac{6 \times 128}{10(100 - 1)}$$

$$= 1 - \frac{768}{990}$$

$$= 1 - 0.776$$

$$= \underline{\underline{0.224}}$$

There seems to be very little correlation between ability in mathematics and ability in economics. However, it may be that the link between them is weak because other factors enter into the picture, e.g. the teaching ability may be variable or the orientation of mathematics students' interest may be biased in favour of academic and science careers rather than towards business.

A third possible situation is when one of the variables is ranked and the other is measured data.

Example 11.4

Seven tyres of similar specification, each from a different manufacturer, were tested to see if price was a good guide to performance:

Manufacturer code	Tyre price (£) (£)	Price ranking	Performance ranking	d	d²
A	23.90	3	2	+1	1
B	22.50	7	7	0	0
C	24.10	2	3	−1	1
D	23.40	5.5	6	−0.5	0.25
E	24.50	1	1	0	0
F	23.40	5.5	5	+0.5	0.25
G	23.80	4	4	0	0
					2.5

In the price ranking we come up against a difficulty caused by two manufacturers giving their products the same price tag, and therefore they are of equal ranking. It is usual to give them the same ranking, calculated by adding up the two ranks and dividing the result by 2. Thus the ranks of 5 and 6 become $\frac{5+6}{2} = \frac{11}{2} = 5.5$. Each is given the rank of 5.5. The next ranking will of course be 7.

Using the formula:

$$R = 1 - \frac{6\Sigma d^2}{n(n^2 - 1)}$$

$$= 1 - \frac{6 \times 2.5}{7(7^2 - 1)}$$

$$= 1 - \frac{15}{336}$$

$$= 1 - 0.04$$

$$= \underline{\underline{+0.96}}$$

The correlation is good and positive, which indicates that as the price increases, so does the performance.

One final note of caution when using limited amounts of data. There is the possibility of the data correlating purely by chance, and this possibility increases as the number of pairs of data decreases. Statisticians use a special test of significance in this situation, but it is beyond the scope of this textbook.

11.4   Exercises on rank correlation

1   The country of Garibaldia has the following record of agricultural consumption over the last decade. Calculate a Rank Correlation Coefficient for home-produced and imported agricultural produce, and comment on the result.

Years	Home-produced consumption (million tonnes)	Consumption of imports (million tonnes)
1	15.5	2.8
2	13.4	3.8
3	14.2	3.3
4	12.6	5.1
5	10.5	4.9
6	11.8	5.6
7	12.6	6.8
8	8.5	9.5
9	7.6	10.2
10	6.5	11.7

2   Student scores in mathematics and physics are found to be as follows in a national examination. Calculate a Rank Correlation Coefficient and comment on the result.

Years	% average in maths	% average in physics
1	76	58
2	72	56
3	65	53
4	58	52
5	59	50
6	63	48
7	66	58
8	71	66
9	72	74
10	73	71

3 The following employees had figures for their average scores in their marketing part-time day-release courses as shown below. Alongside these are their selling achievements to the nearest £1 000 in the same 12 months.

Work out a Rank Correlation Coefficient and assess the adequacy of the course results as an indicator of selling success.

Name of student	Examination score (%)	Sales (£ '000)
Tom	79	194
Dick	52	136
Harry	68	172
Anne	83	165
Maria	75	185
Peter	64	162
Serena	75	138
Abdul	71	179
Malik	63	198
Sean	59	172

4 Two housewives were asked to rank eight washing powders in order of preference, and to give their reasons in writing for choosing their respective first, second and third choices. Their rankings were as follows:

Brand	Housewife 1	Housewife 2
A	8	5
B	2	3
C	1	1
D	7	8
E	6	6
F	5	7
G	3	2
H	4	4

Work out the Rank Correlation Coefficient and comment on it as far as the housewives' agreement or disagreement about the products are concerned. What would be the point of asking for their written reasons for choosing a particular brand as 1, 2 or 3?

11.5   Summary of Chapter 11

1   There are two methods of measuring correlation. They are Pearson's Product Moment Correlation Coefficient and Spearman's Rank Correlation Coefficient.

2   Pearson's Product Moment Correlation Coefficient is usually designated r (little r), and by contrast Spearman's Rank Correlation Coefficient is designated R (big R).

3   The formula for Pearson's Product Moment Correlation Coefficient is

$$r = \frac{n\Sigma xy - \Sigma x \Sigma y}{\sqrt{[n\Sigma x^2 - (\Sigma x)^2]\,[n\Sigma y^2 - (\Sigma y)^2]}}$$

where n is the number of pairs of data, x is the various values of the independent variable, and y is the various values of the dependent variable. (It is worthwhile learning this formula by heart.)

4   The correlation coefficient can vary between -1 and $+1$. Both the values of 1 indicate perfect correlation, with -1 indicating perfect negative correlation. 0 implies that there is no correlation at all, and the closer r is to 0, the weaker the correlation between the two sets of data.

5   Rank correlation is used when precise measurements of data are not possible because the items under consideration are matters of opinion – this wine is better than that, etc. In these cases all we can do is to rank the items in order of preference. If we now compare the rankings given by two different people to find the difference in ranking, we can calculate a measure of their correlation, by the formula:

$$R = 1 - \frac{6\Sigma d^2}{n(n^2 - 1)}$$

where d is the difference in ranking, and n is the number of pairs of data.

12
Time series

12.1 Introduction

Chapter 3 was concerned with an important statistical concept, the frequency distribution. It was stated that frequency distributions are useful where a collection of data *relating to the same period in time* is to be analysed. However, it is often necessary to process data in such a way that comparisons over time are made. There are many examples of such comparisons: the level of registered unemployed, the growth (or contraction) of population, the number of motorcycle registrations, the number of ships built in shipyards – all these can involve the element of time. In circumstances where a comparison over time is important, a frequency distribution is clearly inappropriate; instead a form of presentation known as a **time series** is used. A time series, as the name suggests, relates to a set of data in chronological order. Time series will be found in most businesses under such headings as sales, stock, production, accounts, personnel records, etc. Such sets of data are an aid to management, particularly in the area of business forecasting. All companies must make estimates about future sales, production, manufacturing capacity, cash flow, etc. All governments must assess the future levels of expenditure in social programmes, education, infrastructure development, etc.

Table 12.1 illustrates a simple time series. Such a form of presentation is useful in itself, in that it helps to clarify a mass of figures. However, a time series is chiefly used in an attempt to isolate three main influences upon the data being studied:

1 The trend.
2 The seasonal variation.
3 The random variation.

A fourth influence is the cyclical variation associated with the cycles of business activity, booms and slumps, which have always been a feature of industrial society.

Even just by studying the figures in Table 12.1 we can identify some of these influences which make up the pattern of sales of this 5-year period.

The trend

The sales have increased consistently and provided a satisfactory trend. The trend is the long-term pattern of development of the figures, and we can see that they grow year by year, rising from £8 314 000 in year 1 to £17 400 000 in year 5.

Table 12.1 Sales of Portland cement

Year	Quarter	Sales (£ '000)	Total (£ '000)
1	1	1 084	
	2	1 976	
	3	3 600	
	4	1 654	8 314
2	1	1 179	
	2	2 532	
	3	5 421	
	4	1 965	11 097
3	1	2 021	
	2	3 251	
	3	6 452	
	4	2 348	14 072
4	1	2 136	
	2	3 682	
	3	6 552	
	4	3 217	15 587
5	1	3 000	
	2	4 124	
	3	6 675	
	4	3 601	17 400
Grand total			66 470

The seasonal variations

Clearly sales were best in the third quarter of each year and worst in the first quarter. The second quarter sales were second in value and the fourth quarter sales next. So sales were obviously influenced by the season of the year.

Residual or random variations

Although not immediately apparent from the table, it is unlikely that all the variations which exist can be explained by the seasonal effect. There may be some special influences specific to the product. There may have been short-time working, strikes, natural catastrophes, and so on, all of which could have contributed to the variation in sales. Such variations are often described as **random variations**, because they can occur at any time. There is no special season for natural disasters, and industrial unrest tends to occur at any time, without any particular pattern. The term **residual variations** is also used, because it is possible to remove the seasonal variations and have a set of figures which has no seasonal variations in it at all – but we shall still find there are variations from the trend. It is this residue of variations which are the random ones, and for which we shall find an explanation if we look at our records – a strike, a breakdown of machinery, an earthquake or a flood.

Cyclical variations

If we had the sales data for a longer period than 5 years, it is possible that a fourth component might become apparent. We might find that a succession of good years (in which sales rose year by year) was followed by a number of lean years, when results were not so good. This period of slump might then be followed by another period of expansion. Such cyclical variations may have been associated with changes in the economy, which in turn would affect business statistics. As the economy expands, so sales wound increase, and as the economy contracts, sales similarly would be expected to fall. Cycles may occur about every 5 to 8 years, and you may well be able to offer some explanation for this cycle of events.

We must now study these influences in greater detail, in particular devoting time to the calculation of each of them.

12.2 The trend

The trend may be defined as the long-term pattern of development of the data: the course which the data have followed over a considerable period. For example, is the number of registered unemployed rising or falling? Is the number of motor vehicles being produced increasing or decreasing? What is the *trend* in motorcycle deaths in recent years? Are fatalities increasing, decreasing or constant?

It might be thought that all one needs to do to arrive at the trend is to look over the available data and make a rough 'guesstimate'. This could even be appropriate when only a few figures are available and a *very* rough guide is required. However, more reliable indications of the trend call for calculation. The method used when calculating the trend is that of the **moving average**. This is nothing more than a series of overlapping arithmetic averages. In statistics an average is often spoken of as a 'mean'. Table 12.2 indicates how a moving average is calculated. It shows the quarterly sales of Portland cement over a period of 5 years, as given in Table 12.1. Since most quarterly figures can be analysed best as four quarterly figures averaged together, the procedure is to add up the first four quarters and find the average of them, which comes to £2 078 500. This is the central figure for the four quarters. Its position in the table is explained in the notes below the table.

We now repeat this average calculation for the next four quarters by leaving out quarter 1, year 1 and taking in quarter 1, year 2. The four quarters now give an average of £2 102 250.

What type of moving average should be used depends upon the statistics in use. For example, monthly figures would require us to calculate a moving average based on 12 monthly periods, and quarterly figures would be appropriately analysed on the basis of four quarterly periods being averaged together. In Table 12.2 the quarterly figures given in Table 12.1 have been used to produce a moving average. The method, which is explained in the notes below the table, has to be carried out in two stages, because an average over the first four quarters gives a mean figure which is situated at the date June 30–July 1, i.e. between quarters 2 and 3, and not opposite a quarterly value. This happens successively each quarter. To find an average figure which is positioned opposite a quarterly value we have to take a further average of each pair of averages. This gives us a figure for each period, called the **centred trend**.

In an examination you will often be told what type of moving average (3 years, 4 years, 5 years, etc.) to use, but note that if you have a free choice, it is best to use an odd number, because the resulting average would then be positioned at the midpoint of the group, exactly opposite a figure in the original data. Thus the average of five yearly periods would be correctly positioned opposite the third year figure. With quarterly data the average comes in between two of the original figures and we must find the 'centred trend' by a further averaging process. If you can choose an 'odd' set of averages, there is no need for the 'centred trend' calculation.

The reader should now consider Table 12.2 and the notes below it.

Table 12.2 Sales of Portland cement (£'000)

Year (I)	Quarter (II)	Sales (III)	Four-quarter moving average (IV)	Centred trend (V)
1	1	1 084		
	2	1 976		
			2 078.50	
	3	3 600		2 090.38
			2 102.25	
	4	1 654		2 171.75
			2 241.25	
2	1	1 179		2 468.88
			2 696.50	
	2	2 532		2 735.38
			2 774.25	
	3	5 421		2 879.50
			2 984.75	
	4	1 965		3 074.62
			3 164.50	
3	1	2 021		3 293.38
			3 422.25	
	2	3 251		3 470.12
			3 518.00	
	3	6 452		3 532.38
			3 546.75	
	4	2 348		3 600.62
			3 654.50	
4	1	2 136		3 667.00
			3 679.50	
	2	3 682		3 788.12
			3 896.75	
	3	6 552		4 004.75
			4 112.75	
	4	3 217		4 168.00
			4 223.25	
5	1	3 000		4 238.62
			4 254.00	
	2	4 124		4 302.00
			4 350.00	
	3	6 675		
	4	3 601		

12.3 Exercises on the trend

1 The following data show the quarterly sales (in thousands of pounds) of a company over a 5-year period. You are asked to find the trend in sales, using a four-quarterly moving average, and to plot both the sales and the trend on the same graph.

Company sales (£ '000)

| | Quarters | | | |
	1	2	3	4
Year 1	158	129	149	189
Year 2	179	148	168	207
Year 3	197	166	185	234
Year 4	113	191	200	248
Year 5	236	205	223	270

Notes on Table 12.2 opposite

(a) Column (*III*) is the quarterly total of sales.

(b) Column (*IV*) is the moving average of four quarterly totals. This is found in the following way. Add up the first four quarters, i.e. $1\,084 + 1\,976 + 3\,600 + 1\,654 = 8\,314$. Divide this by 4 to get the average, which gives 2 078.50. This average is positioned at the midpoint of the four quarters, i.e. at the date 30 June–1 July. We now move our average down one quarter, in other words we discard quarter 1, year 1 and include quarter 1, year 2. This gives $1\,976 + 3\,600 + 1\,654 + 1\,179 = 8\,409$. The average is therefore $8\,409 \div 4 = 2\,102.25$. This is positioned at the midpoint of the four quarters, i.e. at the date 30 Sept.–1 Oct. The procedure is continued right down the column. Note that there is no average in the first part of column *IV* or in the very last part of year 5.

(c) As the moving average continues down column (*IV*), discarding the first quarter and picking up the new quarter, the average changes all the way down the table. Each of these averages is positioned at the division between two quarterly figures. This is inconvenient, because it means we cannot compare the actual quarterly figures (*III*) with the moving average in (*IV*). We must therefore find a 'centred' figure which is level with the quarterly figure by averaging the moving averages on either side of the quarterly figures in column III.

(d) Column (*V*) shows this 'centred trend' figure. We can now compare the actual figure in the third quarter of year 1 with the trend in the same quarter. We shall do this later when we are studying seasonal variations.

(e) The effect of calculating a moving average in this way is to smooth out the fluctuations in the original data – whether caused by seasonal factors, random factors or cyclical factors and leave only a 'trend' figure showing the general tendency of the figures, which is in fact a 'steady growth' in sales.

(f) Once calculated, the effect of smoothing the actual statistics can be illustrated by drawing a graph. This is done in Figure 12.1, which demonstrates how the smoothed trend line shows the gradual upward movement of the statistics, as opposed to the indented 'peak-trough' variation in the actual data. (*Now try 12.3 above.*)

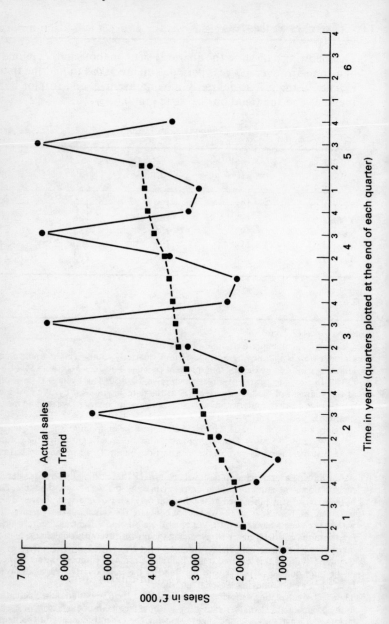

Figure 12.1   Sales of Portland cement: actual and trend

2 The following sales were achieved by a carpet manufacturer over a 4-year period:

Sales of tufted carpets (100 000m)

| | Quarters | | | |
	1	2	3	4
Year 1	248	262	230	283
Year 2	249	265	236	278
Year 3	257	266	259	313
Year 4	313	297	295	353

Source: Monthly Digest of Statistics

(a) Calculate the trend by means of a moving average (correct to two decimal places)

(b) Draw a graph showing the trend and the quarterly figures above.

3 Sales of a manufactured product by Assemblers Ltd over the years have been as follows (figures in £ millions):

Year	£(m)	Year	£(m)	Year	£(m)
1973	150	1979	130	1985	170
1974	100	1980	120	1986	200
1975	90	1981	140	1987	260
1976	140	1982	220	1988	280
1977	180	1983	220	1989	250
1978	160	1984	190	1990	220

You are required:

(a) To calculate the trend, using a 5-year moving average.

(b) To plot both the original data and the trend on the same graph.

4 The following figures relate to the trade in cereals of developing countries, 1979–90. The figures are in million tonnes:

	1979	1980	1981	1982	1983	1984
Exports	17.3	18.9	18.7	14.5	16.9	18.5
Imports	29.3	33.6	36.9	34.5	47.0	48.3

	1985	1986	1987	1988	1989	1990
Exports	15.2	19.6	26.9	22.9	25.8	28.8
Imports	52.9	51.0	49.0	56.8	61.9	63.5

(a) Calculate the moving average trend for both 'exports' and 'imports', using a 5-year moving average in each case.

(b) Display both trends on a suitable graph. (You do not need to display the original data, only the moving average trends.)

12.4 Seasonal variations

There are many instances where the examination of a time series will have as its objects not the trend but the level of seasonal variation. Seasonal variation records to what extent a regular upward or downward character is superimposed on the trend as a result of factors which have a seasonal nature: such factors as the increasing level of unemployment in seaside towns in winter, and the increasing sales of building materials in spring and summer, are very largely, though not exclusively, explained by seasonal events.

It is possible to calculate the degree to which seasonal factors cause distortion from the trend. The work proceeds in three stages, which may be listed as follows:

(a) Calculating the deviation of actual figures from 'trend' figures.

(b) These deviations from trend will partly be caused by seasonal events and partly by random deviations caused by a wide variety of events, such as strikes, natural disasters, changes in taste and fashion, credit availability, etc. To arrive at the best estimate of seasonal influences we *average over the years of the enquiry the seasonal influences for each period.* This is stage (b).

(c) These seasonal fluctuations should, for reasons explained below, cancel one another out. If they do not they must be adjusted until they do. The result will be a 'corrected' seasonal influence which is the best estimate of seasonal variation at which we can arrive.

Such a seasonal variation might be of enormous importance in planning, for example, port activities, transport availability, stock levels required, etc.

Let us now look at each of these stages in turn.

Stage (a) Calculating the deviation of actual data from the trend

It is first necessary to find by how much the actual recorded data deviate from the calculated trend. Using the same data as in Table 12,2, but disregarding Col. *IV* which has served its purposes, we can find the variation of the actual quarterly data from the trend by deducting Col. *V* from Col. *III* (or vice versa), depending on which is the larger. Some quarters' sales are above the trend and some below. The results are shown in Table 12.3. Study these now, and the notes below the table.

Stage (b) Averaging the seasonal influences for each period

The next stage is to calculate the mean deviation from trend for each of the time periods (in our case for each of the quarters). To do this we take the deviation from trend figures for the first quarter of each year, add them together, and divide by the total number of years in which the quarters fall. The process is then repeated for the second, third and fourth quarter. Table 12.4 illustrates this method.

Table 12.3 Sales of portland cement (£'000) (Col. IV omitted)

Year (I)	Quarter (II)	Sales (III)	Centred trend (V)	Deviation of actual from trend (VI)
1	1	1 084		
	2	1 976		
	3	3 600	2 090.38	+1 509.62
	4	1 654	2 171.75	−517.75
2	1	1 179	2 468.88	−1 289.88
	2	2 532	2 735.38	−203.38
	3	5 421	2 879.50	+2 541.5
	4	1 965	3 074.62	−1 109.62
3	1	2 021	3 293.38	−1 272.38
	2	3 251	3 470.12	−219.12
	3	6 452	3 532.38	+2 919.62
	4	2 348	3 600.62	−1 252.62
4	1	2 136	3 667.00	−1 531.00
	2	3 682	3 788.12	−106.12
	3	6 552	4 004.75	+2 547.25
	4	3 217	4 168.00	−951.00
5	1	3 000	4 238.62	−1 238.62
	2	4 124	4 302.00	−178.00
	3	6 675		
	4	3 601		

Notes
(a) The deviations from the trend may be positive (actual figures greater than trend) or negative (actual figures less than trend).

(b) We can see that the third quarter is always a large positive figure (sales of cement in the third quarter being well above trend).

(c) By contrast, in all other quarters the sales are below trend, and the worst quarter for sales is the first quarter of the year. (*Now return to p. 267, stage (b)*.)

Table 12.4   Seasonal variation

Year	Quarter 1	Quarter 2	Quarter 3	Quarter 4
1	—	—	+1 509.62	−517.75
2	−1 289.88	−203.38	+2 541.50	−1 109.62
3	−1 272.38	−219.12	+2 919.62	−1 252.62
4	−1 531.00	−106.12	+2 547.25	−951.00
5	−1 238.62	−178.00	−	−
Totals	−5 331.88	−706.62	+9 517.99	−3 830.99
Mean of quarterly deviation	−1 332.97	−176.66	+2 379.50	−957.75

Stage (c)   Correcting seasonal deviation

The reader might reasonably conclude that the mean of quarterly deviations can be taken as the figure representing seasonal variation for each quarter in the period covered. However, this is not exactly the case. Some error has in fact entered into our calculations. This error is caused by irregular fluctuations which cannot be eliminated by the 'moving average' process. Since the moving average must average whatever figures are there, a succession of years in which seasonal output was steady will be adequately 'smoothed' but a succession of years which were subject to wild fluctuations, due to natural events such as floods, might be less well smoothed in the moving average process. The trend will not be a smooth line, but will have 'humps' and 'hollows'.

That an error does exist can easily be proved because the four averages of quarterly deviation listed in Table 12.4 should altogether come to zero. The reader who finds this point difficult to follow should make a simple calculation which will demonstrate that the figures on either side of an arithmetic mean will sum to zero. For example, take the average of $22 + 14$, $\dfrac{22 + 14}{2} = 18$: 18 is 4 below 22 (-4) and 4 above 14 ($+4$); -4 and $+4$ when added together $= 0$. In Table 12.3 the position is:

+ items	*− items*
+2 379.50 (Quarter 3)	− 1 332.97 (Quarter 1)
	− 176.66 (Quarter 2)
	− 957.75 (Quarter 4)
	−2 467.38

Difference = +2 379.50 − 2 467.38
= − 87.88

Dividing this by four, we have that each quarterly deviation is wrong by −21.97. The **correction factor** is therefore +21.97. Since the negative column in the calculation is larger, giving us a final result of −21.47 per quarterly deviation, we have to add +21.97 to each quarter to make the result come to zero.

Our final calculation of seasonal deviation is therefore in Table 12.5.

Table 12.5 Seasonal variation (*continued*)

	Quarter 1	Quarter 2	Quarter 3	Quarter 4
Mean of quarterly deviation	−1 332.97	−176.66	+2 379.50	−957.75
Correction factor	+21.97	+21.97	+21.97	+21.97
Seasonal Variation	−1 311.00	−154.69	+2 401.47	−935.78

Check: −1 311.00 and −154.69 and −935.78 when added together give −2 401.47. Since quarter 3 has a deviation of +2 401.47 the figures do sum to zero.

The seasonal variation figures from Table 12.5 above can now be used to deseasonalize the data and assist us in calculating the random variation. In fact students should appreciate that working those figures out fully is really an example of **spurious accuracy**. Although the student can follow the figures more easily if they are fully worked out, it is really rather pointless, since the original data were only given to the nearest £1 000, and fractions of £1 000 are therefore really not sensible. Rounding the seasonal variations to the nearest whole number would be good enough.

12.5 Random variations and the de-seasonalizing of data

We have already calculated the trend and also found the degree to which the actual data deviate from the trend. We have seen that these deviations from trend can be due to seasonal variations or other variations termed 'random'.

We must now de-seasonalize the deviations from trend. This means we must subtract the seasonal variations from the deviations from the trend. Any remaining deviation must be explained by random variations. Table 12.6 shows how this is done, and is fully explained in the notes below the table.

Table 12.6   Finding the random variation

Year	Quarter	Sales (£'000)	Trend	Deviation from trend	Season variation	Random variation
1	1	1 084	—			
	2	1 976	—			
	3	3 600	2 090.38	+ 1 509.62	+ 2 401.47	− 891.85
	4	1 654	2 171.75	− 517.75	− 935.78	+ 418.03
2	1	1 179	2 468.88	− 1 289.88	− 1 311.00	+ 21.12
	2	2 532	2 735.38	− 203.38	− 154.69	− 48.69
	3	5 421	2 879.50	+ 2 541.50	+ 2 401.47	+ 140.03
	4	1 965	3 074.62	− 1 109.62	− 935.78	− 173.84
3	1	2 021	3 293.38	− 1 272.38	− 1 311.00	+ 38.62
	2	3 251	3 470.12	− 219.12	− 154.69	− 64.43
	3	6 452	3 532.38	+ 2 919.62	+ 2 401.47	+ 518.15
	4	2 348	3 600.62	− 1 252.62	− 935.78	− 316.84
4	1	2 136	3 667.00	− 1 531.00	− 1 311.00	− 220.00
	2	3 682	3 788.12	− 106.12	− 154.69	+ 48.57
	3	6 552	4 004.75	+ 2 547.25	+ 2 401.47	+ 145.78
	4	3 217	4 168.00	− 951.00	− 935.78	− 15.22
5	1	3 000	4 238.62	− 1 238.62	− 1 311.00	+ 72.38
	2	4 124	4 302.00	− 178.00	− 154.69	− 23.31
	3	6 675				
	4	3 601				

Notes

(a) The seasonal variation has been calculated previously (see Table 12.5) and is the same in all years for each season. Thus the same figures appear in quarter 3, year 1, quarter 3, year 2, etc.

(b) The actual deviation from trend is not the same as the seasonal deviation. This shows that other types of random deviations have crept into the statistics that were collected.

(c) It is easy to see that the amount of these random deviations is the difference between the seasonal variations and the deviations from trend. What is not so easy to understand is which sign the random variation will have. The reader will find the best guide to this is as follows:

(i) Look at the seasonal variation column. In the season under consideration (say year 1 quarter 3) we would have expected the deviation from trend to be seasonal, i.e. 2401.47. In fact, it was only $+1\,509.62$. This means that another variation, a random variation, occurred to reduce the seasonal effect. It must therefore have been a negative variation, i.e. -891.85. By contrast in year 2 quarter 3 the actual deviation, instead of being a seasonal $+2\,401.47$ was even larger $+2\,541.50$. So the random variation of 140.03 was positive i.e. $+140.03$.

(ii) By the same argument, in year 1 quarter 4 we would have expected the deviation from trend to be a seasonal -935.78. In fact, it was less than this; the actual figure was -517.75. This means that a random variation which was positive crept into the statistics to reduce the deficit, $+418.03$. By contrast, in year 2, quarter 4 the seasonal variation we expected of -935.78 was even larger $-1\,109.62$. This means that a negative variation crept in to make the deficit even greater, -173.84.

The nature of random variation

As its name implies, random variation can arise from a variety of causes, many of which are quite unpredictable. Fate knocks on the door of individuals, businessmen, governments and even nations every day. The death of a salesman, the departure of a chief executive or a vital craftsman can adversely affect sales, output, or public confidence. Particular events, like a rise in oil prices, can affect countless businesses, some more than others. Analysis of a series of figures which reveals a particularly sudden random variation may be related to a particular event of this sort. These are often called **special variations**.

Another type of variation is **induced variation**. This induced variation arises because of the averaging process over relatively small groups of numbers.

De-seasonalizing the actual data

It is frequently helpful, e.g. in planning business activities, to de-seasonalize the actual data, i.e. to express the actual figures with the variation due to seasonal fluctuation removed. In order to achieve this the actual figures in Table 12.7 (Sales £'000) have seasonal variation added or subtracted. There is some possible confusion over signs here. If the seasonal variation has a positive sign, this signifies that actual figures for that quarter exceed the trend because of the favourable season: the seasonal variation is therefore *subtracted*. If the amount of seasonal variation has a negative sign, then this means that the actual figures are less than trend and seasonal variation is *added*.

If the actual figures of Table 12.6 (Sales £'000) are seasonally adjusted, they give de-seasonalized data as shown in Table 12.7. Again, there is an element of 'spurious accuracy' in the figures given.

Table 12.7 De-seasonalizing data

Year	Quarter	Sales (£ '000)	Seasonal variation	De-seasonalized data
1	1	1 084	− 1 311.00	2 395.00
	2	1 976	− 154.69	2 130.69
	3	3 600	+ 2 401.47	1 198.53
	4	1 654	− 935.78	2 589.78
2	1	1 179	− 1 311.00	2 490.00
	2	2 532	− 154.69	2 686.69
	3	5 421	+ 2 401.47	3 019.53
	4	1 965	− 935.78	2 900.78
3	1	2 021	− 1 311.00	3 332.00
	2	3 251	− 154.69	3 405.69
	3	6 452	+ 2 401.47	4 050.53
	4	2 348	− 935.78	3 283.78
4	1	2 136	− 1 311.00	3 447.00
	2	3 682	− 154.69	3 836.69
	3	6 552	+ 2 401.47	4 150.53
	4	3 217	− 935.78	4 152.78
5	1	3 000	− 1 311.00	4 311.00
	2	4 124	− 154.69	4 278.69
	3	6 675	+ 2 401.47	4 273.53
	4	3 601	− 935.78	4 536.78

12.6 Seasonal ratios

You may find that seasonal variations are sometimes expressed as ratios. Such a ratio is found by expressing the actual data, e.g. the quarterly sales figure, as a fraction of the trend figure. Using the data already discussed in Table 12.3 but finding a seasonal ratio instead of a seasonal deviation from trend, we have, using the fraction *quarterly data ÷ trend*, seasonal ratios as shown in Col. *VI* opposite:

Table 12.8 Sales of Portland cement (£'000)

Year (I)	Quarter (II)	Sales (III)	Centred trend (V)	Seasonal ratio (VI)
1	1	1 084		
	2	1 976		
	3	3 600	2 090.38	1.722
	4	1 654	2 171.75	0.762
2	1	1 179	2 468.88	0.478
	2	2 532	2 735.38	0.926
	3	5 421	2 879.50	1.883
	4	1 965	3 074.62	0.639
3	1	2 021	3 293.38	0.614
	2	3 251	3 470.12	0.937
	3	6 452	3 532.38	1.827
	4	2 348	3 600.62	0.652
4	1	2 136	3 667.00	0.582
	2	3 682	3 788.12	0.972
	3	6 552	4 004.75	1.636
	4	3 217	4 168.00	0.772
5	1	3 000	4 238.62	0.708
	2	4 124	4 302.00	0.959
	3	6 675		
	4	3 601		

When these ratios are averaged over the years we have:

Year	Quarters 1	2	3	4
1	—	—	1.722	0.762
2	0.478	0.926	1.883	0.639
3	0.614	0.937	1.827	0.652
4	0.582	0.972	1.636	0.772
5	0.708	0.959		
Total	2.382	3.794	7.068	2.825
Average	0.5955	0.9485	1.767	0.7063

The seasonally adjusted data can now be found directly from this ratio. If we take the actual quarterly figure and divide it by the ratio which is appropriate to it, i.e. the first quarter's ratio for any first quarter figure, and so on, we arrive at the seasonally adjusted figure. Thus in year 1 of Table 12.8 the seasonally adjusted figures are:

1   $1\,084 \div 0.5955 = 1\,820.3$
2   $1\,976 \div 0.9485 = 2\,083.3$
3   $3\,600 \div 1.767 \ \ = 2\,037.4$
4   $1\,654 \div 0.7603 = 2\,341.8$

The process should be continued for the other years.

If you compare these seasonally adjusted figures with those calculated in Section 12.4 there clearly are differences. The reason is that in the first method we adjusted each particular quarter by a constant absolute amount, but in the second method we adjusted by a constant ratio. I think that most statisticians would advise the second of the two procedures.

12.7   Exercises on seasonal and random variations

1   Live births in UK ('000s) are as follows:

	Quarters			
	1	*2*	*3*	*4*
Year 1	210	198	192	186
Year 2	188	188	189	174
Year 3	177	180	176	163
Year 4	175	174	170	156

Source: *Monthly Digest of Statistics*

(a) By means of a moving average find the trend and seasonal variations in this data.
(b) Then de-seasonalize the data.

2   Arrange the following data in such a way that you can conveniently calculate:

(a) A moving average which reveals the trend in the statistics.
(b) The seasonal variations from the trend.
(c) The residual variation that exists in the statistics when seasonally adjusted.

Earnings of hoteliers from overseas tourists (£m)

| | Quarters | | | |
	1	*2*	*3*	*4*
Year 1	32	47	160	83
Year 2	37	56	174	96
Year 3	57	80	236	126
Year 4	97	132	341	185
Year 5	128	182	397	227

Make the calculations and comment on the trend and seasonal variations.

3   The following figures relate to the sale of men's pullovers, jumpers and cardigans over a 4-year period. You are required:

(a) By means of a moving average to find the trend and seasonal variations concealed in the figures.

(b) To give the data for year 4 seasonally adjusted (calculations correct to two decimal places).

Sales of male woollen overgarments (millions)

| | Quarters | | | |
	1	*2*	*3*	*4*
Year 1	1.98	2.30	2.44	3.09
Year 2	1.80	2.01	2.23	3.04
Year 3	1.68	1.96	2.10	3.12
Year 4	1.91	2.25	2.43	2.98

Source: Monthly Digest of Statistics

4   The following figures show the sales of ladies' fashions in a large emporium over a 5-year period. Calculate:

(a) The trend in the statistics.

(b) The seasonal variations from the trend.

(c) The residual variations in the statistics once the seasonal variations have been taken into account.

Ladies fashions: sales (£ millions)

	Quarters			
	1	*2*	*3*	*4*
Year 1	42	68	55	71
Year 2	47	73	57	79
Year 3	54	82	63	85
Year 4	56	89	69	87
Year 5	59	91	71	91

12.8 Cyclical variations

A cyclical variation is one that results from the cycle of business activity, which is most popularly characterized as the boom–slump–boom–slump cycle. As such, it is a cycle that operates over a period of years, and we do need a fairly long series of data to detect it. Cyclical variations are detected in the same way as seasonal variations, in that the trend is subtracted from the actual data and the differences averaged. The data will almost always feature annual figures, e.g. annual sales or annual production. The business cycle is rarely less than 5 years, and often more like 8 or 9 years from a peak, or trough, to the next peak, or trough, of activity. An initial guide to the likely length of the cycle can sometimes be obtained from a graph of the data. For example, consider Table 12.9.

Table 12.9 Sales (£'000s): Steady-growth PLC

Year 1	150	Year 10	220
Year 2	100	Year 11	220
Year 3	90	Year 12	190
Year 4	140	Year 13	170
Year 5	180	Year 14	200
Year 6	160	Year 15	260
Year 7	130	Year 16	280
Year 8	120	Year 17	250
Year 9	140	Year 18	220

When plotted on a graph, these figures seem to reach a low point about every 5 years, and a high point about every 5 to 6 years, as shown in Figure 12.2.

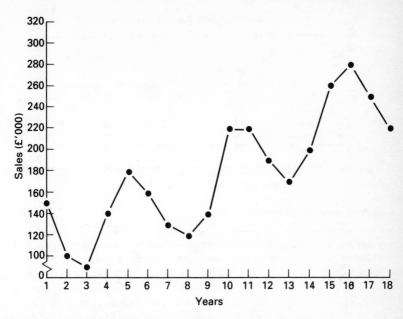

Figure 12.2 High points and low points in cyclical activity

Finding the trend and the variations from the trend, using a 5-year cycle, we have the data as in Table 12.10. Remember that if we decide the cycle is effective over an even number of years (say 6 years) we should need to centre the trend before finding the variations from the trend.

Table 12.10   (*continues on page 278*)

Year	Sales (£'000s)	Trend	Variation from the trend
1	150		
2	100		
3	90	132	−42
4	140	134	+6
5	180	140	+40
6	160	146	+14
7	130	146	−16
8	120	154	−34
9	140	166	−26
10	220	178	+42

11	220	188	+32
12	190	200	−10
13	170	208	−38
14	200	200	−20
15	260	232	+28
16	280	242	+38
17	250		
18	220		

If we now tabulate these variations to show them in each year of the 5-year cycle we have variations as in Table 12.11.

Table 12.11 Table of variations

Year 1 of the cycle	Year 2 of the cycle	Year 3 of the cycle	Year 4 of the cycle	Year 5 of the cycle
–	–	−42	+6	+40
+14	−16	−34	−26	+42
+32	−10	−38	−20	+28
+38	–	–	–	–
Total +84	−26	−114	−40	+110
Average +28	−13	−38	−13.33	+36.67
Correct to nearest whole number				
+28	−13	−38	−13	+37

It therefore appears that we should expect the cycle to affect sales roughly by the amount shown above or below the trend, according to which year of the cycle we are in. Thus a statistician commenting in year 18 on the likely year 20 data (which is the fifth year in a cycle) would, after calculating the trend for year 20, add on £37,000 to get the likely sales figure for that year.

Forecasting from a time series

The method for forecasting cyclical figures from a time series can be studied at this point. Trying to anticipate, in year 18, what the sales figures would be in year 20 we have to decide:

(a) What the trend figure might be for Year 20.
(b) What the cyclical effect will be in that year (we expect this to be + £37,000).

To find (*a*) we use either of the following procedures:

(i) Decide what the trend will be visually, from the graph Figure 12.2. As we can see from each of the peaks in year 5 and year 10, the figures go into decline for 3 years and then recover a little in the fourth year and a good deal in the fifth year – and this can even be maintained into a sixth year. Since the peak of year 15, there have been 2 years of decline, so a third year of decline followed by a year of recovery would give us a figure of, say, £260,000. By adding the cyclical effect of £37,000, we reach a figure of £297,000 for year 20.

(ii) The second method calls for calculation. In this method we deduct the first trend figure (132) from the last one (242) to find the change over the years. This gives a difference of £110,000. Dividing this by 13 (because there are 13 annual changes in 14 trend years), we have an average trend change of +£8 462. Approximating this to £8 500, we add 8.5 successively to the last trend figure of 242 to move the trend figure on for 4 years. This gives us a trend figure in year 20 of 276. With the cyclical adjustment of £37,000 added to this trend figure of £276,000, we have an estimated sales figure in year 20 of £313,000.

12.9 Exercises on detecting cyclical changes

1 The output of Manufacturing PLC over recent years has been as shown below. You are asked:

(*a*) To draw a graph of the data to discover the length of the business cycle (if any).
(*b*) To find the trend over the years and the variations from the trend.
(*c*) To predict the output in Years 21 and 22

Output of Manufacturing PLC (millions of units)

Year 1	280	Year 11	370
Year 2	272	Year 12	358
Year 3	245	Year 13	320
Year 4	265	Year 14	336
Year 5	295	Year 15	399
Year 6	320	Year 16	450
Year 7	310	Year 17	430
Year 8	275	Year 18	376
Year 9	292	Year 19	388
Year 10	345	Year 20	438

2   Sales of Popular Products Ltd are found to have been as follows in recent years:

Sales of Popular Products Ltd (£ '000s)

Year 1	295	Year 11	392
Year 2	301	Year 12	404
Year 3	316	Year 13	413
Year 4	327	Year 14	410
Year 5	339	Year 15	407
Year 6	350	Year 16	430
Year 7	334	Year 17	460
Year 8	319	Year 18	535
Year 9	336	Year 19	554
Year 10	356	Year 20	564

(a) Draw a graph to find the length of the business cycle.
(b) Determine the trend in sales over the years and the variations from the trend.
(c) Find the likely sales figures in years 21 and 22 (correct to the nearest '000).

3   The country of Novindia, a newly industrialized country, has a national income in the last 20 years as shown below. National income is the total wealth created by the citizens of a country.

You are asked:

(a) To draw a graph of the national income figures to discover whether there is any cycle of activity.
(b) To find the trend in the growth of national income and the variations from the trend.
(c) To estimate the national income in Year 21.

National income of Novindia (billions of Novind dollars)

Year 1	300	Year 11	468
Year 2	325	Year 12	449
Year 3	345	Year 13	482
Year 4	320	Year 14	516
Year 5	310	Year 15	547
Year 6	365	Year 16	563
Year 7	399	Year 17	585
Year 8	454	Year 18	556
Year 9	480	Year 19	538
Year 10	495	Year 20	570

12.10 The uses of time series

The main use of time series relates to predicting the future values of the variable in question. This is of obvious use to businesses, governments, and even to individuals. For example, if a manufacturing enterprise can accurately predict demand for its output in, say, 5 years' time, this will obviously help it to plan investment to produce such an output. It may be able to achieve economies by buying up at favourable prices manufacturing or transport and handling equipment which becomes available and is likely to be needed if the observed trend continues. It may be able to phase out other less profitable work to make capacity available when it is required.

As we have seen with cyclical changes, a common way of showing the method of prediction is **extrapolation** of the trend line – carrying over into a future period the calculated trend line. To extrapolate is to carry a graph on into a future period, beyond the points plotted already.

Thus, if the reader refers back to Figure 12.1, let us consider what may happen in years 6 and 7 (see p. 259). Clearly the trend appears likely to continue up towards the upper 4 000 range in year 6 and the 5 000 range in year 7. Because we know the seasonal variations now, we can anticipate sales and set targets for our salesmen in each season of year 6 and year 7.

The reader should realize that extrapolation is a technique which can have dangerous consequences. The trend is only certain within the range already plotted, years 1–5. This is the portion calculated from actual data. Outside this period dramatic changes in events can cause the trend line to vary quite significantly from the extrapolated one. We must watch out for such events and take them into our calculations wherever possible.

In planning ahead it is not only the trend that is useful. The seasonal variations may need to be taken into account. For example, targets for the sales force will not just take account of the trend in the figures, but superimposed upon the trend will be the quarterly variations. A salesperson may be set a target based on his/her share of the trend sales to be achieved, but increased (or decreased) by the seasonal variation anticipated. A target based on the trend above would mean the salesperson under-achieving in a favourable season and quite unable to achieve the target when the seasonal influence was adverse.

Similarly the purchase of raw materials and components at a busy season will be much greater than in a slack season. Many enterprises using JIT techniques (just-in-time techniques) endeavour to order supplies so that they reach the factory just before they are needed. A regular monthly delivery of the same quantity each month is no good to such manufacturers – they will need warehouse space in the slack times and be short of requirements at busy times.

Although we can obtain a rough idea of future needs by pondering the trend figures, as we did when considering Figure 12.1, a more accurate calculation can be arrived at if we use the technique described earlier (Chapter 10) to work out the equation of the trend line. Of course the trend line may not be straight, but a straight 'line of best fit' can be calculated and used to give us a reasonably accurate prediction of the trend line. Consider Example 12.1.

Example 12.1

Using the method of least squares, obtain the equation of the trend line for a company's profits given from year 1 to year 10 below. Plot the data and the trend on a graph and estimate the profits for year 11.

Company profits

	(£'000)		(£'000)
Year 1	100	Year 6	139
Year 2	111	Year 7	152
Year 3	123	Year 8	159
Year 4	125	Year 9	165
Year 5	129	Year 10	171

You will recall that the equation of a straight line is $y = a + bx$, and we used two equations to obtain the values of a and b

$$a = \bar{y} - b\bar{x}$$

$$b = \frac{n\Sigma xy - \Sigma x \Sigma y}{n\Sigma x^2 - (\Sigma x)^2}$$

In this example the independent variable (x) will be the years, the dependent variable (y) the profits, and n the number of sets of data, i.e. ten.

The calculations are as follows:

Years x	Profits (£000) y	xy	x^2
1	100	100	1
2	111	222	4
3	123	369	9
4	125	500	16
5	129	645	25

(*continues opposite*)

6	139	834	36
7	152	1 064	49
8	159	1 272	64
9	165	1 485	81
10	171	1 710	100
$\Sigma x = 55$	$\Sigma y = 1\,374$	$\Sigma xy = 8\,201$	$\Sigma x^2 = 385$

Therefore:

$$b = \frac{10 \times 8\,201 - 55 \times 1\,374}{10 \times 385 - 55^2}$$

$$= \frac{82\,010 - 75\,570}{3\,850 - 3\,025}$$

$$= \frac{6\,440}{825}$$

$$= \underline{\underline{7.81}}$$

$$a = \frac{1\,374}{10} - \left(7.81 \times \frac{55}{10}\right)$$

$$= 137.4 - 42.96$$

$$= \underline{\underline{94.44}}$$

Therefore the equation of the trend line will be:

$$y = a + bx$$

$$\therefore \ y = 94.44 + 7.81x$$

In order to estimate profits for year 11, substitute 11 in the equation for x.

$$y = 94.44 + (7.81 \times 11)$$

$$= 94.44 + 85.91$$

$$= \underline{\underline{180.35}}$$

i.e. approximately £180 000 profit for year 11. So that we can plot the trend line, we need two points. One can be the profit estimate for year 11 and the other can be the profit for year 1. Calculating these we have:

$$y = 94.44 + (1 \times 7.81)$$
$$= 102.25$$

The graph would then be as shown in Figure 12.3

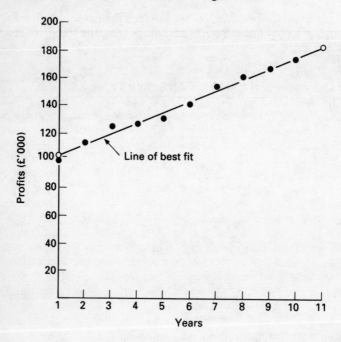

Figure 12.3   Finding the line of best fit for a trend by the method of least squares

We can now predict the trend for future years by extending the trend line (always bearing in mind, that extrapolation can never be absolutely certain).

If the data was given quarterly, the same procedure could be used by renumbering the quarters, as follows:

Years	Quarters		Sales
1	1	1	1 084
	2	2	1 976
	3	3	3 600
	4	4	1 654

2	1	5	1 179
	2	6	2 532
	3	7	5 421
etc.			

Having found the trend figures, we can then predict seasonalized figures by taking account of quarterly deviations from the trend, as described earlier.

12.11 Summary of Chapter 12

1 A set of data showing the changes in output, sales, etc. over a period of time is called a time series.

2 By analysing the data we can discover the trend over the years. The trend is found by calculating a moving average, which smooths out variations in the data due to seasonal or other variations, and reveals the general growth or decline over the years.

3 If we plot the actual data on the same graph, we can see the general pattern of changes very clearly.

4 Once we have the trend, we can find the deviations from the trend. If we then take these deviations for each quarter of the year and average them, we can find the average deviation for the quarter. These average deviations need to be corrected by a 'correction factor', and when this has been done, we have the 'seasonal variation'.

5 We can then de-seasonalize the data. Any remaining deviation from the trend must be the result of random variations (residual variations) which can arise from a variety of causes.

6 Calculating trends and de-seasonalized data can be helpful in planning business activities, e.g. in setting achievable objectives for sales personnel, output targets, etc.

7 Seasonal variations can also be expressed as ratios, by calculating the actual figure e.g. the quarterly sales figure, as a fraction of the trend figure.

8 Cyclical variations are variations due to changes in the cycle of business activity. They are of interest to economists, but they require a fairly lengthy series of data before any discernible cycle of trade can be seen. When this cycle can be observed (say a 5-year or a 7-year cycle), we can calculate the trend and the variations from that trend. We can then use the trend to predict future business activity.

13
Index numbers

13.1 What are index numbers

A major problem in statistical work is to arrange a collection of data in such a way that it becomes easier to interpret. We have seen that an array can be cumbersome. A single average figure often conveys the essence of the contents of the array quickly, and in a form which makes possible a comparison with other sets of figures.

Index numbers are, in a sense, a continuation of the process of rendering large masses of figures intelligible. In this process they play a special role:

(a) They allow the expression of different standards of measures in one figure.
(b) They make possible the comparison of information over time.

As an example of (a), an index number may reduce to a single statistic the price of a basketful of goods which includes a kilogram of potatoes, 16 litres of petrol, a dozen eggs, 5 metres of curtain material and similar items which do not 'mix' in the ordinary way. As an example of (b), we may quote the basketful of goods already referred to, priced on a given date in each year over the period of the enquiry. What did they cost in year 1, year 2, etc. ?

An index number may be defined as a statistic which indicates the level of prices, wages, outputs and other variables at given dates, relative to their level at an earlier date which is taken as a base or standard.

Before considering index numbers in more detail, it is first necessary to explain the special role of the base, and to outline some symbols peculiar to index numbers.

The base

Since index numbers compare information over a period of time, it is usual for one of the points in time to be taken and used as a base. For example, if the price of copper is to be compared in 3 years (year 1, year 2 and year 3), the price in year 1 may be assigned the notional value of 100. Then if the price increases by, say, 10 per cent from year 1 to year 2 and 20 per cent from year 1 to year 3, the year 2 index will be 110 and the Year 3 index 120 (both being based upon the index of 100 for year 1).

Because most people are familiar with percentages and can easily understand changes in terms of parts of 100, it is almost universal for index numbers to have a base of 100.

Symbols used in calculating index numbers

The following symbols are used in calculations relating to index numbers:

w = weight (the emphasis or importance given to an item).
q = quantity of individual commodities or items.
q_0 = quantity of individual commodities or items in the base year.
$q_{1,2,3}$, etc. = as above, but in subsequent years.
p = price of individual commodities or items.
p_0 = price of individual commodities or items in the base year.
$p_{1,2,3}$, etc. = as above but in subsequent years.

Let us consider the simplest type of index number or price relative.

13.2   A simple index or price relative

If on the 1 April petrol cost £1.80 per gallon and on 1 May the same year £1.98 per gallon, this represents a rise in price of 10 per cent. By terming 1 April the base, 100, then the price on 1 May is 110. We have here the basis of a simple index. This is often referred to as a **price relative**, since it shows how the *price* in a *one-item* index changes over time, relative to its price at a base date.

The formula for a simple price index (price relative) is:

$$\frac{p_1}{p_0} \times 100$$

where p_1 is the month or year under scrutiny and p_0 is the base date.
Use of this is demonstrated in Example 13.1.

Example 13.1
Taking year 3 as base year, calculate a petrol price index for years 1–11 inclusive (answers correct to one decimal place).

The price of petrol

Year	Price	Calculation $\left(\dfrac{p_1}{p_0} \times \dfrac{100}{1}\right)$	Price index
Year 1	125	$\frac{125}{133} \times 100$	94.0
Year 2	130	$\frac{130}{133} \times 100$	97.7
Year 3	133	$\frac{133}{133} \times 100$	100
Year 4	136	$\frac{136}{133} \times 100$	102.3
Year 5	138	$\frac{138}{133} \times 100$	103.8
Year 6	140	$\frac{140}{133} \times 100$	105.3
Year 7	180	$\frac{180}{133} \times 100$	135.3
Year 8	190	$\frac{190}{133} = 100$	142.9
Year 9	185	$\frac{185}{133} \times 100$	139.1
Year 10	180	$\frac{180}{133} \times 100$	135.3
Year 11	182	$\frac{182}{133} \times 100$	136.8

Notice that any year can be chosen as the base year, and the index can be calculated for prices in subsequent years and earlier years. In inflationary times, since a base year is 100, subsequent years will tend to show an index above 100 and earlier years an index below 100.

13.3   Exercises: simple index numbers

1   Over an 8-year period the price of a certain metal per tonne on the London Market averaged out as follows: year 1 £230; year 2 £250; year 3 £320; year 4 £340; year 5 £825; year 6 £900; year 7 £940; year 8 £1 000. At the end of year 4 a civil war broke out in a major producing country, and this caused the sudden rise in prices. Calculate a price index for the metal with year 4 as 100 (calculations correct to one decimal place).

2   Over a 5-year period the price of standard rubber per kilogram on the London Rubber Market was as follows: year 1: 53 pence; year 2: 54 pence; year 3: 47 pence; year 4: 45 pence; year 5: 44 pence. The ending of a cartel agreement in certain countries led to the fall in price in year 3. Using year 3 as a base year, calculate a price index for Standard Rubber for these 5 years (calculations correct to one decimal place).

3   The price of wheat on the London markets is quoted as £ per tonne. The prices for September onwards are quoted as follows: September £85.05; October £86.20; November £87.45; December £90.30. Using

September as the base month, calculate a price index for wheat for the rest of the year (calculations correct to one decimal place).

4 The coffee market quotes prices in £ per tonne. In four successive days prices are as follows: day 1 £1 180; day 2 £1 210; day 3 £1 225; day 4 £1 272. Using day 1 as a base, calculate a price index for coffee for the period shown (calculations correct to one decimal place).

13.4 Average price relative index numbers

So far we have calculated index numbers for a single commodity whose price changes over a period of time, but it is more likely that we will be interested in quantifying changes of a group of related products. In the General Index of Retail Prices we may look at changes in individual product prices, e.g. the cost of diesel fuel, but will probably find of greater interest changes in the cost of the whole range of goods and services which are associated with road transport. This requires that we calculate individual price relatives and average them.

Example 13.2

Calculate the group index numbers for the following group of products in 19.0, 19.1 and 19.2, if the base year is 19.0.

Product	Price per unit in pence		
	19.0	*19.1*	*19.2*
A	10	15	20
B	15	18	24
C	20	25	30

Index numbers calculation (19.0 base period = 100):

19.1 Product A $\dfrac{15}{10} \times \dfrac{100}{1} = 150$

Product B $\dfrac{18}{15} = \dfrac{100}{1} = 120$

Product C $\dfrac{25}{20} \times \dfrac{100}{1} = \underline{125}$

Total $\underline{\underline{395}}$

Group index number $= \dfrac{395}{3} = \underline{\underline{131.67}}$

Note that the average is calculated as for the mean, i.e. the price relatives are totalled and divided by three (three products A, B, C)

19.2   Product A $\dfrac{20}{10} \times \dfrac{100}{1} = 200$

Product B $\dfrac{24}{15} \times \dfrac{100}{1} = 160$

Product C $\dfrac{30}{20} \times \dfrac{100}{1} = \underline{150}$

Total $\underline{\underline{510}}$

Group index number $= \dfrac{510}{3} = \underline{\underline{170}}$

The index numbers are therefore 100, 131.7 and 170 for 19.0, 19.1 and 19.2 respectively.

13.5   Exercises on average price relative index numbers

1   Calculate the group index numbers for the following group of products in 19.3, 19.4, 19.5 and 19.6, given that year 19.3 is the base year (answers correct to 1 decimal place).

Product	Price per unit in (£)			
	19.3	19.4	19.5	19.6
A	15	17	19	20
B	18	22	25	30
C	3	4	6	8

2   Calculate the group index numbers for the following group of products in year 1, year 2 and year 3, given that year 1 is the base year (answers correct to 1 decimal place)

Product	Year 1	Price per kg in pence Year 2	Year 3
M	17	19	24
N	5	6	8
O	5	4	3
P	16	25	36

13.6 Weighted index numbers

Although a simple index, as outlined in Example 12.1 above, is easy to calculate, for practical purposes the real values of index numbers is in the comparison of 'unmixables'. For example, how will a rise in the price of synthetic rubber and plastics and a fall in the price of copper affect the price of a family motorcar? The student might thank that the answer lies in taking the rise in the prices of synthetic rubber and plastics, adding them together, and then subtracting the fall in the price of copper. This would, in fact, be the correct method if all three commodites were used in exactly the same proportions. Consider the information given in Example 13.3 below.

Example 13.3
Raw materials in motor vehicles:

Raw material	Quantity used per car (kg)	Original price per kg (£)	Price change per kg
Synthetic rubber	10	1.60	+£0.20
Plastic	10	1.00	+£0.15
Copper	10	1.80	−£0.10

From the table we can work out that synthetic rubber costs 200p (10 × 20p) more; plastic 150p (10 × 15p) more; and copper 100p less (10 × −10p). The extra cost of producing the vehicle is therefore 200p + 150p − 100p = 250p. A quicker way of finding this would be take the price increases 20p + 15p = 35p and subtract the decrease −10p. The result, 25p, is then multiplied by the quantities involved (10 kg in each case) to find the overall price effect, an increase of 250p.

Unfortunately this simple approach has one very serious drawback – it is not realistic. Different commodities are usually used in varying proportions to each other, in the manufacture of outputs. It is to be expected that the quantities of synthetic rubber and plastic would exceed that of copper in the manufacture of a modern motorcar. This will mean that, although copper has fallen in price (Example 13.2), the significance of that price fall will be diminished, since a relatively small amount of the commodity is used. Another example, often quoted in economics in the study of price elasticity of demand, is from the kitchen: a fall of 5p in the price of a carton of cooking salt will not offset a rise of 5p in the price of a pint of milk. The typical family consumes many more pints of milk in a year than it does cartons of cooking salt!

To overcome this problem, **weighting** is used. We have already seen how a weighted arithmetic mean is calculated (see p. 143) and the method used to weight index numbers is an extension of the process. The principle of weighting is quite simple – it seeks to give extra emphasis to an item or items because of their greater significance in terms of quantity. If twice as much synthetic rubber as copper is used in the manufacture of a modern motorcar, then the weights assigned to each must be in the ratio 2:1. In Example 13.2 above the weights 2:1 would not be appropriate, because we still have to accommodate plastic. Assuming that half as much again of plastic compared to copper is used, the weights used could be as shown in Example 13.4, where a weighted index is calculated.

Example 13.4

Commodity	Weight	Year 1 Price per kg (£)	$p_0 \times w$	Year 2 Price per kg (£)	$p_1 \times w$
Rubber	4	1.60	£6.40	1.80	£7.20
Plastic	3	1.00	£3.00	1.15	£3.45
Copper	2	1.80	£3.60	1.70	£3.40
			£13.00		£14.05

The weighted index number can now be calculated by taking the sum of the year 1 column and making it the base 100. The sum of the year 2 column can then be expressed as a proportion of the base column.

The formula $\frac{p_1}{p_0} \times 100$ now has to be modified to take account of the weighting, and becomes:

$$\text{Index} = \frac{\Sigma(p_1 \times w)}{\Sigma(p_0 \times w)} \times 100$$

$$= \frac{£14.05}{£13.00} \times 100$$

$$= \underline{\underline{108}}$$

In this calculation the units being used (in other words the £ signs) cancel out and leave us with an index which is independent of monetary units.

To sum up, then, the method for calculating a weighted index number is as follows:

1 List in a table the constituent items in the basket of goods and their prices.
2 Choose the weights required.
3 Multiply the prices by their respective weights (this process is known as weighting).
4 Add together these products ($p \times w$) for every item for each year (this process is known as aggregating).
5 Divide the total for the 'new' year by the total for the base year and multiply by 100 to express the new year as an index number of the base year.

13.7 Exercises: weighted index numbers

1 A motor-vehicle component consists of 3kg ferrous metals, 2kg non-ferrous metals and 1kg other materials. In the year the prototype was made the ferrous metals used cost £1.30 per kg, the non-ferrous metals £3.25 per kg and other materials £0.75 per kg. In the following year the prices rose respectively to £1.65, £3.85 and £0.95. Calculate a weighted price index for the component (correct to one decimal place).

2 An aerospace component consists of 50kg copper, 20kg aluminium and 30kg other materials. In the year the prototype was made the copper cost £7.30 per kg, the aluminium £3.20 per kg and other materials £1.20 per kg. In the following year the prices of the copper and the aluminium rose respectively to £8.50 and £3.50. The cost of the other materials fell to £1.00 per kg. Calculate a weighted price index for the component (correct to one decimal place).

3 The average price of wheat, barley and oats per tonne in three successive years is given in the table below. The proportions of these grains being used in cereal products are the ratios 10 for wheat, 4 for barley and 6 for oats. Take the prices in year 1 as 100 and

calculate a price index for cereal products over the 3-year period (correct to one decimal place).

Cereal grain prices (£ per tonne)

	Year 1	Year 2	Year 3
Wheat	83	84.50	89
Barley	75	78	85
Oats	68	78	81

4   A contractor uses a standard mixture which consists of 2 parts ballast, 1 part sand and 1 part cement. Prices per tonne in 3 years delivered to site were as follows:

	Year 1 (£)	Year 2 (£)	Year 3 (£)
Ballast	140	150	180
Sand	180	200	220
Cement	200	270	280

Compute a price index (correct to one decimal place) for the mixture, using the year 1 figures as base 100.

13.8   Chain index numbers

The indices used so far have all been fixed base ones, i.e. they have all had a particular period (say year 1) as the point of reference: each year has related back to this one starting point. However, it is possible to construct an index where the base changes annually (or each time period). Such an index uses the previous period as base. There are some advantages with this kind of index:

(a)   It is a good way of showing the *rate* of change occurring, i.e. whether prices, outputs, etc., are falling, rising or remaining constant.

(b)   It is possible to incorporate new items into this kind of index without the necessity of recalculating the whole of the previous period's figures. For example, an index started some years ago and still based upon the typical 'basket of goods' would not reflect changes in task, fashion and lifestyle. An index that included record players and not compact discs, or black and white television sets with no weight given to videos, would be outdated.

Since the chain index is effectively recalculated for each year (time period), this problem is avoided.

Example 13.5 shows how a chain index can be calculated for a single commodity (synthetic rubber).

Example 13.5
A chain index for synthetic rubber prices.

Year	Price (in pence) per kg	Calculation
Year 1	74	100
Year 2	76	$\frac{76}{74} \times 100 = 102.7$
Year 3	80	$\frac{80}{76} \times 100 = 105.3$
Year 4	100	$\frac{100}{80} \times 100 = 125$
Year 5	130	$\frac{130}{100} \times 100 = 130$
Year 6	160	$\frac{160}{130} \times 100 = 123.1$
Year 7	170	$\frac{170}{160} \times 100 = 106.2$
Year 8	177	$\frac{177}{170} \times 100 = 104.1$

The method here is to:

(a) List in a table the price of the commodity each year.
(b) Find the price relative for each year using the previous year's price as base.

Question: Why does this particular index number eventually fall even though the price continues to rise?
Answer: Because a chain index brings out the 'rate of change' of prices. Although prices are still rising they are not rising as fast as in the peak year (year 5), when they rose 30 per cent in the year.

A weighted multi-product chain index

It is also possible to construct a chain index which takes into account more than one product, and which can be weighted. Such an index is demonstrated in Example 13.6.

Example 13.6
Finding a weighted chain index of prices for commodities (see Table 13.1).

Table 13.1 Example 13.6: finding a weighted chain index of prices for commodities

Commodity	Year 1			Year 2			Year 3		
	Weight	Price (pence per kg)	Base	Price (pence per kg)	Calculation	Index No. × weight	Price (pence per kg)	Calculation	Index No. × weight
Synthetic rubber	4	180	100	185	$\frac{185}{180} \times 100 \times 4$	411.1	187	$\frac{187}{185} \times 100 \times 4$	404.3
Plastic	3	105	100	111	$\frac{111}{105} \times 100 \times 3$	317.1	115	$\frac{115}{111} \times 100 \times 3$	310.8
Copper	2	180	100	177	$\frac{177}{180} \times 100 \times 2$	196.7	170	$\frac{170}{177} \times 100 \times 2$	192.1
Total	9					924.9			907.2

$924.9 \div 9 = 102.8$
on base of year 1

$907.2 \div 9 = 100.8$
on base of year 2

The index for all commodities is thus 100; 102.8; and 100.8 over the period.

The method here is:

(a) List in a table the commodities, their prices for each year and their weights.
(b) Give the base year (year 1 in Table 13.6) the value 100.
(c) Find the price relative for each commodity for each year, using the previous year as the base year, and multiply this by its weight.
(d) Add together the price relatives × weight for each commodity.
(e) Divide the answer, which is the total for all commodities for each year by the sum of the weights, to find the index number.

13.9   Exercises: chain index numbers

1   The price of petrol (in pence per litre) at the pumps over a 5-year period was as follows:

Year 1	33.0
Year 2	35.5
Year 3	37.2
Year 4	40.3
Year 5	41.8

Calculate a 'chain' index number for the price of petrol which begins year 1 = 100, etc. (calculations correct to one decimal place).

2   (a) The price of tin (£ per tonne) on the London Metal Exchange over a 5-year period was as follows:

Year 1	1 568
Year 2	1 632
Year 3	1 988
Year 4	2 362
Year 5	1 890

Calculate a 'chain' index number for the price of tin which begins with year 1 = 100 (correct to one decimal place).
(b) In year 1 the price of tin was £1 568 per tonne and in year 5 it was £1 890 per tonne. Explain the index number for year 5 in the light of these prices.

3   The information given below refers to three commodities used in the manufacture of a popular food product. The weighting is shown, and the price changes for a 3-year period. You are asked to calculate a weighted chain index for the food product over the period (correct to one decimal place).

	Weight	Year 1	Year 2	Year 3
Commodity A	4	£1.20	£1.45	£1.95
Commodity B	2	£3.50	£3.35	£3.20
Commodity C	1	£2.20	£2.45	£2.85

4 The information given below refers to three commodities used in the manufacture of a popular food product, the weighting shown, and the price changes for a 3-year period. You are asked to calculate a weighted chain index for the food product over the 3-period (correct to one decimal place).

	Weight	Year 1	Year 2	Year 3
Commodity A	4	£1.60	£1.80	£1.95
Commodity B	3	£2.50	£2.65	£3.20
Commodity C	2	£2.40	£2.45	£2.95

13.10 Linking index numbers

You are sometimes required to change the basis of calculation of an index number in order to compare it with another index number which has been obtained using a different base structure, e.g., reconciling index numbers using a fixed base period with others obtained from a chain base. See Example 13.7.

Example 13.7

Given the following index numbers obtained using a chain base, recalculate, using a base year of 19.0:

Year	19.0	19.1	19.2	19.3
Index	100	120	125	120

The price relatives, i.e. before multiplying by 100, would be:

| | 1.00 | 1.20 | 1.25 | 1.20 |

The new series of index numbers based on 19.0 will be:

19.0		100
19.2	$(1.00 \times 1.20) \times 100$	= 120

19.2	$(1.00 \times 1.20 \times 1.25) \times 100$	$= 150$
19.3	$(1.00 \times 1.20 \times 1.25 \times 1.20) \times 100$	$= 180$

You can check the accuracy of this procedure by doing your own calculations, using the original price data of:

19.0	*19.1*	*19.2*	*19.3*
10p	12p	15p	18p

The other main type of linking index numbers is illustrated in the next two examples.

Example 13.8

The index number in 19.3 of a commodity, taking 19.0 as base, is 125. Calculate the 19.0 index number referred to 19.3 as base:

Year	*19.0*	19.3
Index	100	125
Price relative	1.00	1.25

If 19.3 is to be the base year for recalculating the 19.0 index, it is clear the new index for the year 19.0 will be smaller than 100.

The new 19.0 index will be calculated as follows:

$$\text{New index} = \frac{1.00 \times 100}{1.25} = 80$$

Therefore the new indices are

Year	*19.0*	*19.3*
Indices	80	100

Example 13.9

Indices for a product, taking 19.5 as the base year, are as follows:

Year	*19.5*	*19.6*	*19.7*	*19.8*	*19.9*
Index	100	105	120	130	150

Recalculate the indices with 19.7 as the base year. The procedure is to take the index number of the new base year (in this case $19.7 = 120$) and divide it into each other index number in the series and multiply by 100. This gives us index numbers as follows:

300   *Statistics for Business*

Year	Index: base 19.5	New index: base 19.7
19.5	100	$\frac{100}{120} \times \frac{100}{1} = 83.33$
19.6	105	$\frac{105}{120} \times \frac{100}{1} = 87.5$
19.7	120	$\frac{120}{120} \times \frac{100}{1} = 100$
19.8	130	$\frac{130}{130} \times \frac{100}{1} = 108.33$
19.9	150	$\frac{150}{120} \times \frac{100}{1} = 125$

Equally we could have used price relatives as in the previous example:

Year	Index: base 19.5	Index: base 19.7
19.5	100	$\frac{1}{1.2} \times \frac{100}{1} = 88.33$
19.6	105	$\frac{1.05}{1.2} \times \frac{100}{1} = 87.5$
etc.		

13.11   Exercises on index linking

1   A chain-based index reads as follows:

19.1	19.2	19.3	19.4	19.5
100	106	105	110	103

  (a) What would the price relatives be from year to year?
  (b) What would be the index number for these years based on the first year, 19.1? (Answer correct to 1 decimal place.)

2   A chain-based index reads as follows:

19.4	19.5	19.6	19.7	19.8	19.9
100	110	120	125	140	160

  (a) What would the price relatives be from year to year?
  (b) What would the index numbers be if recalculated relative to year 19.4, and not on a chain basis?
  (c) Explain why your answers to (b) are so much larger after the first year than the chain-based indices given above.

3   An index number in 19.7 is 145, relative to a base year 19.1. What would be the index for 19.1 if it was decided to recalculate the index table, using 19.7 as the base year, and treat the index for 19.7 as 100? (Answer correct to 1 decimal place.)

4   An index number in 19.9, which is based on a base year 19.5, is 164. What would the index for the year 19.5 be if it was decided to make

19.9 the base year and recalculate all the indices relative to that new base? (Answers correct to 1 decimal place.)

5 The average weekly wage is shown below over a period of 7 years

19.0	19.1	19.2	19.3	19.4	19.5	19.6
£136	£154	£162	£169	£174	£186	£195

(a) Calculate an index, based on 19.0 as 100, for average weekly wages over the period.

(b) Now calculate a second index, based on 19.3 as 100 (Answers correct to 1 decimal place.)

13.12 Base-year and current-year weightings

We have seen that simple index numbers, i.e. unweighted index numbers, are of limited use, because they assume that all items in the index are of equal importance. It is more likely that the quantity purchased and the amount spent on each of the products will be different. Let us suppose that three products, A, B and C, are all vegetables, respectively cabbage, broccoli and asparagus. The prices will not be the same, and it is probable that we will purchase more of the cheaper vegetables. If the prices change relative to one another, then our purchases are also likely to change particularly if (using the economists's jargon) demand is more elastic for one product than another. A doubling of the price of a dearer commodity (say asparagus) could well eliminate it from our food expenditure budget altogether, whereas we may still purchase quantities of a cheaper commodity which has risen in price although at a lower level. If the price of potatoes increases dramatically, the demand will fall. People will substitute bread, pasta or rice in order to keep their level of expenditure on food at a satisfactory level. Therefore in calculating an index number we must take into account the relative importance of the various items within the group and we use weights to reflect this importance.

The main problem with weighting is (a) what to use as weights and (b) from which period of time. The answer to both questions rather depends on the use to which the index is to be put, but certain points can be made.

Expenditure index

Many of our index numbers (in particular the Retail Price Index Number) are concerned with changes in the level of expenditure on a fixed basket of goods over a period of time, and therefore it would seem reasonable to use expenditures as the basis for our calculation. Consider Example 13.10, in which our basket consists of only three products, A, B and C.

Example 13.10

Product	Year 0		Year 1	
	Price per unit P_0	Quantity purchased q_0	Price per unit P_1	Quantity purchased q_1
A (per kilo)	80p	2	85p	4
B (per litre)	40p	8	90p	5
C (number)	10p	4	10p	4

You will notice that we have used p to denote price, p_0 for the base year price and p_1 for the current year (current year simply means the year for which the index is being calculated). Similarly, we have used q_0 and q_1 for the quantities purchased.

The amount of expenditure in year 0 was:

$$(80 \times 2) + (40 \times 8) + (10 \times 4) = 520p, \text{ i.e. } £5.20$$

In year 1 the expenditure was:

$$(85 \times 4) + (90 \times 5) + (10 \times 4) = 830p, \text{ i.e. } £8.30$$

We can calculate an *expenditure index* for Year 1 based on Year 0 as follows:

$$\frac{\Sigma p_1 q_1}{\Sigma p_0 q_0} \times 100 = \frac{830}{520} \times \frac{100}{1} = \underline{\underline{159.62}}$$

which shows that expenditure in year 1 was 59.62 per cent higher than in year 0. The method employed in the calculation was similar to that used in Example 13.4, and is known as the weighted aggregate method. The weights used were quantities and were taken from both year 0 and year 1.

Price index

Expenditure is made up of price and quantities purchased, and the explanation for any change in the expenditure index could be in variations of either price or quantities or both. In order to obtain a **price index** we will need to hold quantities constant, and then any change in expenditure will be due to price variations. We could take the quantities bought in year 0 or year 1 as our constant amount, but in Example 13.11 let us use year 0 quantities as the weight.

Example 13.11
Using base year weights, calculate a price index for year 1 based on the base year 0.

Expenditure in year 0 was:

$$(80 \times 2) + (40 \times 8) + (10 \times 4) = 520p$$

Expenditure in year 1, using the same quantities as the base year 0, was:

$$(85 \times 2) + (90 \times 8) + (10 \times 4) = 930p$$

Using the same symbols, our calculation will be:

$$\text{Index} = \frac{\Sigma p1q0}{\Sigma p0q0} \times 100 = \frac{930}{520} \times \frac{100}{1} = 178.85$$

When one calculates an index using only the weights in the base year, it is known as a **Laspeyre's Index**. This index shows that the cost of purchasing a basket of goods as used in the base period will have changed by a certain percentage if purchased in another period. In our example, on average, prices for products A, B and C will have increased by 78.85 per cent if the same quantities are brought in year 0 and year 1. However, it is unlikely that quantities purchased remain unchanged, because the buyer will tend to react to variations in price, and also tastes alter. As already mentioned, when the price of potatoes increases considerably, quantities bought decrease. If we used a base year of 1968, then sales of black and white television sets were more important than sales of colour televisions, video recorders were hardly known and micro-computers a dream. Today few black and white television sets are sold and both video machines and micro-computers are a significant factor in the purchasing pattern of the average family and must be taken into account. Therefore a Laspyre's Index based on 1968 might give a wrong impression of price increases in a period of rising prices, because it ignores product substitution.

By contrast, we can prepare an index using weights based upon the current year. Such an index is called a **Paasche Index**.

This time our calculation will be based on the formula:

$$\text{Index No} = \frac{\Sigma P_1 Q_1}{\Sigma P_0 Q_0} \times 100$$

$$= \frac{(85p \times 4) + (90p \times 5) + (10p \times 4)}{(80p \times 4) + (40p \times 5) + (10p \times 4)} \times 100$$

$$= \frac{340p + 450p + 40p}{320p + 200p + 40p} \times 100$$

$$= \frac{830p}{560p} \times 100$$

$$= \underline{\underline{148.2}}$$

Laspeyre's Index suggested a price rise of 78.85 per cent whereas the Paasche Index shows only 48.2 per cent. It may be that you consider the latter figure to be more indicative of what actually happened because it has taken into account the fact that quantities of A increased and B decreased as a result of price changes between year 0 and year 1. Unfortunately it only does this by assuming that the quantities purchased in year 0 at the lower prices were the same as those quantities purchased in year 1, and again this is unlikely. As the Laspeyre Index tends to overstate the price increase, so the Paasche Index tends to understate the increase. You will not be surprised to learn that there has been some attempt to arrive at an 'ideal' index based on both methods, but it has created almost as many problems as it has solved. The two main 'ideal' index numbers are the Irving Fisher Index and the Marshall-Edgeworth Index, but both are outside the level of this book. The current General Index of Retail Prices is a compromise between the two main methods, and is discussed in detail in the next section

There are two other disadvantages to the Paasche method. It is not a pure price index, because over the course of several years not only the price but the quantities change. Secondly, it can be a long and expensive job obtaining repeated up-to-date weights. With the Laspeyre Index the weights are known at the start, but they do become increasingly unrealistic as the years pass.

Obviously the choice of the base period will have an effect on the value of the index both with regard to the price relative and to the expenditure weight. In examinations there is no problem because the question must indicate the base period, but in real-life practice it is advisable to take a normal period as the base, although what is 'normal' can be very subjective and lead to abuse.

A quantity index

The most important index is the price index, both in examinations and in practice, but we can obtain a quantity index by using the same procedure. The weights are again expenditure weights, but instead of using price relatives, we use quantity relatives, as in Example 13.12.

Example 13.12
Calculate quantity index numbers for year 1 and year 2, using the
Paasche method. The base year is year 0.

| Product | Price per unit (p) | | | Quantity purchased | | |
	Year 0	Year 1	Year 2	Year 0	Year 1	Year 2
A (per kilo)	80	82	83	2	3	4
B (per litre)	40	60	75	8	6	5
C (number)	10	12	12	4	5	5

The expenditure weights will be as follows using year 2 for the
current-year quantities and prices required for a Paasche Index.

A $\quad 83 \times 4 = 332$
B $\quad 75 \times 5 = 375$
C $\quad 12 \times 5 = \;\;60$

Quantity index number: year 1

Price relative	Weight
A	$\frac{3}{2} \times 332 = 498$
B	$\frac{6}{8} \times 375 = 281.25$
C	$\frac{5}{4} \times \;\;60 = \;\;75$
	$\overline{767} \quad \overline{854.25}$

Quantity index no. for year 1 $= \dfrac{854.25}{767} \times \dfrac{100}{1} = \underline{\underline{111.38}}$

Quantity index number: year 2

Price relative	Weight
A	$\frac{4}{2} \times 332 = 664$
B	$\frac{5}{8} \times 375 = 234.375$
C	$\frac{5}{4} \times \;\;60 = \;\;75$
	$\overline{767} \quad \overline{973.375}$

$$\text{Quantity index number for year 2} = \frac{973.375}{767} \times \frac{100}{1} = \underline{\underline{126.91}}$$

Example 13.13

Using the same data as in the previous example, calculate a Laspeyre quantity index for year 1 and year 2. Base year is year 0.

The expenditure weights will be (using base-year quantities and prices)

A $80 \times 2 = 160$
B $40 \times 8 = 320$
C $10 \times 4 = 40$

Index number - year 1

A $\dfrac{3}{2} \times 160 = 240$

B $\dfrac{6}{8} \times 320 = 240$

C $\dfrac{5}{4} \times 40 = 50$

             $\underline{\underline{520}}$ $\underline{\underline{530}}$

$$\text{Index for year 1} = \frac{530}{520} \times \frac{100}{1} = \underline{\underline{101.92}}$$

Index number: year 2

A $\dfrac{4}{2} \times 160 = 320$

B $\dfrac{5}{8} \times 320 = 200$

C $\dfrac{5}{4} \times 40 = 50$

             $\underline{\underline{520}}$ $\underline{\underline{570}}$

$$\text{Index for year 2} = \frac{570}{520} \times \frac{100}{1} = \underline{\underline{109.62}}$$

Laspeyre and Paasche will differ significantly in their results if (*a*) price rises are considerably larger for some items, and (*b*) changes have occurred in the ratio of quantities bought. This has been the case in our example particularly with product B.

13.13 Exercises on base-year and current-year weightings

1 What is an expenditure index? Calculate an expenditure index for a product which rises in price from year 1 £1 000 to year 5 £1 450 but in which a manufacturer's requirements rise from 400 units in year 1 to 1 250 units in year 5.

2 The table below shows the quantities of four raw materials used by a manufacturing company annually, and the average prices payable per unit (£) in year 1 and year 5.

Commodity	Year 1		Year 5	
	Quantity	Price	Quantity	Price
A	12	24	18	38
B	8	20	10	36
C	4	30	4	48
D	10	12	16	24

Calculate an index number for prices for year 5, with year 1 as a base year, (*a*) base-year weighted and (*b*) current-year weighted. (Answers correct to one decimal place).

3 The table below shows the weights of various metals used by an engineering company in years 1 and 6 of its activities, all quantities being in metric tonnes. Prices of the metals are in pounds sterling per tonne.

Metal	Year 1		Year 6	
	Quantity	Price	Quantity	Price
Copper	15	650	25	1 000
Tin	20	1 250	40	1 400
Lead	12	1 500	10	1 825
Zinc	8	750	16	950

Calculate an index number for prices for year 6, with year 1 as the base year, (*a*) base-year weighted and (*b*) current year weighted (answers correct to one decimal place). Comment on your results.

4   (*a*) Briefly explain the advantages and disadvantages of Laspeyre's and Paasche's price index numbers.
   (*b*) Calculate Laspeyre's and Paasche's price index numbers for the following holdings of shares, with year 1 = 100 as base year (answers correct to one decimal place).
   The weighting are the decimal holdings by an investor.

Share	Year 1 Price (p)	Quantity (q)	Year 5 Price (p)	Quantity (q)
X	75	4 000	125	2 000
Y	70	2 500	35	4 500
Z	165	850	470	1 000

13.14   The General Index of Retail Prices

This chapter so far has been concerned with the weighted aggregative type of index – an index which is weighted by volume and which uses the formula

$$\text{Index} = \frac{\Sigma(p_1 \times w)}{\Sigma(p_0 \times w)} \times 100$$

Some effort has already been made to point out that there are many alternative types of index, and in the United Kingdom one of these in particular deserves more detailed consideration. This is the weighted average of price relatives index, one which is particularly suited to value, as opposed to volume, weighting. It is of importance to us here because the General Index of Retail Prices, probably the best known index in the country, is calculated by means of this method.

The method of calculation of an index using the weighted average of price relatives is simple. We first have to return to the price relatives we discussed in the early part of this chapter. These are essentially one-item index numbers. If we take a number of these one-item relatives and average them, we effectively have a composite index number. Once again an item's importance in the series can be taken account of by a process of weighting. The following example indicates how the process works.

Example 13.14

Item	Year 1 (base year) price (£)	Year 2 price (£)	One-item price relative $\frac{p_1}{p_0} \times 100$	Weight	Price relative × weight
Fuel and light	28	36	129	15	1 935
Housing	160	198	124	30	3 720
Food	30	49	163	55	8 965
				100	14 620

$$\therefore \quad \text{Composite index number} = \Sigma \frac{\left(\frac{p_1}{p_0} \times 100 \times w\right)}{\Sigma w}$$

$$= \frac{14\,620}{100}$$

$$= 146.2$$

The General Index of Retail Prices is one of the most important of the Government's statistical publications and is certainly the best known and most widely used.

Historically there have been many attempts to estimate the general level of prices from Tudor times through to the start of the First World War in 1914. Remarkably, the general level would appear to have changed very little between 1800 and 1914, although there were some quite violent swings up and down during the period. It was in 1914 that an index was set up to measure changes in the prices of essential goods bought by working people, and it was based on their pattern of expenditure in that year of 1914. It was a much more narrowly based index than we use today, because it included a much smaller list of goods and services, and a rather limited number of the population were involved. Nevertheless, this index (called the Cost of Living Index) continued until 1947, although it had been planned to introduce changes to its form about 1939. In 1937 an enquiry was held into the family budgets of manual workers and certain non-manual workers whose wages or salaries were not over £250 a year, and the results were to have been used to update the index. Unfortunately the war years of 1939–45 delayed any changes, and it was not until 1947 that the Cost of Living Advisory Committee (since renamed the Retail Price Index

Advisory Committee) considered the matter. It recommended that the results of the 1937–8 enquiry should form the basis of an interim index until such time as a comprehensive household expenditure survey could be undertaken under more stable economic conditions. The Interim Index of Retail Prices began in 1947, with the average level of prices at 17 June being taken as the base.

The committee judged that in 1951 some sort of normality had returned, and recommended that certain modifications should be made to the weighting pattern used in the construction of the interim index. It also suggested that a comprehensive enquiry be held in 1953–4 and the results used for weighting a new Index of Retail Prices as from January 1956. The next year saw the beginning of the Family Expenditure Survey (FES), which has been carried on continuously since that date, although changes have been made to its form.

A new index series was started in 1962, with 16 January taken as 100. It was decided that 3 successive years of the FES should be used to reweight the index annually and this practice was continued until 1975, when the results of one year's FES were used. A new base date was established in 1974 (15 January), only in its turn to be replaced by the current index from 1 January 1987.

The role of the RPI

It is a measure of the changes of the prices most people pay for the goods and services they buy. Therefore it is a consumer price index and purports to measure changes in retail prices for an average 'basket' of consumer items. It is *not* a cost-of-living index nor a measure of inflation, although it is frequently used for this purpose, mainly because it is the best available measure. It is a weighted index, and there are several problems associated with the selection of the base period and the weights and the method of calculation. It is to these problems that we now turn our attention.

The average basket

In theory all items of household expenditure should be included in the index, but clearly it would be impracticable to collect prices every month for each commodity purchased and service utilized. Also certain payments are excluded because of the variable nature of some services and the difficulty of identifying a unit of price which could be measured from month to month, e.g. income tax, national insurance contributions and life insurance, betting payments, etc.

Therefore a selection of commodities and services for regular pricing is made in such a way that any changes which occur are representative of price movements of commodities and services as a whole. Some 350 items are priced and combined into 83 sections, which in turn are collected into 14 main groups. These groups are food, catering, alcoholic drink, tobacco, housing, fuel and light, household goods, household services, clothing and footwear, personal goods and services, motoring expenditure, fares and other travel costs, leisure goods and leisure services. The motoring expenditure group has, for example, sections concerned with the purchase of motor vehicles, maintenance of motor vehicles, petrol and oil and vehicle tax and insurance. Obviously it is necessary to ensure that the index basket reflects as far as possible the proportion of average spending devoted to the different commodities and services. It was to this end that the FES was introduced.

The Family Expenditure Survey

This survey is very important because it not only supplies information on how people spend their money but also on the source of their income. About 10,000 households are selected at random from the Register of Electors, and interviewers call at the chosen addresses to ask for cooperation in the survey.

Those households which take part are asked to give details of their income from all sources and are required to record all payments made during a 14-day period. Information is also sought about certain payments which occur fairly regularly over longer periods, e.g. rent, gas and electricity accounts, and so on. The data given are kept confidential, in that the names and addresses are removed from the original source documents and are not sent to any other Government department. The survey itself is conducted by the Social Survey Division of the Office of Population Censuses and Surveys on behalf of the Department of Employment, which is responsible for publishing the results.

Numerous articles are written in the *Employment Gazette* which explain and detail some of the results taken from the annual report of the FES. This selection includes tables which cover the size and composition of households; some limited information about the employment of members of the household; average household expenditure under group headings, household composition, regions, etc.; and details of the expenditure of one-person and two-person pensioner households. For example, data are provided about the proportion of expenditure on transport and vehicles according to area, family size, work status, income, and so on. Such information is of great importance to the transport operator, as well as to local and regional planning authorities. This wide variety of data derived from the survey is of great value to workers in market research, social security and taxation, both in the private and public sectors. It provides unique economic and social data which can be used to assess the economic and social effects of changes in benefits and taxes on different types of households and to study the relation between income and expenditure on particular goods and services, such as different forms of transport and fuel.

However, its primary purpose is in the calculation of weights for use in the Index of Retail Prices. These weights are adjusted annually and are based on the pattern of expenditure of the average household in the previous 12 months (in the case of pensioner households, a 3-year period is used). The average expenditure per week is calculated and all the items whose prices are included in the index are given weights which reflect the proportion spent on them on average each week. The total weights are 1 000. Both these weights and the Index since January 1987 are reproduced in Tables 13.2 and 13.3.

Table 13.2   General Index of Retail Prices

Groups of items	Weights
1 Food	158
2 Catering	47
3 Alcoholic drink	77
4 Tobacco	34
5 Housing	185
6 Fuel and light	50
7 Household goods	71
8 Household services	40
9 Clothing and footwear	69
10 Personal goods and services	39
11 Motoring expenditure	131
12 Fares and other travel costs	21
13 Leisure goods	48
14 Leisure services	30
	1 000

Prices

The prices of about 350 different items are collected each month from various parts of the country. Staff from some 200 offices of the Department of Employment contact various retailers and organizations and record prices of these selected items on a Tuesday nearest to the middle of each month. They are supplemented by information given by certain organizations, and the combined data supplies some 150,000 individual prices.

Table 13.3 General Index of Retail Prices
(Prices at Junuary 1974 – 100)

Year	Jan.	F3b.	Mar.	Apr.	May	June	July	Aug.	Sept.	Oct.	Nov.	Dec.
1974	100.0	101.7	102.6	106.1	107.6	108.7	109.7	109.8	111.0	113.2	115.2	116.9
1975	119.9	121.9	124.3	129.1	134.5	137.1	138.5	139.3	140.5	142.5	144.2	146.0
1976	147.9	149.8	150.6	153.5	155.2	156.0	156.3	158.5	160.6	163.5	165.8	168.0
1977	172.4	174.1	175.8	180.3	181.7	183.6	183.8	184.7	185.7	186.5	187.4	188.4
1978	189.5	190.6	191.8	194.6	195.7	197.2	198.1	199.4	200.2	201.1	202.5	204.2
1979	207.2	208.9	210.6	214.2	215.9	219.6	229.1	230.9	233.2	235.6	237.7	239.4
1980	245.3	248.8	252.2	260.8	263.2	265.7	267.9	268.5	270.2	271.9	274.1	275.6
1981	277.3	279.8	284.0	292.2	294.1	295.8	297.1	299.3	301.0	303.7	306.9	308.8
1982	310.6	310.7	313.4	319.7	322.0	322.9	323.0	323.1	322.9	324.5	326.1	325.5
1983	325.9	327.3	327.9	332.5	333.9	334.7	336.5	338.0	339.5	340.7	341.9	342.8
1984	342.6	344.0	345.1	349.7	351.0	351.9	351.5	354.8	355.5	357.7	358.8	358.5
1985	359.8	362.7	366.1	373.9	375.6	376.4	375.7	376.7	376.5	377.1	378.4	378.9
1986	379.7	381.1	381.6	385.3	386.0	385.8	384.7	385.9	387.8	388.4	391.7	393.0
1987	394.5	396.1	396.9	401.6	402.0	402.0	401.6	402.8	404.0	405.9	407.9	407.5

(Prices at January 1987 – 100)

Year	Jan.	Feb.	Mar.	Apr.	May	June	July	Aug.	Sept.	Oct.	Nov.	Dec.
1987	100.0	100.4	100.6	101.8	101.9	101.9	101.8	102.1	102.4	102.9	103.4	103.3
1988	103.3	103.7	104.1	105.8	106.2	106.6	106.7	107.9	108.4	109.5	110.0	110.3
1989	111.0	111.8	112.3	114.3	115.0	115.4	115.5	115.8	116.6	117.5	118.5	118.8
1990	119.5	120.2	121.4	125.1ˈ	126.2	126.7	126.8	128.1	129.3	130.3	130.0	129.9

Of course there are problems with quality, special offers, discounting, credit transactions, product changes, etc., but as far as possible the items priced are chosen to be representative of the section or group from which they are taken. Any changes in quality are taken into account, and only cash transaction prices are used.

Calculating the Index

The first step is to calculate the average percentage change in price since the base date for each separate commodity and service in each of the 200 areas. These indices are combined to form a national item index and then a section index. Finally, the indices are weighted to form the group index numbers. For example, the price relatives for a particular item whose price had been collected from five shops in an area might be 440.3, 439.9, 440.2 and 440.1 and 440.2. These would be combined with other price relatives for the same item from the other areas to give a national price relative. Similarly all other items would be combined into their respective sections.

Under group 11, motoring expenditure, there are four sections: purchases of motor vehicles, maintenance of motor vehicles, petrol and oil and vehicle tax and insurance. In March 1990 the respective price relatives based on January 1987 = 100 were 114.8; 123.7; 108.7; and 125.9. The weights were 58, 20, 33 and 20. In order to obtain the group index, each price relative is multiplied by its weight. The results are totalled and divided by the sum of the weights, 131. The results are:

$$
\begin{aligned}
114.8 \times 58 &= 6\,658.4 \\
123.7 \times 20 &= 2\,474.0 \\
108.7 \times 33 &= 3\,587.1 \\
125.9 \times 20 &= \underline{2\,518.0} \\
&\quad\; 15\,237.5 \div 131 = 116.3
\end{aligned}
$$

In order to calculate the percentage change in prices over 1 month use the following method:

All items index of retail prices:

$$13 \text{ January } 1987 = 100$$

$$\text{Index in March } 1990 = 121.4$$

$$\text{Index in Feb } 1990 = 120.2$$

$$\text{Percentage change in month} = \frac{\text{difference in the indices}}{\text{starting index}} \times \frac{100}{1}$$

$$= \frac{1.2}{120.2} \times 100$$

$$= 1.0\%$$

Similarly, the percentage change in prices over 12 months would be:

1990	March	121.4
1989	March	112.3

$$\text{Percentage change} = \frac{121.4 - 112.3}{112.3} \times \frac{100}{1} = \frac{9.1}{112.3} \times \frac{100}{1} = 8.1\%$$

This is called the inflation rate (the rise in prices from one year to the next). It is widely used in wage negotiations as an argument for a 'fair' wage settlement.

13.15 Exercises: index numbers

1 Describe the construction and use of the General Index of Retail Prices. To what extent does the General Index of Retail Prices measure changes in the 'cost of living'?

2 Calculate the General Index of Retail Prices for all items for year 3, with January year 1 = 100 (answer correct to one decimal place).

Group		Weights	Price relatives February, year 3 (year 1 = 100)
1	Food	158	117.7
2	Catering	47	122.4
3	Alcoholic drink	77	117.8
4	Tobacco	34	108.4
5	Housing	185	151.0
6	Fuel and light	50	110.1
7	Household goods	71	113.9
8	Household services	40	116.8
9	Clothing and footwear	69	113.3
10	Personal goods and services	39	120.2
11	Motoring expenditure	131	116.0
12	Fares and other travel costs	21	121.5
13	Leisure goods	48	111.0
14	Leisure services	30	120.0
		1 000	

3 Calculate the General Index of Retail Prices for all items for June, year 4, with January, year 1 = 100 (answer correct to one decimal place).

Group		Weights	Price relatives June, year 4
1	Food	158	111.3
2	Catering	47	118.0
3	Alcoholic drink	77	114.7
4	Tobacco	34	106.4
5	Housing	185	138.2

6	Fuel and light	50	109.0
7	Household goods	71	110.9
8	Household services	40	113.2
9	Clothing and footwear	69	111.0
10	Personal goods and services	39	115.6
11	Motoring expenditure	131	115.1
12	Fares and other travel costs	21	116.3
13	Leisure goods	48	107.8
14	Leisure services	30	117.2
		1 000	

4   The Prime Minister declares that the year-on-year rate of inflation
is only 3.2 per cent and gives as proof the Retail Price Index for
the previous month (119.5) and the same month 1 year ago (115.8).
Is the statement correct? Show your calculations.

5   What is the year-on-year rate of inflation if the retail price index
rises from 136.8 in May 19.1 to 147.5 in May 19.2.

6   Calculate the index of industrial production (*a*) for all industries,
and (*b*) for manufcturing industries (correct to one decimal place)
from the following data.

Industry	Weights	Index December 19.5 (19.0 = 100)
Mining and quarrying	37	103
Manufacturing		
Food, drink and tobacco	84	105
Chemicals	65	119
Metals	57	74
Engineering	319	98
Textiles	76	94
Other manufacturing	144	100
Construction	146	89
Gas electricity and water	72	161

Source: *Monthly Digest of Statistics*

13.16   Summary of Chapter 13

1   An index number is a statistic which indicates the level of a variable
(such as prices, wages, industrial output, etc.) at a given date,
relative to the level at an earlier, basic date.

2   The base period is the starting point. So far as possible a base date should be chosen for its relative normality (since if we choose an abnormal starting points, the figures resulting from it will not give a true impression). However, it is difficult to know what is normal.

3   A simple price relative is found from the formula

$$\frac{P_1}{P_0} \times 100$$

where $P0$ is the base year and $P1$ is the current year, i.e. the year we are interested in.

4   If a number of variables enter into the matter under discussion, e.g. in running a car there are many costs, we may need not a simple price relative but an average price relative, taking all the component changes in costs into account. To find this we find the price relative for each component, and then find the average of these.

5   That is all very well, but the 'weighting' then comes into the picture. Some costs may be relatively more important than others, and the question 'What weights, or emphasis, shall we give to each component', arises. For example, in the Retail Price Index we have to carry out a special survey, the Family Expenditure Survey, to find out what 'basket of goods' the average family is buying.

6   A chain index number is one where the base year changes each year, and we measure the changes this year compared to last year.

7   A base-year weighted index is called a Laspeyre Index, We work out the increased costs in an expenditure index of this sort using the base-year pattern of expenditures. This gives a simple index, but it does get increasingly out of date as quantities purchased change and new products enter into the picture.

8   By contrast a Paasche Index is one based on the pattern of purchases in the current year, but this requires constant recalculation of the pattern of purchases. This procedure is very expensive, as we need to survey the situation again each year.

9   The Index of Retail Prices takes account of changes in the prices of all the items in the basket of goods purchased by an average family. It is a weighted index, with 1 000 weights in all allocated to various classes of goods in 14 main groups, with 350 items altogether.

10   The inflation rate can be calculated from the Retail Price Index, using the formula:

$$\frac{\text{Change in Index over 12 months}}{\text{Index of 1 year ago}} \times \frac{100}{1}$$

14
Sources of statistics

14.1 Official sources of statistics

Although the enumeration of populations by means of a census is as old as Government itself, the systematic collection of statistics is a relatively recent development. The first Census of Population in the United Kingdom was made in 1801 and has continued every 10 years since that date, except for the year 1941, when war intervened. Sample surveys are even more recent, and at first were privately conducted by interested individuals rather than officials. Charles Booth's Victorian enquiry, *Labour and Life of the People of London*, filled seventeen volumes. It was followed by another famous enquiry. Seebohm Rowntree's study of poverty amongst the working classes in York, published in 1901. This type of social enquiry continues today in an official way. The Social Survey Division of the Office of Population Censuses and Surveys conducts both standing and *ad hoc* enquiries to meet the needs of Government.

Most official statistics are a by-product of Government and local government activity in the economic, social and cultural fields. While statistics collected for one purpose (for example, the National Health Service) may not be absolutely appropriate for other purposes, there are many cases where they are good enough, and probably more comprehensive than any private enquiry could afford to collect. There are several periodicals containing monthly and quarterly statistics, and others which give annual figures. A further range of publications deals with historical statistics, and with regional data in the four broad regions of England, Scotland, Wales and Northern Ireland. Local authority statistics form a further field. Certain topics, such as education, health, prices and consumer protection, etc., are of wide general interest, and detailed analysis of trends and developments are available, while more specialized topics, such as weights and measures, industrial safety, distribution, etc., are also well documented.

It is impossible to describe many of these sources in detail in a book of this sort. The Central Statistical Office, which was originally part of the Cabinet Office and was set up in 1941 by Sir Winston Churchill, publishes the *Guide to Official Statistics*, a comprehensive guide to the literature available. The latest edition is in every public library reference section and should be available in every college and school, for it is an invaluable reference work for students.

Purists might hold that there is something intrinsically unsatisfactory about having a Central Statistical Office so closely identified with the Cabinet Office, since it might be suspected of introducing a bias into the data to meet Government policies. There may be some truth in this criticism. Against this argument it must be said that almost all parties agree these days that the management of prosperity is an essential function of Government, even if some Governments feel that the best way to achieve prosperity is by decentralization rather than centralized control. If prosperity is to be managed, the collection of reliable collections of data cost money, and require compulsory completion of questionnaires on a regular basis, the Government is the best organization both to provide the funds and compel performance. We must perhaps remind ourselves that the very word 'statistics' means 'data of interest to the state'.

Perhaps to meet the criticisms mentioned earlier, in April 1990 the Central Statistical Office ceased to be part of the Cabinet Office and became a separate Government department, responsible to the Chancellor of the Exchequer. Other statistical sections under the control of the Department of Trade and Industry, and the Department of Employment have been amalgamated with the new Department. The Director of the CSO said at the time: 'The main reason for the change is to bring under one management more of the work underlying the compilation of macro-economic statistics. This should make it possible to decide priorities and tackle problems in a more effective and co-ordinated way'.

Besides the *Guide to Official Statistics* referred to above, all statistical publications are made available through Her Majesty's Stationery Office. The best way to get hold of anything you require from HMSO is to phone the telephone ordering service in London on 071 873 9090. You will have to pay by credit card if you do not have an account with them, and must be ready to give your card details, the name and address of the person to whom the publications are to be sent and exact details of the title and numbers of each item required.

Alternatively you can order by post from HMSO, PO Box 276, London SW8 5DT, or from the HMSO bookshops at:

(a) 49 High Holborn, London WC1V 6HB, 071-873-0011 (counter service only).
(b) 258 Broad Street, Birmingham B1 2HE, 021-643 3740, and other addresses (see your local telephone directory).

How to find what you want

The most recent *Guide to Official Statistics* available at the time of writing explains this as follows:

> For anyone coming new to government statistics, the first thing to grasp is that each department prepares and publishes its own statistics – via HMSO in the case of most printed publications.
>
> If the series is of sufficient interest, it may emerge first in summary form as a press notice. A more detailed treatment is given in the department's own publications, such as *Business Monitors* and *Business Bulletins*, which are purely statistical reports. Finally, it may be included in all embracing statistical periodicals like the *Monthly Digest of Statistics* or the annual *Social Trends*, again often in a more summarized form.
>
> It may be that your needs can be met from one of these sources; or you have to consult the special departmental publication; or you may have to go further still and seek a special tabulation – at a cost – from the department. If the published source does not yield what you want it is usually worth checking with the department to see if they can help you.
>
> The following pages list the main publications. Current copies of selected series can be referred to at many public reference libraries, at the Central Statistical Office Library, Newport, Gwent, and at the Export Market Information Centre, 1–19 Victoria Street London SW1H 0ET.
>
> In summary:
> - Look at the published source
>   at your local reference library
>   or the Central Statistical Office Library
>   or the Export Market Information Centre
>   or by purchasing from HMSO or through booksellers.
> - For further information
>   phone or write to the appropriate department
> - If in doubt:
>   (*a*) *consult the Guide to Official Statistics*, or
>   (*b*) phone or write to the Central Statistical Office.

Students should certainly buy for their own use at least one copy of the *Monthly Digest of Statistics*, so that they can absorb the spirit behind a well-presented set of national statistics. Students of economics who can afford them should also buy at least one copy of the *Blue Book on National Income and Expenditure* and the *Pink Book on the Balance of Payments*. To buy such publications every year, and thus be really up to date, is perhaps beyond the pockets of most students, but employers running in-house training schemes and trainers offering business studies' courses should certainly place a standing order and build up a library for employee and student use. Even top management can learn a lot by regular perusal of the CSO's publications.

14.2 Regular publications by the Central Statistical Office (CSO)

For the student the provision of up to date statistics is essential, and several series of statistics are issued on a regular basis. A word of warning here. Tables for these regular sources are revised and redefined at intervals to suit current needs. This means that tables may not have a long run, especially in inflationary times. Thus a retail price index may have a 6-year or 8-year run and then the 'basket of goods and services' on which it is based is reassessed. The new table will not be strictly comparable with the old and a new base year will therefore be designated. Students, particularly those interested in modern history, will find it helpful to keep issues of the *Monthly Digest of Statistics* even if they appear out of date. To throw away such data when, in 10 years' time, it might be of great interest, is unwise.

The chief regular series of statistics are the following.

Monthly Digest of Statistics

This monthly publication is the major source of statistical material for students. It contains about 175 tables covering the main statistical series for which monthly and quarterly figures are available, besides the vital statistics (births, marriages and deaths), social services, entertainment and the weather.

Annual Abstract of Statistics

This weighty volume extends the figures available in the *Monthly Digest of Statistics* to cover 400 tables, over a 10-year period. Almost every Government department contributes to the *Abstract*, as well as other organizations. Statistics cover area and climate, population and vital statistics, social conditions, education, labour, production, transport and communications, retail distribution and miscellaneous services, external trade, balance of payments, national income and expenditure, etc.

Employment Statistics

A monthly publication, the *Employment Gazette* includes articles, and charts on manpower, employment, unemployment, hours worked, earnings, labour costs, retail prices, strikes and other disputes. It also features the wide variety of detailed reports about manpower skills, etc., which appear at both regular and irregular intervals.

The Census of Population

The Office of Population Censuses and Surveys (OPCS) is one of the two big collection agencies of the Government Statistical Service (GSS). The other is the Central Statistical Office itself. OPCS is responsible for collecting statistics on population and households. Its chief source of data is the population census held in the first year of every decade, i.e. 1961, 1971, 1981, 1991, etc. In Scotland and Northern Ireland the census is conducted by the Registrar General for each area. It takes most of the 10 years between censuses to analyse and publish the detailed results. For example, statistics from the 1981 Census are available in reports for each county in England and Wales (Regions and Island Areas in Scotland) and in a national and regional report. The same range of statistics is available for small areas (*Small Area Statistics*) throughout Britain. There are also summary reports of key statistics for local authorities, towns and cities, parliamentary constituencies and wards. Full details of these are given in the annual notebook *Government Statistics: a brief guide to sources*.

There is a series of national reports on particular topics, including family statistics (birth, marriage, divorce), mortality, morbidity (including cancer, infectious diseases and congenital malformations), abortion, international migration, vital statistics (population, births, deaths and internal migration) and electoral statistics (based on electoral rolls).

The official term for population statistics is **vital statistics**, implying the statistics of births, marriages and deaths. This term should not be confused with the more popular 'vital statistics' of the female figure.

The Blue Book on National Income and Expenditure

National Income has been defined as 'the aggregate net product of, and the sole source of payment for, all the factors of production'. If we are to know how much wealth we have created, and how to share it most fairly, we must have reliable data about the National Income. This celebrated *Blue Book*, published annually, gives data under thirteen main headings about production, capital investment, private expenditure and public sector expenditure on a rolling 11-year basis. Thus the 1990 edition contains the figures for 1979–89.

The Pink Book on UK Balance of Payments

Always a topic of enduring interest, the balance of payments of the United Kingdom is fully documented in this *Pink Book*. Published annually, on the same rolling 11-year programme as the *Blue Book* mentioned above, the statistics are grouped under fourteen headings, including visible trade, invisible services, transactions in UK external assets and liabilities, exchange rates, etc. It is essential reading for all business students and especially for those interested in the export fields.

Economic Trends

Published monthly, this publication reviews economic developments as they occur, giving not only the data, but interpretations of them and presentations in diagrammatic form. It is most informative and instructive.

Social Trends

This is a similar publication, published annually dealing with social developments and giving official analyses of many situations. It is of the very greatest use to those studying sociological aspects of United Kingdom life.

Financial Statistics

This publication gives a full account of the financial sector activities, state of the National Debt and similar matters.

Transport Statistics of Great Britain

This is an invaluable collection of data for transport students, updated annually, which covers all aspects of transport by road, rail, inland waterway, sea and air.

Government Statistics: a brief guide to sources

A useful guide which is updated annually and is free from the Central Statistical Office, Press Publications and Publicity Dept, Great George Street, London, SW1P 3AQ.

14.3 Occasional official data

Some data, of an historical nature, are not published on a regular basis, since they do not lend themselves to updating in the same way as the regular tables described in Section 14.2 above. A more occasional treatment only is necessary. The *Abstract of British Historical Statistics* and the *Second Abstract of British Historical Statistics* give as long a period of statistics as can be made available in most subject areas. Most series start in the nineteenth century, but some start much earlier. The first volume brings data up to 1938, and the second up to 1965.

Lectures and teachers may find a recent publication, *Using Statistics in Economics*, very helpful. It has been developed by the Central Statistical Office in collaboration with other Government departments and a panel of educational advisers. Purchasers are invited to photocopy any extracts needed for class use, or may order further copies as required.

It may be obtained from the Central Statistical Office, Great George St., London, SW1P 3AQ.

14.4   Other sources of data

Almost all major business institutions provide sets of data which are of interest to students of business activity, finance, economics, and social and environmental studies.

Bank of England Quarterly Bulletin

This invaluable publication not only includes a statistical section with the most pertinent financial statistics but a range of articles and authoritative accounts of the financial scene which are most informative to those studying business subjects. It is available in most libraries and may be purchased by anyone on an annual subscription basis by writing to the Economics Division, Bank of England, London, EC2R 8AH (Phone 071-601-4030).

The World Bank publications

These are excellent publications on a wide range of topics, made available in the United Kingdom through Microinfo Ltd, PO Box 3, Omega Park, Alton, Hampshire, GK34 2PG (Tel: 0420 86848). A list of publications is available on request. One particularly useful publication for students is *World Tables*, published annually.

Euro-statistics

The growing and important field of statistics relating to the European Community is best approached by studying *Euro-statistics: data for short-term economic analysis*. Tables are in two sections, Community Tables and Country Tables. *Eurostatistics* is available from the Statistical Office of the European Community, Batiment Jean Monnet, Plateau de Hirchberg, Boite Postale 1907, Luxembourg.

14.5   Exercises: official statistics

1   Describe in some detail *one* of the following:

   (a) The *Monthly Digest of Statistics*.
   (b) The *Annual Abstract of Statistics*.
   (c) The *Abstract of British Historical Statistics*.

2 Describe in some detail two of the following:

(*a*) The Census of Production.
(*b*) The Census of Distribution.
(*c*) The Census of Population.

3 What is the difference between a census and a survey? In which situations is a census preferable to a survey? Describe in some detail any published census or survey with which you are acquainted.

4 Describe two of the following briefly:

(*a*) *The Blue Book of the National Income.*
(*b*) *The Pink Book of the Balance of Payments.*
(*c*) *Economic Trends.*
(*d*) *Social Trends.*

5 Describe one of the following bodies in some detail:

(*a*) The Social Survey.
(*b*) The Central Statistical Office.

15
Some end-of-course examination papers

15.1 Examination preparations

Those who study steadily throughout a year of preparation for an examination will have an excellent chance of passing when the time comes. In statistics there are several factors to bear in mind when preparing for the examination:

1 There is a lot to learn, and real facility in handling formulae and calculations cannot be developed overnight. Practice makes perfect.
2 The separate elements in a course which make up the chapters of a book will be examined in some way in nearly every paper. Don't spend too much time on a specialist area – revise the whole syllabus and make sure you know how to tackle each type of question.
3 Revise an area one night, try questions on it the next night and invent further practice exercises, where you feel uncertain, to do the next night. Then move on to another area.
4 Work as many past papers as you can, from the particular examinations for which you are preparing. The rest of this chapter consists of typical 'past papers'. However, in most examinations you are given some choice, and only have to answer, say, five questions out of eight. In Past Paper No. 1 there are only five questions. You are therefore forced to try them all.
5 Some examination bodies insist on at least some part of the paper being in the form of a 'case study'. The merit of such questions is that they change statistics from being a purely theoretical study into 'applied statistics'. One such paper is included in Section 15.7 below.

15.2 Past paper No. 1

1 What is the difference between primary and secondary data? Give examples of each? Why is it important for the statistician to make this distinction?   (10 marks)

Prepare a draft for a short manual of guidance on questionnaire
construction. Make sure adequate reasons are given for any
suggestions you make. (10 marks)

2 One hundred men working at the same process were timed (to the
nearest minute) over a sample period chosen at random, with the
following results:

34	30	28	28	31	29	33	29	31	30	28	30
30	30	30	32	30	33	30	29	29	32	30	31
35	32	30	29	30	30	31	33	35	29	31	30
30	30	32	31	30	29	30	31	36	31	31	30
30	31	31	36	30	30	30	30	30	30	29	30

30	30	31	30	30	32	29	31	31	31	30	34
29	32	29	30	32	30	30	29	33	35	30	30
32	34	31	30	30	30	31	29	35	30	30	30
30	30	31	30

(a) Arrange the above data into a grouped frequency distribution
of about 9 or 10 groups. (4 marks)
(b) Draw a histogram to illustrate this distribution. (10 marks)
(c) How would your procedure have differed if the final class interval
had not been of constant size? (6 marks)

3 (a) Describe any four commonly used methods of sample selection.
(12 marks)
(b) Give the relative advantages and disadvantages of each and the
circumstances in which they may be used. (8 marks)

4 The data below is taken from the factory maintenance department's
records:

Age of machine (in months)	Number of hours of maintenance per month
4	8
19	11
14	12
11	12
20	18
32	19
15	20
29	24
34	29
39	30

(a) Plot the above figures on a scatter diagram.   (4 marks)

(b) Express the relation between age of machine and hours of maintenance in the form of a regression equation.   (14 marks)

(c) Estimate the hours of maintenance required for a machine 30 months old.   (2 marks)

5   The values of a random sample of sales invoices are recorded below:

Value (£)	Number of invoices
0 to under 10	5
10 to under 20	6
20 to under 30	7
30 to under 40	8
40 to under 50	9
50 to under 60	13
60 to under 70	18
70 to under 80	32
80 to under 90	34
90 to under 100	3
100 to under 110	1
110 to under 120	1

Calculate:

(a) The mean sales value.   (5 marks)

(b) The standard deviation.   (8 marks)

(c) The coefficient of variation   (2 marks)

(d) Explain the usefulness of the coefficient here.   (5 marks)

Also indicate its use in general, explaining when it is to be preferred to the standard deviation as a measure of variability.

15.3 Past paper No. 2

Answer all questions.

1 *Index of industrial production*   *Average 19.0 = 100*

Textiles, leather and clothing	*Sub-group weights*	*Unadjusted indices for October 19.7*
Textiles	49	102
Leather, leather goods and fur	3	97
Clothing and footwear	24	146

Source: *Monthly Digest of Statistics*, December 19.7

(a) Explain what is the difference between adjusted and seasonally adjusted index numbers, and how seasonally adjusted indices are calculated. (5 marks)
(b) Calculate the group index number for October 19.7 (5 marks)
(c) Explain how the sub-group indices and the sub-group weights are arrived at for the index of industrial production, and comment on any difficulties in obtaining the data for them. (10 marks)

2 The table below shows the number of trade unions and their total membership, according to the *Department of Employment Gazette*:

Year	*No. of unions at end of year*	*Membership at end of year (to the nearest thousand)*
1	622	10,259
2	604	10,188
3	583	10,191
4	562	10,470
5	540	11,178
6	522	11,126
7	504	11,351
8	515	11,447
9	501	11,755
10	492	12,184
11	462	12,376

(a) Using a 3-year moving average, calculate the trend of both the number of the unions and membership. (6 marks)

330 Statistics for Business

(b) Plot both trends on the same graph. (7 marks)
(c) Estimate both the number of unions and their membership for
   year 12. (2 marks)
(d) Comment on your results. (5 marks)

3 One of the most important Government statistical publications is
   the *Department of Employment Gazette*.

   (a) How often is it published, why is it important and to whom?
       (4 marks)
   (b) There are four main sections. What are they? Give a summary
       of the main information contained in them. (16 marks)

4 An investigation was undertaken to see if there was any relation
   between the rate of output of components from a particular machine
   and the quality of these components measured by the proportion
   of parts which are off tolerance. The following observations were
   made:

Observation number	Production rate	Quality percentage
1	150	87
2	200	82
3	250	88
4	300	76
5	350	73
6	400	74
7	450	74
8	500	72
9	550	67
10	600	76

   (a) Calculate the product moment coefficient of correlation.
       (16 Marks)
   (b) Comment on your results. (4 marks)

5 The table below represents the results of a series of blood alcohol
   tests on motorists stopped on suspicion of driving while 'under the
   influence':

Blood alcohol (milligrams per millimetre)	Frequency
0 to under 10	5
10 to under 20	6
20 to under 30	7
30 to under 40	8
40 to under 50	9
50 to under 60	13
60 to under 70	18
70 to under 80	32
80 to under 90	34
90 to under 100	3
100 to under 110	1
110 to under 120	1

Calculate:

(a) The mean blood alcohol level. (6 marks)
(b) The standard deviation. (8 marks)
(c) The coefficient of variation. (2 marks)

Explain the use of the coefficient of variation. (4 marks)

15.4 Past paper No. 3

Answer all questions.

1 Explain the method of construction, using rough sketches to illustrate and the principal uses of any two of the following:

(a) Gantt chart. (5 marks)
(b) Lorenz curve. (5 marks)
(c) Scatter chart. (5 marks)
(d) Z chart. (5 marks)

2 The *Monthly Digest of Statistics* gave the following aircraft kilometres flown per month, in millions of kilometres:

	J	F	M	Ap.	M	J	Jul.	Au.	S	O	N	D
Year 1	19.7	20.3	23.6	25.6	25.8	30.6	28.8	28.9	31.0	25.0	21.7	25.0
Year 2	21.8	21.2	25.1	24.7	25.6	29.9	28.1	28.0	30.8	26.1	23.0	25.6

(a) Calculate the trend using a 6 monthly average.   (8 marks)
(b) Plot the trend and the original series on the same graph.
(8 marks)
(c) Comment on the results with particular reference to any seasonal influences.   (4 marks)

3   The annual sales for 1 000 products in a factory's range are tabulated below:

Annual sales	Number of products
0 but less than 100	18
100 but less than 200	40
200 but less than 300	61
300 but less than 400	93
400 but less than 500	168
500 but less than 600	183
600 but less than 700	191
700 but less than 800	156
800 but less than 900	83
900 and over	7
	1 000

(a) Graph the data, using a cumulative frequency curve.
(8 marks)
(b) From it obtain the median sales and the quartile sales.
(6 marks)
(c) Estimate the percentage of products which have sales of less than 250 per annum.   (2 marks)
(d) Why is the median a more appropriate average than the mean for this set of data?   (4 marks)

4   Describe the method of construction and calculation of the Index of Retail Prices. What part does the Family Expenditure Survey play and how is it organized?   (20 marks)

5 'Opinion Polls are inaccurate and therefore misleading'. Discuss this statement, illustrating your answer with examples.

(20 marks)

15.5 Past paper No. 4

1 Three gangs of workmen on a similar repetitive job were timed (to the nearest minute) over a sample period, with the following results:

Gang A
```
32  30  28  26  31  29  33  29  31  30  29  31  31  28
28  31  29  30  29  31  31  29  30  29  33  28  29  31
27  32  30  34  30  33  29  32  30  32  30  27  30  32
30  32  29  30  27  30  28  27
```

Gang B
```
30  30  29  30  31  30  31  29  30  30  31  30  31  30
30  31  28  29  30  30  30  31  30  29  30  30  28  30
30  29  30  29  29  30  31  30  30  30  30  32  31  28
32  30  30  30  30  29  31  30
```

Gang C
```
29  30  30  30  31  33  30  31  30  32  34  30  35  30
30  32  29  32  32  31  31  30  29  35  33  36  31  30
34  30  32  31  34  30  35  30  36  31  33  30  33  31
31  30  29  29  30  30  32  35
```

(a) Arrange each set of data into an ungrouped frequency distribution. (6 marks)
(b) Illustrate each by the appropriate diagram. (9 marks)
(c) Comment on the results, with particular reference to points of statistical interest, indicating what further steps of analysis you might take. (5 marks)

2 With reference to the most recent Census of Population, answer the following questions:

(a) Why did we need a census? (3 marks)
(b) What were the main questions asked? (6 marks)
(c) What were the main duties of the census officer? (3 marks)
(d) What did the enumerator have to do? (3 marks)
(e) What problems arose in connection with the collection of the data? (5 marks)

3 An investigation into the germination interval (interval between sowing and appearance above ground) and soil temperature was

conducted in twelve plots of winter wheat with the following recorded results:

Mean soil temperature at 4 inches (°C)	Interval (days)
13	10
6	20
4	41
6	29
7	27
6	27
7	19
5	18
8	19
7	30
6	29
5	33

(a) Plot the above figures on a scatter diagram.   (4 marks)
(b) Calculate the regression equation and mark the regression line on your diagram.   (14 marks)
(c) Use it to estimate the germination interval for a mean soil temperature of 9°C   (2 marks)

4   The following percentage yield was obtained from individual items of raw material used in a production process:

Percentage yield	Number of items
Under 56	2
56 and under 57	6
57 and under 58	18
58 and under 59	30
59 and under 60	38
60 and under 61	26
61 and under 62	12
62 and under 63	6
63 and under 64	3
64 and under 65	2

65 and under 66	1
66 and over	1
	145

Calculate:

(a) The mean percentage yield. (6 marks)
(b) The standard deviation and variance. (9 marks)
(c) Comment on the characteristics of the distribution and the merits of the two measures used to describe it. What characteristics of the distribution have you not measured? (5 marks)

5   A clothing manufacturer wished to know the length of time that sewing machines were out of action due to breakdown, and a record was kept for a month:

Duration (*minutes*)	Frequency
Less than 10	4
10 and less than 15	5
15 and less than 20	12
20 and less than 25	19
25 and less than 30	28
30 and less than 35	16
35 and less than 40	8
40 and less than 45	2
45 or more	1

Calculate:

(a) The mean stoppage time. (5 marks)
(b) The standard deviation and variance. (8 marks)
(c) Explain, without calculations, the principles on which a measure of skewness of this distribution can be obtained. Why do you think skewness is much less frequently measured than the position and the dispersion of a distribution? (4,3 marks)

15.6   Past paper No. 5

1   An investigation by a transport company into the effects of operator performance on unit costs of repair gave the following results:

Performance (BSI)	Cost per standard hour (£)
54	15.60
57	13.20
65	11.00
68	12.80
69	12.00
72	10.80
73	12.60
74	12.50
75	12.70
76	12.40
77	11.10
78	12.50
79	10.60
81	11.50
82	11.20

(a) Calculate the rank correlation coefficient. (12 marks)

(b) Comment on the results. (8 marks)

2 A random sample was taken of the daily temperature at noon and the number of road accidents reported to the police between 6am and 6pm on the same day:

Temperature (°C) (x)	Number of accidents (y)
13	10
6	20
4	41
6	29
7	27
6	27
7	19
5	18
8	19
7	30
6	29
5	33

Calculate the product moment correlation coefficient.

(20 marks)

3 (a) Explain, with examples, the meaning of the following terms: (i) negatives correlation, and (ii) spurious correlation. Illustrate with scatter graphs where appropriate.   (4 marks)

   (b) Draw a scattergraph and calculate the rank correlation coefficient of the following data. Comment on the results and explain what alternative measure is available for examining the relation between these two sets of figures.

Family No.	Rent per week (£)	Rent arrears at referral (to nearest £)
1	16.25	65
2	13.30	63
3	17.55	85
4	17.05	30
5	15.85	2
6	12.45	0
7	15.00	11
8	14.30	10
9	13.80	0
10	16.20	25
11	15.60	100
12	12.85	8
13	13.85	75
14	13.60	62
15	14.60	109
16	15.20	114

Source: A Local Authority Welfare Department.

   Scattergraph.   (6 marks)
   Rank correlation coefficient.   (6 marks)
   Comment.   (2 marks)
   Alternative.   (2 marks)

4 Company sales, in thousands, over a period of 4 years were as follows:

Year	1st Quarter	2nd Quarter	3rd Quarter	4th Quarter
19.1	692	242	137	503
19.2	708	248	134	534
19.3	698	261	130	540
19.4	692	272	134	538

(a) Calculate the trend by use of moving averages.   (9 marks)
(b) Compute the average seasonal differences.   (7 marks)
(c) Estimate the sales for the four quarters of 19.5 (answers in thousands, correct to 1 decimal place).   (4 marks)

5   Consider the following data:

Grade of Labour	19.1, number employed	Average weekly wage (£), 19.1,	19.9, number employed	Average weekly wage (£), 19.9
A	200	90	190	240
B	175	115	140	300
C	110	120	100	310
D	94	130	103	320
E	266	155	358	360
F	24	190	42	420

(a) Calculate a base-weighted index number of the wage rates paid in the factory, using the aggregate method,
   (i) for 19.9, using 19.1 as the base year.   (7 marks)
   (ii) for 19.1, using 19.9 as the base year.   (7 marks)
(b) Account for the infrequent use of current weighted indices. Have they any advantages and what are they?   (6 marks)

15.7   Applied statistics module: a case study

Time allowed: 3 hours.

Instructions to candidates

A   Answer ALL questions. All questions are equally weighted.
B   The use of non-programmable electronic calculators is permitted. All working at intermediate stages of problems should be shown on the answer paper; failure to do so could result in a loss of marks.

C   Marks will be awarded for the logical development of solutions, for the clarity of English, and for the neat presentation of work generally.

Calculators may be used.

Situation description

Rex King set up in business in 1947 as a general carpenter and joiner. He bought a small factory in East London, built about 1920, which had been damaged by bombs in the Second World War. This he repaired with the aid of war damage compensation, and then proceeded to prosper, doing similar repair work for others and sub-contract jobs for the building and furniture trades.

In 1955 this type of business was declining, and so after much deliberation he decided to start manufacturing caravans. Again he prospered, and to meet the ever-increasing demand which occurred during the 1960s, the factory was continually enlarged as far as the site allowed.

In 1965 he formed a private limited company, with members of his family as directors, so that today Mr King (aged 60) is the managing director, his eldest son (aged 33) is the production director, his younger son (aged 32) the sales director, and his daughter-in-law (aged 34) the company secretary.

During recent years the market has become more difficult, owing to inflation, increased competition and the growth of other leisure activities, but there has been an increase in demand for luxury caravans. This recent move into a new and improved range of caravans has proved very successful and it has once again brought to the fore the problem of lack of space both for production and supporting activities. Proposed plans for increasing production of existing models and the development of new models are dependent on finding a new site. So far there has been one concrete offer, from Thetford, but there are other options available to the Company.

The following information is available:

Table 15.1   UK sales of caravans, 19.0–19.9

Year	Total UK	Company
19.0	86 023	17 200
19.1	78 160	15 319
19.2	84 751	16 441
19.3	126 433	24 401
19.4	151 511	28 787

19.5	146 628	27 272
19.6	161 290	30 544
19.7	180 645	38 515
19.8	195 097	49 967
19.9	210 705	58 763

Table 15.2   Company sales by model

	A (Cheapest)	B (Medium priced)	C (Expensive)
19.0	10 320	5 150	1 730
19.1	9 038	4 595	1 686
19.2	9 700	4 932	1 809
19.3	14 275	7 320	2 806
19.4	16 840	8 636	3 311
19.5	15 817	8 182	3 273
19.6	16 478	9 000	5 076
19.7	16 836	10 900	10 779
19.8	18 469	11 692	19 806
19.9	19 737	13 547	25 479

Table 15.3 was extracted from the company's payroll, and shows the distributions of weekly earnings among the factory operatives for 19.9.

Table 15.3   Payroll data

Weekly earnings (£)	No. of operatives
Less than 100	2
100 and less than 120	60
120 and less than 140	123
140 and less than 160	260
160 and less than 180	197
180 and less than 200	165
200 and less than 220	118
220 and less than 240	51
240 and over	14

Your task is to complete the following:

1   The company is considering the introduction of a profit-sharing scheme and wishes to know the reactions of the staff to the idea.

You have been asked to conduct a sample survey amongst the 1 500 staff employed.

(a) Which type of sample design would you use and give reasons for your choice?
(b) Design an appropriate questionnaire.
(c) Briefly describe how you would conduct the survey.

2 Using the UK sales of caravans from 19.0 to 19.9 (Table 15.1), calculate an equation of the trend line, using the least squares method.
   Estimate sales for the coming year 19.0.
   Why is it important to calculate the correlation coefficient when making predictions using this equation?
3 Using the company payroll data in Table 15.3, calculate the arithmetic mean and standard deviation weekly earnings of the factory operatives. Are there any advantages in using the median and quartiles to analyse this distribution?
4 One of the most important government surveys is the 'earnings survey'.

(a) Describe when and how the survey is organized and give a brief summary of the main information collected.
(b) How is the data published, and to whom is this information important?
(c) What use can this information be to this particular company?

5 (a) Plot the data in Tables 15.1 and 15.2 on the same ratio graph, using the semi-logarithmic graph paper provided.
(b) Write a brief report to the sales director, advising him on what the graph reveals.
(c) What are the advantages of using this particular graph in these circumstances?

Answer section

Section 1.10

Questions (1)–(5) do not have numerical answers. (6) 7.3; 6.9; 7.8; 4.3; 5.6; (7) (*a*) -242; (*b*) -26; (*c*) $+579$; (*d*) -7. (8) (*a*) 2750 ± 25; (*b*) 1600 ± 50; (*c*) 7000 ± 500; (*d*) 2765 ± 2.5. (9) (*a*) 2.38%; (*b*) 1.11%; (*c*) 0.14%; (*d*) 0.47%. (10) (*a*) 149570 ± 555; (*b*) 4275 ± 102.5. (11) (*a*) 25030 ± 55; (*b*) 25100 ± 100; (*c*) 25345 ± 52.5. (12) (*a*) 14000000 ± 375000; (*b*) 472500 ± 15500. (13) (*a*) 17.20 ± 0.54; (*b*) 15.36 ± 0.73.

Section 2.7

The questions in Chapter 2 do not require numerical answers.

Section 3.5

(1) Total = 12 310 therms. (2) Total = 11 814 cattle. (3) Total annual sales ('000m^2) = 226 904. (4) Total exports year 1, £15 657 million; year 2 £26 366 million.

Section 3.10

(1) 17 cars had 1 occupant; 14 had 2, 5 had 3, 3 had 4 and only 1 car had 5 occupants. (4) It would be wrong to specify the classes as shown in the question as the groups would be ambiguous, e.g. we would not know whether a person earning £130 came in Group 1 or Group 2. (6) Answer to (*d*) = 44.6%.

Section 5.2

No numerical answers required.

Section 5.5

No numerical answers required.

Section 5.8

(1) (*a*) £190 000; (*b*) £140 000; (*c*) loss of £35 000. (2) (*a*) £1 080 000; (*b*) £680 000; (*c*) break-even output = 3 000 units. (3) (*a*) £305 000; (*b*) £170 000; (*c*) £19 000 (answers within £1 000 acceptable). (4) The 34th unit will pass the break-even point for takings. (5) (*a*) Break-even point is at a sales volume of 230 000 units and a value of £920 000 (answers within 5 000 units or £5 000 acceptable); (*b*) Volume of 205 000 at sales worth £828 000 (answers within 5 000 either way are acceptable); (6) (*a*) Break-even point is at sales of 430 000 units worth £357 500; (*b*) Break-even point is at sales of 347 500 units worth £287 500 (answers within 2 500 units or £2 500 either way acceptable).

Section 5.10

No numerical answers required.

Section 5.12

No numerical answers required.

Section 5.14

No numerical answers required.

Section 5.16

No numerical answers required.

Section 6.3

(1) 34 826 units. (2) 27.8 yrs. (3) 1 120.2 books. (4) 50 981 m. (5) 288 kg.

Section 6.5

(1) 72.9 m^2. (2) £2 282. (3) 1 202 kg. (4) £7.74.

Section 6.7

(1) 22 litres. (2) 11 days absent. (3) £30 300. (4) £25 800. (5) £285.45. (6) £222.47.

Section 6.9

(1) £23 300. (2) 59 cm. (3) 454.1 km. (4) £107.69. (5) 89.9 cm.

Section 6.11

(1) Brown 70.3%, Dark 60.3%. (2) Lark 54.7%, Sparrow 77.4%. (3) Y = 67.5% Z = 77.3% and hence Mr Z was the better competitor. (4) A 78.3%, B 83.4%, C 82.7%, and hence B was best in show.

Section 6.13

(1) 236 hours. (2) 193.5 eggs. (3) £14 250. (4) £16 626.50.

Section 6.15

(1) £86.39. (2) £184.97. (3) 353. (4) The total frequency is 13 231 and the median cost is £200.74.

Section 6.17

Answers given below have been read from the author's own ogive curves. Answers within the + or − figures shown are acceptable. (Thoughtful students might like to work out the calculations exactly to see how closely they succeeded in reading off the median correctly.)

No.	Cumulative total	Median	Error permitted
1	1 102	£88	(+ or − £1)
2	16 000	29.6 years	(+ or −0.5 year)
(3)(*a*)	250	£104 500	(+ *or* − £500)

(*b*) Lower quartile £65 400 (+ or −£100). Upper quartile £117 100 (+ or − £100). (*c*) Tenth percentile £49 350 (+ or − £100). Sixtieth percentile £110 750 (+ or − £100).

Section 6.19

(1) A 27 runs, B 5 runs, C 36 runs. (2) A 4 wickets, B 2 wickets, C 1 wicket and 3 wickets – a bimodal series. (3) 3 bedrooms. (4) The formula answer is £515.38. Histogram answers within + or − £5 acceptable. (5) The formula answer is £10 055. Histogram answers within + or − £30 acceptable.

Section 6.21

(1) 10.0 tonnes. (2) mean = 8, median = 7, mode = 6. (3) (*b*) 30 years. (4) (*a*) mean = £426.2; median = £432.40.

Section 7.4

(1) No numerical answer required. (2) (*a*) 5 339 units; (*b*) 385 – 10 000 units: a range of 9 615 units. (3) (*a*) 6 124 spectators; (*b*) 1 569 – 12 726; a range of 11 157 units. (4) (*a*) 753 and 590, (*b*) 0 – 84 (a range of 84) and 24 – 36 (a range of 12); (*c*) Mr A = 47 units, Mr B 29.5 units; (*d*) Mr A = 68 units, Mr B = 4.75 units, (*e*) Mr A = 34 units Mr B = 2.375 units; (*f*) Very helpful. Despite his bad attendance Mr A is the more productive employee. (5) (*a*) 4 808; (*b*) £20 053; (*c*) £15 174 and £32 370; (*d*) £17 196; (*e*) £8 598. (6) (*a*) £81; (*b*) 20.82; (*c*) M = £17; $Q1$ = £9.75, $Q3$ = £26.25; (*d*) £16.50; (*e*) £8.25. (7) (*a*) 122 outlets; (*b*) 38.8 outlets; (*c*) $Q1$ = 16, $Q3$ = 54½; (*d*) 38.5 outlets; (*e*) QD = 19.25 outlets. (8) (*a*) 58.7 marks; (*b*) $Q1$ = 48.2 marks, $Q3$ = 71 marks; (*c*) 22.8 marks; (*d*) = 11.4 marks. (*Note*: as these answers are read off a graph, errors of 0.5 are allowable, either + or –.) (9) QD = 6.3 seats.

Section 7.6

(1) Mean income £11 290; mean deviation £4 789. (2) Mean tonnage 114 000 tonnes; mean deviation 55 500 tonnes. (3) Mean age = 45.67 years; mean deviation = 21.11 years. (4) (*a*) Mean sales = $49 500; mean deviation = $20 300. (*b*) We understand that the average sales in the USA by these representatives was $49 500, and the average variation from this figure was $20 300.

Section 7.10

(1) Mean £3,980; SD = £3,542. (2) Mean = 30.85 hours; SD = 12.49 hours. (3) Mean = 51.40 marks; SD = 14.19 marks. (4) Mean = 1.80 metres; SD = 0.11 metres. (5) CV = 12.1 % and 25.4 % respectively. This tells us that the demand for 'deep pan' pizzas is more than twice as unpredictable as the demand for 'thin and crispy' pizzas. (6) CV = 6.0 % and 32.3 % respectively for Garages A and B. This seems to tell us that the class of repair done by Garage A is fairly uniform and tends to be fairly high priced, whereas repairs done by Garage B are on average cheaper but do vary from relatively small jobs to quite expensive big repair jobs.(7) See text.

Section 8.5

(1) See text. (2) SK = – 1.3. It tells us that the data are negatively skewed to the extent of 1.3 standard deviations. (3) SK = 0.67. It tells us that the data are positively skewed to the extent of .67 of a standard deviation. (4) (*a*) See text; (*b*) because the No. 1 coefficient uses the mode, which is an inconvenient average, since there may be no mode, or several modes; (*c*) (i) 2.7 (ii) 2.8. (5) Mean = 55.0; Med. = 54; SD = 12.13.

Coefficient of skewness = 0.13. (6) Median = 54; Q3 = 64; Q1 = 47; SK = 0.353. (7) Median = 49.95; $Q3$ = 58.23; $Q1$ = 42.28; SK = 0.08.

Section 9.5

(1) (a) 0.019; (b) 0.077; (c) 0.25. (2) (a) 0.2; (b) 0.25; (c) 0.05. (3) 0.22. (4) 0.923. (5) 0.204. (6) (a) See text; (b) 0.5; (c) 0.5; (d) 1.0. (7) (a) See text; (b) 0.154; (c) 0.308. (8) (a) 0.028; (b) 0.005. (9) 0.14. (10) 0.3. (11) (a) 0.2; (b) 0.032; (c) 0.0035.

Section 10.4

(4) Regression equation is $y = 1.11 + 2.32x$.

Section 11.2

(4) $r = 0.93$. (5) $r = 0.99$. (6) $r = -0.13$.

Section 11.4

(1) $R = -0.9$. (2) $R = 0.764$. (3) $R = 0.212$. (4) $R = 0.81$.

Section 12.3

(1) Trend figures are 158.875, 163.875, 168.625, 173.25, 177.75, 182.25, 186.625, 192.125, 197.5, 202.625, 207.625, 211.25, 215.875, 220.5, 228.125 and 230.75. (2) Trend readings are as follows: 255.88, 256.38, 257.50, 257.62, 258.00, 259.12, 262.12, 269.38, 280.75, 291.62, 300.00, 309.50. (3) Trend figures are 132, 134, 140, 146, 154, 166, 178, 188, 200, 208, 220, 232, 242. (4) Exports vary: 17.26, 17.5, 16.76, 16.94, 19.42, 20.62, 22.08, 24.8; imports rise: 36.26, 40.06, 43.92, 46.74, 49.64, 51.60, 54.32, 56.44.

Section 12.7

(1) (a) Trend readings ('000s) are as follows: 193.75, 189.75, 188.125, 186.25, 183.375, 181.0; 178.375, 175.375, 173.75, 172.75, 171.25, 169.625. Seasonal variations are as follows: 1st quarter 0.865; 2nd quarter 3.698; 3rd quarter 2.156; 4th quarter −6.719; (b) De-seasonalized data: 209.135, 194.302, 189.844, 192.719, 187.135, 184.302, 186.844, 180.719, 176.135, 176.302, 173.844, 169.719, 174.135, 170.302, 167.844, 162.719. (2) (a) Trend readings are as follows: 81.125, 82.875, 85.75, 89.125, 93.25, 98.75, 109.5, 121.0, 129.75, 141.25, 160.875, 181.375, 192.625, 202.75, 216.00, 228.25; (b) Seasonal variations are as follows: 1st quarter −£60.516m, 2nd quarter −£39.672m, 3rd quarter +£106.328m, 4th quarter −£6.141m. (c) Random variations are as follows: −£27.453m, +£6.266m,

+£11.766m, +£6.547m, −£25.578m, +£3.391m, +£8.016m, −£1.328m, −£0.078m, −£9.109m, −£3.359m, −£9.703m, +£42.047m, −£11.609m, −£27.484m, −£6.578m. (**3**) Trend readings are as follows: 2.43, 2.37, 2.31, 2.28, 2.26, 2.23, 2.21, 2.20, 2.24, 2.31, 2.39, 2.41. Seasonal variations are as follows: 1st quarter −0.51, 2nd quarter −0.22, 3rd quarter −0.05, 4th quarter +0.78; (*b*) Data for year 4 seasonally adjusted: 1st quarter 2.42, 2nd quarter 2.47, 3rd quarter 2.48, 4th quarter 2.20. (**4**) (*a*) Trend figures: 59.625, 60.875, 61.75, 63.0, 64.875, 66.875, 68.75, 70.25, 71.25, 72.375, 74.0, 75.0, 75.625, 76.25, 76.75, 77.5; (*b*) Seasonal variations are: 1st quarter −16.453, 2nd quarter +12.172, 3rd quarter −6.984, 4th quarter +11.266; (*c*) Random variations are as follows: +2.359, −1.141, +1.703, −2.172, −0.891, +0.859, +1.703, −0.422, −1.266, +1.359, −1.547, +1.828, +0.359, −0.516, −1.297, +1.328.

Section 12.9

(1) (*a*) Trend rises from 271.4 to 416.4 (5-year cycle); (*b*) variations in the 5-year cycle: years 1, 6, 11, 16 = +37.32, years 2, etc. = 15.12, years 3, etc. = −34.14, years 4, etc. = −25.747, years 5 etc. = +7.453; (*c*) output in year 21, 482.7, year 22, 482.7. (2) (*a*) Trend rises from 323.14 to 480.00 (7-year cycle); (*b*) variations in the cycle: years 1, 8, 15 = −24.04, years 2, 9, 16 = −19.39, years 3, 10, 17 = −9.68, years 4, 11, 18 = +14.83, years 5, 12, 19 = +18.83, years 6, 13, 20 = +19.61, years 7, 14, 21 = −0.17; (*c*) output in year 21 = £528 000 and in year 22, £564 000. (3) (*a*) Trend rises from 337.71 to 553.57 (a 7 year cycle); variations in the cycle: years 1, 8, 15 = +23.38, years 2, 9, 16 = +28.10, years 3, 10, 17 = 31.96, years 4, 11, 18 = −14.47, years 5, 12, 19 = −46.62, years 6, 13, 20 = −19.62, years 7, 14, 21 = −2.76, (*c*) National income in year 21 = 617 billion N dollars.

Section 13.3

(1) 67.6, 73.5, 94.1, 100, 242.6, 264.7, 276.5, 294.1. (2) 112.8, 114.9, 100, 95.7, 93.6. (3) 100, 101.4, 102.8, 106.2. (4) 100, 102.5, 103.8, 107.8.

Section 13.5

(1) 100, 122.9, 155.2, 188.9. (2) 100, 117.0, 146.6.

Section 13.7

(1) 122.0. (2) 112.9. (3) Index reads 100, 105.7, 111.6. (4) Index reads 100, 116.7, 130.3.

348   *Statistics for Business*

Section 13.9

(1) Chain index reads 100, 107.6, 104.8, 108.3, 103.7. (2) Chain index reads 100, 104.1, 121.8, 118.8. 80.0. (3) Chain index reads 100, 112.3, 120.7. (4) Chain index reads 100, 108.0, 115.2.

Section 13.11

(1) (*a*) Price relatives: £1.00, £1.06, £1.05, £1.10, £1.03; (*b*) indices based on year 1: 100.0, 106.0, 111.3, 122.4, 126.1. (2) (*a*) Price relatives: £1.00, £1.10, £1.20, £1.25, £1.40, £1.60; (*b*) indices based on year 19.4: 100, 110, 132, 165, 231, 369.6. (3) 19.1 = 69.0. (4) 19.5 = 61.0. (5) (*a*) Index based on 19.0 = 100, 113.2, 119.1, 124.3, 127.9, 136.8, 143.4; (*b*) Index based on year 19.3 = 80.5, 91.1, 95.8, 100, 102.9, 110.1, 115.4.

Section 13.13

(1) Expenditure index = 453.1. (2) Laspeyre 170.9; Paasche 171.6. (3) Laspeyre 123.4; Paasche 122.7. (4) Laspeyre 160.4; Paasche 139.3.

Section 13.15

(1) No numerical answer required. (2) 122.5. (3) 117.4. (4) The answer is 'yes'. (5) 7.8%. (6) (*a*) 102.0, (*b*) 98.8.

For Chapter 15 only the numerical answers have been given. Refer to the text for other answers.

Section 15.2

(1) See text, via index. (2) Groups 27.5–28.5, etc.; frequencies 3, 13, 45, 18, 8, 4, 3, 4, 2. (3) See text, via index. (4) *b*) $y = 0.599x + 5.3$; (*c*) 23.27 hrs. (5) (*a*) Mean sales value £63.18; (*b*) £24.08; (*c*) CV = 38.11%.

Section 15.3

(1) (*b*) 115.70. (2) (*c*) say 455 and 12 578 000. (4) ,−0.79. (5) (*a*) 63.18 mg; (*b*) 24.08 mg; (*c*) 38.11%.

Section 15.4

(1) See text, via index. (3) (*b*) M = 565, QD = 138; (*c*) 8.8%.

Section 15.5

(3) (*b*) $y = -2.651x + 42.84$; (*c*) 19 days. (4) (*a*) 59.58%; (*b*) SD = 1.85%, var = 3.435%. (5) (*a*) 25.82 mins; (*b*) SD = 8.066 mins, var = 65.06 mins.

Section 15.6

(1) (*a*) $R = -0.49$. (2) $r = -0.73$. (3) $R = 0.39$. (4) (*a*) Trend rises by 1.25 a quarter on average; (*b*) 1st quarter $+294.0$, 2nd quarter -146.3, 3rd quarter -269.3, 4th quarter $+121.5$; (*c*) sales 707.0, 267.9, 146.1, 538.2. (5) (*a*) (i) 247.42, (ii) 40.95.

Index